Dark Logic

Dark Logic

**TRANSNATIONAL CRIMINAL TACTICS
AND GLOBAL SECURITY**

Robert Mandel

Stanford Security Studies, An Imprint of Stanford University Press
Stanford, California

Stanford University Press
Stanford, California

Special discounts for bulk quantities of Stanford Security Studies are available to corporations, professional associations, and other organizations. For details and discount information, contact the special sales department of Stanford University Press. Tel: (650) 736-1782, Fax: (650) 736-1784

Printed in the United States of America on acid-free, archival-quality paper

Library of Congress Cataloging-in-Publication Data

Mandel, Robert
    Dark logic : transnational criminal tactics and global security / Robert Mandel.
        p.   cm.
    Includes bibliographical references and index.
    ISBN 978-0-8047-6992-1 (cloth : alk. paper) — ISBN 978-0-8047-6993-8 (pbk. : alk. paper)
    1. Transnational crime.   2. Organized crime.   3. Corruption.   4. Violence.
5. Security, International.   I. Title.
    HV6252.M36   2010
    364.1'35—dc22

                                                 2010021704

Typeset by Motto Publishing Services in 10/14 Minion

CONTENTS

ILLUSTRATIONS

Figures

Tables

ACKNOWLEDGMENTS

THIS STUDY OF TRANSNATIONAL ORGANIZED CRIME—my tenth book—is the product of years of deep pondering. My continuing concern with post–Cold War global disorder has appeared in several articles and in five books published over the last decade: *Deadly Transfers and the Global Playground: Transnational Security Threats in a Disorderly World* (Praeger, 1999); *Armies without States: The Privatization of Security* (Lynne Rienner, 2002); *Security, Strategy, and the Quest for Bloodless War* (Lynne Rienner, 2004); *The Meaning of Military Victory* (Lynne Rienner, 2006); and *Global Threat: Target-Centered Assessment and Management* (Praeger Security International, 2008). Although appearing on the surface to be a quite narrow topic, in reality transnational organized crime is linked with today's most pressing global security concerns.

An investigation of this magnitude can rarely be executed successfully alone. I wish to thank my two undergraduate student research assistants, Lila Wade and Sarah Patterson, for considerable help with the case studies and for refinement of some of the general ideas. My conversations with Phil Williams at the University of Pittsburgh were invaluable, with Phil radiating the highly unusual combination of keen insight and kind encouragement. Beyond examining the published literature, numerous conversations with several colleagues in government intelligence and defense organizations have significantly contributed to my thinking, and they all deserve thanks. Finally, I wish to express special appreciation to Geoffrey Burn, the editor with whom I worked at Stanford University Press—his integrity, directness, enthusiasm, warmth, and humor made this publishing experience the best I have ever had so far. I also very much appreciated the considerable help from Jessica Walsh, his editorial assistant. I take full responsibility, however, for any egregious errors found in this volume.

This book is dedicated to global law enforcement and defense officials who endeavor to the best of their abilities to monitor, apprehend, and prosecute members of transnational criminal organizations. These officials toil without ceasing to comprehend, adjust to, and overcome the ever-changing challenges posed by these ruthless and unruly forces. The diligence and sincerity of effort among them should not be underestimated.

Dark Logic

1 INTRODUCTION

The Central Question

SINCE THE END OF THE COLD WAR, transnational nonstate forces have been a major source of global instability, and many ominous disruptive flows of people, goods, and services have moved readily across international boundaries. Deflecting attention away from transnational organized crime as a primary facilitator of these critical disruptive flows was first the sense of euphoria associated with the fall of the Berlin Wall in 1989 and then later the focus on transnational terrorism triggered by the 9/11 terrorist attacks on the United States in 2001. Although some analysts go too far in claiming that currently "the dimensions of global organized crime present a greater international security challenge than anything western democracies had to cope with during the Cold War,"[1] the transnational criminal threat is nonetheless highly insidious at a lower level. There is now a pivotal hole in our understanding of transnational criminals' decision making about the means to pursue their illicit ends and the security implications of these decisions.

This investigation begins to remedy this crucial analytical deficiency. Challenging puzzles requiring probing investigation surround the pervasive yet clandestine presence of transnational organized crime in the contemporary world, and focusing on these puzzles provides deeper insight into the nature of its operations and their consequences. So little is known about the modus operandi of transnational criminal organizations, and what little understanding does exist rarely distinguishes among their disruptive tactics or links these tactics to different kinds of security impacts. Consequently, an urgent need exists to explore within the contemporary international relations environment the dark logic behind transnational organized crime, its

1

subtle fluid patterns, and the resulting interference with effective security protection.

Proper appraisal of the disruptive tactics, security impacts, and corrective responses pertaining to transnational organized crime involves considerable complexity. Indeed, upon closer scrutiny, many conventional assumptions about the causes, consequences, and cures of transnational criminal activities prove to be controversial, wrongheaded, or ill-advised. Disagreements abound among experts even about the most basic issue of whether transnational organized crime is worthy of security attention. Today many global political leaders possess conflicting conceptions and misunderstandings about how to gauge the elusive dangers involved, and, as a result, their policy responses have generally failed to achieve stated goals. This investigation's primary aim is to shed significant new light on the topic to create a more coherent and probing comprehension of the operational dynamics of transnational organized crime, the ways in which it disrupts security, the reasons for its success and the failure of attempts to constrain it, and some fresh ideas to help those responsible to grapple more successfully with this global threat.

THE NATURE OF THIS STUDY'S CENTRAL QUESTION

This study focuses on two particular issues: (1) *when and how* transnational criminal organizations choose corruption and violence tactics and (2) *when and how* transnational criminal activities generate individual/human and national/state security impacts. The specific central question is as follows:

> Under what conditions is it most likely that transnational criminal organizations choose to rely primarily on *corruption* versus *violence* in their illicit cross-border transactions, and under what conditions is it most likely that transnational criminal activities primarily influence *individual security* versus *state security*?

This constitutes the first major study showing (1) when corruption and violence are most likely to be used, (2) when transnational criminal activities are most likely to affect individual security and state security, and (3) when the negative consequences of these tactics and activities can be most successfully combated. The presumed sequence is that first transnational criminal organizations select tactics to use in their activities, and then these activities generate security impacts, and discerning the criminal choice of tactics and their security impacts relies more on tangible observable behavior rather than elusive underlying motivations.

At this juncture, one might well ask, Why is the distinction between the criminal tactics of corruption and violence worthy of investigation? Certainly it could be argued that, because both tactics represent unruly disruptive behavior, those wishing to combat transnational organized crime would incur an equal responsibility to minimize each, thus making fine distinctions between the two unnecessary (in the colloquial words of one defense analyst, "since both are bad, let's just stamp them both out"). As illustrated in later chapters, however, (1) the vulnerabilities that facilitate widespread criminal corruption are quite distinct from those that facilitate widespread criminal violence, (2) the targets for corruption differ markedly from the targets for violence, and, as a result, (3) the means for containing corruption differ markedly from the means for containing violence.

Similarly, one might ask, What is the rationale for differentiating between the influence of transnational organized crime on individual/human security and the influence of transnational organized crime on national/state security? One could readily assert that the most important issue—given the magnitude of the dangers involved—is to reduce the aggregate threat transnational organized crime poses with regard to any form of security, and that attempting to separate its impact on different types of security is like splitting hairs. Some analysts argue that, especially within democracies, promoting state security automatically enhances individual security, and most analysts of transnational organized crime make little distinction among different types of resulting security implications. Again, as discussed in later chapters, (1) the criminal threat to individual and societal well-being is vastly different from the criminal threat to government functioning; (2) the individual/human and national/state security impacts can occur in substantially different areas, taking advantage of different kinds of vulnerability and using substantially different disruptive techniques; and, consequently, (3) the means for protecting individual/human security are quite distinct from the means of protecting national/state security.

Because of the interconnections with broader security issues, this analysis emphasizes, wherever possible, how the patterns of transnational criminal use of corruption and violence tactics and individual/human and national/state security impacts are both causes and consequences of other more widely studied recent global security transformations. In the end, any attempt to alter the modus operandi of transnational organized crime would require both a full understanding of these relationships and an ability and willingness to address and transform the key security parameters directly facilitating criminal behavior. It is worth noting at the outset that, on occasion, such willingness may necessitate compromising the principles embedded in enlightened liberal democratic values situated within an open globalized world.

Typical of a newly resurgent area of investigation, much existing research on transnational organized crime has been largely descriptive, serving primarily to outline the general scope and nature of the threat. Although these insights are important, as this unruly activity has evolved and proliferated, there is a need for much more refined and differentiated analysis. Despite their significance, little attention has focused on contrasting the transnational criminal tactics of corruption and violence: a few analyses scrutinize violence and corruption separately, without identifying when each tactic is selected; most studies of transnational organized crime simply give anecdotal evidence of the occurrence of the two activities across time, organizations, and locations, without identifying specific conditions under which each is likely to be chosen.[2] Similarly, few existing publications carefully differentiate between the individual security impacts and the state security impacts of transnational organized crime, preferring instead simply to describe emerging dangers in broad general terms. Furthermore, relatively few studies carefully situate the challenges associated with transnational organized crime explicitly within the broader international security context. There is certainly considerable value in providing colorful illustrations of how transnational organized crime operates worldwide and generates threat; however, not identifying overarching patterns and conditions surrounding tactics and impacts, not linking these with broader security issues, and not providing differentiated policy prescriptions can inadvertently condemn victims and observers alike to passive acceptance of seemingly inevitable dangers.

RATIONALE FOR SELECTION OF THE CENTRAL QUESTION

This study analyzes transnational criminal tactics explicitly from a security perspective—rather than from the popular alternative perspectives of international political economy and public administration—because the criminal choice of corruption or violence in its most extreme form appears to have the most direct influence on individual, state, and global security and because these security impacts seem to be more important than any other consequences of criminal activity. In today's world, "when the situation deteriorates to a point at which criminal organizations can undermine a government's ability to govern, as in Italy, Russia, Colombia, and elsewhere, then the problem goes beyond a law-and-order [or economic] issue and becomes a national and international security concern."[3] Given the frequency and severity within the last two decades of disruptive transnational criminal incidents, fears have intensified about the loss of protection and the potential coercive destruction of the political system, civil society norms, and persons and property. The disruptions generating these security-oriented fears appear to involve more far-reaching pernicious consequences—meriting both increased understanding and improved management—than those concerning economic downturns and disparities or administrative inefficiencies in carrying out essential functions. Nonetheless, even with its emphasis on security, this book makes a concerted effort to integrate insights from scholarly works approaching the topic from many different angles, in the process linking together especially the rather divergent perspectives of law enforcement and national defense.

Examining in detail the patterns of transnational organized crime's corruption and violence tactics and the resulting individual and state security impacts provides a unique lens—in many ways, a behind-the-scenes lightning rod—for analyzing today's global security dilemmas. Through this lens, one can grapple with fundamental security questions in international relations about the level and type of aggregate threat posed by (1) transnational organized crime in comparison to other unruly nonstate forces (such as terrorism), (2) disruptive nonstate groups in comparison to disruptive states (such as rogue states like Iran or North Korea), and, finally, (3) security challenges in the current international system in comparison with security challenges in previous global settings (such as that during the Cold War). This lens also permits analysis of the preparedness of targets vulnerable to transnational organized crime in comparison with targets vulnerable to other disruptive nonstate groups and to disruptive states or, alternatively, with targets in previous international systems. Placing the answers to this study's central question within this broader context of threat, vulnerability, and preparedness seems helpful to understand fully how the dynamics of transnational organized crime interrelate with those of other pressing security issues, especially how criminal dynamics influence and are influenced by other sources of disruption within international relations.

More specifically, exploring the central question highlights several fundamental conceptual controversies. These include (1) how the nature of sovereignty is changing in today's world; (2) how globalization can facilitate undesired transmissions across national boundaries; (3) how the increasingly intertwined nature of public and private authority structures has dramatically decreased accountability for the actions undertaken; (4) how government officials and private citizens often resist curtailing these unsanctioned transfers, revealing the moral murkiness in any condemnation; (5) how observers and participants alike find it troublesome to distinguish between legitimate and illegitimate enterprise in a world embodying multiple contrasting value systems; (6) how restraining authorities find it difficult to separate narrow law-and-order concerns and broader defense concerns; (7) how backfire effects are likely if knee-jerk responses to illicit criminal cross-state transfers are undertaken; and (8) how the tight and growing links among disruptive transnational nonstate forces in international relations, especially between terrorists and criminals, make orderly management much more complicated. Together these issues create challenges for security policy that call for major analytical shifts and significant deviation from standard responses.

This study's central question also highlights the covert security vulnerabilities of potential transnational criminal targets. Unlike a conventional military threat, transnational organized crime undermines the physical security of countries—including the economic, cultural, and political dimensions—in ways that are largely invisible until the intrusion is well advanced and difficult to reverse: "Rather like some diseases in the early stages, a response is easy but detection is difficult; when detection becomes easier, the cure is much more difficult."[4] Because vulnerabilities are so multifaceted and intertwined with normal societal interaction patterns, they are frequently quite difficult to pinpoint and overcome.

More broadly, the study sheds light on how nonstate sources of insecurity work today within and across states. When does transnational organized crime work in a top-down (affecting first society and then government) versus a bottom-up (affecting first government and then society) manner? When does this phenomenon operate well within and radically outside of prevailing security norms? The answers to these questions shed more light on exactly how transnational disruptions function within the current global security environment and how those vulnerable to such disruptions should prepare for them.

Finally, this study reinforces the need to consider underground cross-border activities to discern what is really transpiring in the world today. For example, looking at published trade figures dealing with legitimate businesses transporting well-accepted commodities misses the boat on much of what really drives the global economy and what really creates security disruptions within affected societies. It is somewhat puzzling that so many international relations analysts look only at aboveboard international transactions representing blatant threats when so much significant activity goes on beneath the surface in the world with such a monumental influence on global trends.

IMPEDIMENTS TO INVESTIGATING
THE CENTRAL QUESTION

Despite its overall importance, three primary obstacles impede investigation of this study's central question: the absence of hard data, the difficulty of defining transnational criminal activities, and the ambiguity in attempting to isolate transnational criminals and their organizations. Although such obstacles are not unique to this topic, the elusive nature of transnational organized crime amplifies the challenges involved considerably. Together these three impediments have created chaos in much existing research on transnational organized crime, fostering "many inaccuracies, simplifications, exaggerations, and misconceptions."[5]

First, unreliable information surrounds transnational organized crime. Firsthand accounts are unrepresentative and tainted with bias and subjectivity, and broad impersonal generalizations are overly sweeping and do not capture the subtle distinctions among groups or their activities. Even with completely impartial researchers, the results from direct interviews with transnational criminals are of questionable value because of open questions about the credibility—and intentional use of deception—of the people being interviewed. There are no reliable aggregate data—qualitative or quantitative—on the global pattern of transnational criminal behavior. Little cross-checking or accountability exists when nobody has a systematic way of verifying claims. For example, estimates of the revenues or profits of different kinds of criminal activities vary widely. Both law enforcement groups and the criminals themselves closely guard data relevant to transnational organized crime.[6] The reality that both those engaged in this illicit activity and those attempting to restrain it are opposed to transparency—for differing reasons—creates a nearly insurmountable obstacle for those attempting to investigate the subject.

Second, precisely defining the activities associated with transnational organized crime is a daunting task, in terms of both delineating the scope of activity covered and using the appropriate terminology to do so.[7] Perhaps the most overarching definition of "transnational organized crime" is "systematic illegal activity for power or profit"[8] across national boundaries, but that in many ways seems too broad. Simply listing the types of illicit activities covered[9] as a definitional mode is thwarted by their continual transformation. Undermining use of the definition "acts that are offenses in one state that involve actions or actors in another state" are many states' weak or poorly defined criminal codes that do not find uniform guidance about what constitutes an "offense"; in this regard, ambiguities are not eliminated by substituting "acts that entail avoidable or unnecessary harm to society, which are serious enough to warrant state intervention, and similar to other kinds of acts criminalized in some countries."[10] In reality, what is acceptable within states in the major realms of transnational criminal activities varies markedly. Equally problematic is determining whether transnational criminal activity is "organized": many serious cross-border crimes are initiated by individuals,[11] and, even when they are not, determining a minimum number of associated criminals or discerning the degree of required premeditation or coordination is difficult. Finally, complexities surround the meaning of "transnational," including whether perpetrators cross national boundaries, illicit products are smuggled out of a country, people enter a state illegally, proceeds move through foreign jurisdictions, or digital violations involve virtual boundary crossings.[12]

Third, it is challenging to differentiate among the various roles of the different shady and not-so-shady players involved in transnational criminal activity. In today's globalized world, a depressing widespread belief is that nobody is considered to be completely pure, honest, trustworthy, and aboveboard, and everyone seems willing to consort with virtually anyone else in undertaking cross-border transactions.[13] Moreover, "the identities of terrorists, guerrilla movements, drug traffickers, and arms smugglers are becoming more slippery," with considerable "identity mutation" apparent.[14] Transnational criminals work quite hard to conceal their true nature:

> International organized crime in its highest form is far removed from the streets. These groups are highly sophisticated, have billions of dollars at their disposal, are highly educated, and employ some of the world's best accountants, lawyers, bankers and lobbyists. They go to great lengths to portray themselves as legitimate businessmen and even advocates/benefactors for the local populace and others.[15]

The perpetrators of transnational crimes are not necessarily sinister outfits with dastardly motivations and goals, as sometimes "legitimate organizations in pursuit of otherwise legal business goals" engage in criminal activities.[16] Because illicit networks are tightly intertwined with both legitimate activities in the private sector and government entities in the public sector, globally "there is an enormous gray area between legal and illegal transactions, a gray area that the illicit traders have turned to great advantage."[17] Moreover, interdependencies between "dirty" and "clean" markets have become increasingly significant:[18] transnational criminals have partnered with "governments, financial institutions, mining companies and traders, security companies, mercenaries, and even non-governmental organizations."[19] Indeed, transnational criminals "can acquire, sometimes as a result of a definite 'public relations' strategy, a degree of public legitimacy, whether this is through fostering a myth of community spirit (as witnessed by the Yakuza's prompt dispatch of aid to the survivors of the 1995 Kobe earthquake) or by posing as champions of national or cultural identity (whether in Kosovo, Chechnya, or Kurdistan)."[20]

Although some attempts have been made to establish precise criteria for differentiating transnational criminal activity from legitimate business operations—such as "the covert nature of its operations, its reliance on violence and intimidation to protect and develop its market share, its access to capital which is not necessarily encumbered as in legitimate financial dealings, its interests in monopoly market structures, its use of corruption to strengthen its market relationships, and its resistance to external regulation"—in this effort "the separation between legitimate and illegitimate commerce may not be neat."[21] Even with perfect information, one could deem a transnational business activity either legitimate or illegitimate depending on its context. Although norms sanctioning violence differ across societies, isolating corruption in particular can be culturally relative, as "the cost of doing business in many parts of the world includes bribery of those (mostly in government) in charge of granting access, franchises or rights of exploitation."[22]

METHOD OF INVESTIGATING THE CENTRAL QUESTION

Because the three major obstacles to systematic research on transnational organized crime are so formidable, in investigating corruption versus violence tactics and individual versus state security impacts, this study seeks to circumvent these impediments more by minimizing their intrusion than by eliminating them completely. To reduce the impact of the often-unreliable data on transnational criminal organizations and their activities, this investigation emphasizes highlighting ongoing controversies and differences of opinion and multiple diverse sources for any firm conclusions reached. To overcome the difficulties of precisely delineating transnational criminal behavior, this study concentrates on the three major transnational criminal activities. To avoid being hampered by the ambiguity surrounding isolating transnational criminal organizations—and trying to separate them from legitimate businesses—this research effort focuses on the five major transnational criminal organizations. Finally, to increase the validity of the findings, this study tracks comparative cross-sectional patterns associated with transnational organized crime longitudinally across a couple of decades (specifically from the early 1990s until today), rather than examining these patterns at a single point in time. The intrusion of the research obstacles concerning transnational organized crime should be reduced, if not eliminated, using this combination of strategies.

This study's research methodology makes the underlying assumption that transnational organized crime, although not chaotic and disjointed, is not a collection of static monolithic entities that have operated in the same way across time and that have uniform and universal standard operating procedures controlling their global decision making. There are significant variations evident during different historical periods, within different geographical regions, across different types of transnational criminal organizations, and for different forms of transnational criminal activity. Nonetheless, a crucial premise of this undertaking is that enduring patterns do exist surrounding transnational criminal tactics and their security impacts that merit identification and analysis. Exploring these patterns should allow for much deeper understanding of the roots of transnational criminal behavior, better anticipation of what transnational criminal organizations might do in the future in response to the differing opportunities and countermeasures they encounter, and, ultimately, sounder ideas about effective containment of transnational organized crime. Nonetheless, the primary thrust of the book is more explanatory than predictive or prescriptive.

This study uses comparative case study analysis to investigate the central question posed earlier. It appears crucial in this investigation to explore the nature of both the transnational criminal organization perpetrators and the transnational criminal activities these perpetrators undertake, in order to analyze the patterns surrounding corruption versus violence and individual security versus state security. Although a burgeoning set of local, national, and international criminal groups exist, the emphasis here is on the major longstanding transnational criminal organizations exhibiting the greatest worldwide power: for well over two decades, these have been the "Big Five"[23]—the Chinese triads, the Colombian cartels, the Italian Mafia, the Japanese Yakuza, and the Russian Mob. Similarly, although the scope of transnational criminal activities has certainly grown, expanding well beyond the traditional focus on easy-to-monopolize vice goods and services to encompass a wide range of illicit activities, this study's focus is on the three activities representing the largest global illicit markets[24] and exhibiting the greatest potential for security disruption:[25] illicit arms transfers, illicit drug transfers, and illicit human transfers. In undertaking this comparative case study analysis, there is extensive reliance on secondary sources because of the scarcity of primary materials, but—as noted earlier—key findings receive support from multiple independent sources so as to increase their validity.

Given that transnational organized crime operates throughout the world rather than confining itself within particular regions, the geographical scope of this study is explicitly global. This means that there is no special focus on transnational criminal organizations and activities within any one country or on any one country's security interests, including the United States. Moreover, there is neither a summary of trends by country or region nor a comparative analysis of crime across countries or regions, for patterns uncovered clearly transcend national borders. The expansion of criminal operations to include different parts of the world and forms of illicit commerce has made encompassing this international scope—incorporating both advanced industrial societies and the developing world—essential to capture appropriately ongoing security implications.

Because of the major impact of the end of the Cold War upon (1) the dramatic transformation of transnational organized crime, (2) the increased volatility of the global security context, (3) the heightened vulnerability of potential targets to transnational criminal intrusion, and (4) the intensified security policy maker needs for assistance in dealing with the criminal threat, the time span for this investigation is the post–Cold War global security environment. For both organizations and activities, it appears crucial to analyze those that have been prominent during the entire post–Cold War period, instead of those that have surfaced only very recently, so as to be able to examine adaptation to changing circumstances. Many of the groups and activities explored have transformed dramatically to adapt to the new opportunities present within the contemporary global security environment. The roughly two decades since the fall of the Berlin Wall allow sustained reflection about both how the emerging patterns have changed over time since the early 1990s and how current tactical choices and security impacts are likely to be altered in the near future.

ORGANIZATION OF THE BOOK

The general organization of this volume is to present the changing nature of the transnational criminal threat, conceptual framing of the choice of tactics by transnational criminal organizations and the security impacts of transnational criminal activities, case analyses revealing empirical evidence surrounding these choices and impacts, identification of overarching patterns revealing when they are most likely to occur, links between transnational organized crime and transnational terrorism, and ways to manage the transnational criminal threat. Each chapter builds on the discoveries and findings of those that preceded it; to facilitate comprehension, comparison, and integration of key insights, these chapters make extensive use of illustrations to summarize key points. Wherever possible, the study earnestly endeavors to avoid leaving the reader with just sweeping generalizations and instead to uncover specific conditions under which the patterns it identifies and the conclusions it reaches are most and least likely to occur.

More specifically, this introductory chapter explains and defends the study's central question. Then chapter 2 analyzes the nature of the recent transformation in transnational organized crime; the origins of the transformation; the relationship of the transformation to the clash among sovereignty, anarchy, and interdependence; the emerging security threat; the debate surrounding the dangers associated with this transformation; and the ultimate resulting security disruption. With respect to the disruptive tactics of corruption versus violence and the disruptive security impacts of individual security versus state security, chapter 3 provides an overview of their global significance, the means of gauging their severity, their different orientations, and their particular relationship to transnational organized crime.

At this point, this book presents in two stages a detailed case analysis focusing on corruption versus violence and individual security versus state security. Chapter 4 explores the general organizational background, the choice of tactics of corruption versus violence, and the impact on individual/human security versus national/state security pertaining to the five major transnational criminal organizations—Chinese triads, Colombian cartels, Italian Mafia, Japanese Yakuza, and Russian Mob. Chapter 5 explores the general scope and nature of each activity, the roots of and responses to each activity, the key subcategories of each activity, the choice of tactics of corruption versus violence, and the impact of each activity on individual security versus state security pertaining to the three major transnational criminal activities— illicit arms transfers, illicit drug transfers, and illicit human transfers. Chapter 6 then analyzes the general patterns evident from these cases, including identifying the conditions under which transnational criminal organizations are likely to choose to resort primarily to corruption versus violence and the conditions under which transnational criminal activities are likely to generate primarily individual/human security impacts versus national/state security impacts. Chapter 7 places transnational organized crime in the context of other transnational disruptive nonstate forces and identifies its similarities and dissimilarities with transnational terrorism, the connections between criminals and terrorists, the modes of criminal facilitation of terrorism, and the security implications of this relationship. Finally, chapter 8 concludes by identifying security paradoxes in addressing transnational organized crime, the changes in orientation needed to overcome these concerns, and, ultimately, a concrete set of specific policy recommendations for managing transnational organized crime.

TARGET AUDIENCE OF THE BOOK

This study takes a fresh integrative conceptual look at the choice of tactics by transnational criminal organizations and the security impacts of transnational criminal activities so as to analyze and address the opportunities and limitations surrounding the ensuing global dangers. As such, this study is not designed to provide an encyclopedic empirical review of existing knowledge pertaining to the history and operations of transnational organized crime, but rather to generate new conceptual insights pertaining to its central question about corruption versus violence as transnational criminal tactics and individual security and state security as transnational criminal impacts in contemporary international relations.

Even though delving into transnational organized crime can be a jolting experience, this study makes every effort to maintain a detached and balanced analytical perspective. Rather than presenting insights from a particular normative vantage point that is subtly imposed on the reader, the patterns discovered regarding corruption versus violence and individual security versus state security are evaluated explicitly without an effort to judge the extent to which they are normatively objectionable. Rather than leading readers down a rigid linear path to produce a certain interpretation of these patterns, the focus here is to make transparent the logic of both transnational criminal thought processes and the author's thought processes (which are assumed to be quite different) so that readers can decide for themselves how these modes of analysis fit with their own values and beliefs. Rather than taking a distinctly American perspective on the patterns identified, this study attempts to take into account differing political and cultural perspectives on illicit cross-national transactions.

Thus this study is aimed at readers who are intelligent critical thinkers interested in reaching their own conclusions and ready to be exposed to open controversies, instead of being passively led by the nose or expecting definitive sweeping black-and-white answers to questions raised. However, there is no underlying assumption concerning readers' background knowledge about transnational organized crime, corruption and violence, or individual and state security. For readers new to the topic, they should discover sufficient context that they will begin to be able to grapple with the complexities and paradoxes surrounding the underlying issues. For readers knowledgeable and experienced on the topic, they should find traditional ways of thinking called into question and fresh modes of analysis and response proposed. In either case, rather than simply being exposed to interesting empirical examples of how this threat operates in today's world, readers will be encouraged to engage in a concerted rethinking of commonly held assumptions about the ways in which transnational organized crime operates within today's global security setting. If, after finishing this book, readers end up questioning prevailing beliefs, then this book has truly accomplished its mission.

This book is thus designed to speak to students, international relations scholars, and security analysts and policy makers about (1) transnational organized crime, (2) corruption and violence, and (3) individual/human and national/state security. Bridging the gap between academic and government security studies is highly challenging, but absolutely crucial to increase sensitivity to and cross-fertilization of the different perspectives involved and to allow each group to benefit directly from the findings of the other. In keeping with this broad target audience, this study makes every effort to avoid reliance on scholarly or policy-making jargon, unexplained acronyms, or implicit assumptions of any prevailing school of thought. Given that the threat associated with transnational organized crime can endanger the average citizen just as much as government officials (or academic experts), it appears imperative to write in a way that is intelligible to all affected parties.

2 TRANSNATIONAL ORGANIZED CRIME'S CHANGING THREAT

THIS CHAPTER EXPLORES the recent transformation of transnational organized crime. It analyzes the nature of this transformation; the origins of this transformation; the relationship of this transformation to the clash among anarchy, sovereignty, and interdependence; the emerging security threat; the debate over the dangers associated with this transformation; and the ultimate resulting security disruption. The emphasis throughout is on how challenges are evolving within the contemporary security environment.

THE NATURE OF CHANGE IN TRANSNATIONAL ORGANIZED CRIME

During the spring of 2009, unprecedented world attention was focused on the growing scope and power of organized crime reflected through two startling predicaments, summarized here to illustrate the current pervasiveness of the threat. The first predicament centered on Mexico's war on its powerful drug cartels—the primary suppliers of cocaine, marijuana, and methamphetamine to the United States (which brings in about $38 billion a year)—declared by President Felipe Calderón in 2007.[1] About 60,000 Mexican police are fighting five major drug cartels, which are struggling hard to maintain control of key areas. In 2008, nearly 6,300 people were killed in this war, many through gruesome means—including kidnappings, torture, and beheadings—by the ruthless criminals armed with assault and sniper rifles, grenades, and missile and rocket launchers (most acquired in the United States).[2] During the first eight weeks of 2009, over 1,000 people were killed in Mexico in drug-related violence.[3] The susceptibility to bribes of many Mexican police, law enforcement, and judicial institution officials has compounded the problem and impeded its resolution.[4] The United States became so concerned with the instability and the escalation of the violence that, on March 24, 2009, it announced plans for a massive crime-fighting operation targeting the Mexican drug cartels "on a scale not seen since the battles against the US mafia": in addition to dispatching more than 100 customs officers to the border, the U.S. government is providing $700 million to the Mexican government for five new helicopters, a surveillance aircraft, and other crime-fighting equipment.[5] Despite this action, many Mexican citizens bemoan that there is little chance of civic order being restored because of the strength of the cartels, and illicit drug transfers are escalating rapidly.

The second predicament, which involved the ongoing threat of Somali piracy in the Gulf of Aden, reached a fever pitch at around the same time. Maritime piracy has been thriving recently off the coast of East Africa, with the number of attacks growing from 41 in 2007 to 122 in 2008;[6] in 2008, there were 42 successful hijackings by pirates off the coast of Somalia, and in 2009, that number rose to 47,[7] despite reduced global shipping and a multicountry naval military force aimed at stemming piracy in the region. The Somali government has been too weak—it sees the pirates as more powerful than it is— and too corrupt to do anything about this illegal activity. Somalia's poverty and the past success of pirate operations have attracted many young Somali men to join the pirates in a quest for wealth and power that could facilitate entrance into elite circles.[8] On April 8, 2009, four Somali pirates tried to seize the ship *Maersk Alabama* carrying, among other cargo, 5,000 metric tons of relief supplies bound for Somalia, Uganda, and Kenya, and managed to capture and hold hostage for five days its American captain Richard Phillips. After a tense set of encounters, on April 12 U.S. Navy SEAL snipers killed three pirates holding the captain after determining that his life was in danger. Even the U.S. Navy, however, found itself initially hamstrung in its attempt to take effective counteraction. Moreover, since that incident, there has been little indication that the pirate activity is subsiding; "left unchallenged, piracy is spiraling out of control, and now threatens the sea-lanes that transport almost half the world's cargo."[9] Both the Mexican and the Somali cases display a mixture of corruption and violence that has led to relatively intractable individual, state, and international security dilemmas.

Taking a broader longitudinal view, organized crime has been around for many centuries and is by no means a new phenomenon. Indeed, "criminal groups operating across distances existed prior to the emergence of the modern nation-state," as, for example, "groups of highwaymen robbed and extorted money from travelers in Europe, often using the borders between European city-states and regal territories to their advantage."[10] After the end of the Cold War, however, there has been a noticeable resurgence and expansion of a new variety of transnational organized crime.

Transnational organized crime has been mushrooming specifically since the early 1990s, as local criminal groups expanded across national boundaries and formed tactical and strategic regional and international alliances.[11] The scope of this formidable challenge has recently widened, reflected by the substantial diversification of transnational criminal organizations and activities and the huge increase in the number of countries impacted by transnational organized crime.[12] The value of illicit criminal financial flows across national boundaries in the late 1990s ranged from $800 billion to $1.5 trillion, and transnational criminal activities consume roughly between 5 and 20 percent of the world's gross domestic product per year.[13] In many ways, criminal aspirations have become limitless in both time and space, with no means or ends out of bounds. The geographical extension of the reach of criminal groups has in itself led to a dramatic expansion of the range of criminal activities. According to a 2008 survey, the top ten countries with the highest levels of organized crime—based on perceived organized crime prevalence, the extent of the shadow economy, grand corruption, money laundering, and unsolved murders per 100,000 people—are (in order) Haiti, Paraguay, Albania, Nigeria, Guatemala, Venezuela, Russia, Angola, Ukraine, and Colombia.[14]

Today most organized crime is decidedly transnational.[15] Typically, local crime is more "predatory," involving forcible or fraudulent wealth redistribution, episodic time spans, and little infrastructure, whereas transnational organized crime is more involved in "market-based offences" involving longer planning horizons, more complex infrastructure, and the production and distribution of illegal goods and services to willing consumers.[16] In addition, typically more locally oriented criminal groups heavily rely for their source of power on controlling populations and territories within a specific region, whereas, in contrast, more transnational criminal organizations heavily rely for their source of power on global networking for trading and smuggling purposes.[17]

Within the post-9/11 global security environment, transnational organized crime has flourished heavily covertly, reflecting subtle "informal penetration"[18] across borders by nonstate groups. Criminal syndicates have at times engaged in purposely flagrant acts of violence, often so as to establish their turf within a particular geographical region, exemplified by the early Colombian cartels and the ongoing clash among drug lords in Mexico. Once transnational criminal organizations have firmly established themselves within an area, however, they usually prefer to operate without being seen and to embed their operations within legitimate and quasi-legitimate enterprises. Despite these "under-the-radar" characteristics, global crime has gone from previously having little political impact to now more than occasionally subverting not only state authority but also the very foundations of democratic governance.[19] As a result, many states are now concerned more about "cross-border law evasions rather than military invasions."[20] Indeed, this illicit transnational activity has caused the long-standing implicit social contract between the rulers and the ruled to become considerably more limited, fragile, and tenuous.

Since the early 1990s, transnational criminal organizations have employed more dispersed, decentralized, adaptable, and fluid strategies[21] than ever before, and they have moved away from fixed centralized hierarchies toward sophisticated decentralized networks, from controlling leaders seeking hegemony toward multiple loosely linked cells, and from rigid lines of control and exchange toward shifting transactions as opportunities arise.[22] Aided by advancements in transportation and communication facilitating the evasion of state regulation, transnational criminal organizations have realized "that networking, flat hierarchies, and small working units would enable them to adapt more quickly and more efficiently than large cartels."[23] Exemplifying this sophisticated network structure are the Colombian cartels: "Their structure is compartmentalized, and mimics a large, multinational corporation— with the home-based president and vice-presidents making decisions, monitoring and managing the acquisition, production, transportation, sales and finance for the drug-trafficking 'business,' and the overseas cells handling the import, storage and delivery of the product, as well as money laundering."[24] Any assumption by onlookers about uniformity in these transnational organized crime structures is extremely dangerous: different conditions lead to different types of criminal networks with different modes of operation, and these generate different types of security problems, which elicit different types of management responses. Modern global criminals mobilize extensive cross-border linkages and thus can flexibly challenge both national and supranational authorities.[25] Indeed, today Western powers "confront a new breed of smart enemies that are network-based, transnational in scope, highly flexible and adaptable in their operations, learn from their mistakes, have an ability to both exploit and embed themselves in social and financial institutions in ways that are virtually undetectable, and possess a capacity for regeneration even when they have suffered considerable degradation."[26]

The largely clandestine, transnational, and fluid nature of post–Cold War criminal activity has caused it to fall between the cracks of government agencies designed to protect against this kind of threat. Traditional distinctions are now blurring between military and police activities, between defense and law enforcement functions, and between internal and external security.[27] Facets of the murky military/police divide include the recently emerging pattern of military forces becoming more involved in domestic security missions such as border control; policing functions becoming more internationalized and militarized; the police and the criminal justice system relying more heavily on the military/war model for their rationale and policy dealing with crime, drugs, and terrorism; and criminality often being redefined as insurgency and crime control often being redefined as low intensity conflict.[28] The cause of this convergence of key elements of internal and external security appears to be the surge of transnational security threats, including that posed by organized crime;[29] and the result of this convergence challenges the fit and appropriateness of many existing administrative structures. Indeed, the nature of transnational criminal activity makes the bureaucratic dividing line between narrow law-and-order issues and broader national defense concerns increasingly artificial and difficult to delineate, causing, in turn, vital security threats to fall between the bureaucratic cracks: one example of such fragmented management of transnational organized crime occurs within the United States, where addressing this set of dangers requires sustained cooperation among the Organized Crime and Racketeering Section of the Department of Justice's Criminal Division; the Federal Bureau of Investigation; U.S. Immigration and Customs Enforcement; the Internal Revenue Service; the Postal Inspection Service; the Secret Service; the Drug Enforcement Administration; the Bureau of Alcohol, Tobacco, Firearms and Explosives; the Bureau of Diplomatic Security; the Department of Labor/Office of the Inspector General; and components of the State Department, the Treasury Department, and the intelligence community.[30] Because the institutional adjustments to changing security challenges have consistently been rather limited,[31] it is no coincidence that the scope of today's transnational security threats does not conform to the scope of agencies responsible for security regulation.

The challenge posed by transnational organized crime thus has changed significantly since the early 1990s, and table 2.1 summarizes both the nature of this transformation and its broad security implications. Looking first at changes in the nature of transnational organized crime, during the early 1990s transnational organized crime was characterized more by fixed centralized hierarchies, controlling leaders seeking monopolies, local ties, slow unreliable proximate interaction, rigid lines of exchange, short planning horizons, and domestic and regional scope; after 9/11, however, transnational organized crime was characterized more by decentralized fluid networks, loosely linked cells used to competition, mobilization of external cross-border linkages and alliances, instantaneous secure remote communication, shifting transactions as opportunities arise, longer planning horizons, and transnational and global scope. Transnational organized crime today is much less predictable and uniform than it was during earlier decades.

Table 2.1. Changes over time in transnational organized crime

1990s time period	Post-9/11 time period
Nature of transnational organized crime	
Fixed centralized hierarchies	Decentralized fluid networks
Controlling leaders seeking monopoly	Loosely linked cells used to competition
Local ties	Extensive cross-border linkages and alliances
Slow unreliable proximate interaction	Instantaneous secure remote communication
Rigid lines of exchange	Shifting transactions as opportunities arise
Shorter planning horizons	Longer planning horizons
Domestic and regional scope	Transnational and global scope
Broad security implications	
Disruption of economic system	Disruption of economic, political, and social systems
Stretching of police forces	Overwhelming/blurring of military and police forces
Reconfiguring of national power distribution	Reconfiguring of global information distribution
Form of governance left largely intact	Democratic governance significantly undermined
Social contract between rulers and ruled maintained	Social contract between rulers and ruled limited
Challenge to local authorities	Challenge to national and international authorities
Easier monitoring and management	More convoluted monitoring and management

Turning to the broad security implications of these changes, during the early 1990s transnational criminal activities caused economic system disruption, stretching of police force capacities, reconfiguring of national power distribution, and challenges to local authorities, but these activities had little effect on the form of governance, allowed the social contract between the rulers and the ruled to continue, and were easier to monitor and manage. In contrast, after 9/11, transnational criminal activities caused economic, political, and social system disruption, overwhelming and blurring military and police force capacities, reconfiguring global information distribution, significantly undermining democratic governance, limiting the social contract between the rulers and the ruled, challenging national and international authorities, and making monitoring and management more convoluted. Despite the best efforts of the authorities, transnational organized crime appears now to be both more damaging and more evasive than in the past.

ORIGINS OF THE CHANGE IN TRANSNATIONAL ORGANIZED CRIME

Given the sovereignty-challenging open global playground[31] setting, numerous elements have fostered the recent growth of transnational organized crime. On an individual level, criminals and their collaborators seem increasingly motivated by a burning desire for money, power, and fame; by fear; or by strong cultural or family connections.[33] On a state level, the aggressive international expansion of criminal laws and prohibition policies aimed at eradicating transnational organized crime's illicit market activities[34] ironically has tended to push undesired activity underground into criminal hands. On an international level, the differences in values and norms pertaining to illicit cross-border activities allow transnational criminal organizations considerable latitude about where to base their operations. Aside from these stimulants, three interrelated systemic background conditions seem particularly important in facilitating the recent changes in transnational organized crime: (1) intensified economic globalization, (2) proliferating politically fragile or failing states, and (3) accelerating technological transformation.

Intensified Economic Globalization

First, through promoting permeable national borders and foreign disruption of domestic economies, economic globalization has amplified the potential for outside criminal manipulation. Any system that opens its doors to a large volume of goods, services, and people flowing into and out of countries relies on the premise that most involved in this activity will abide by established rules and procedures. What this logic downplays is that many people are clever enough to understand the fragility of this assumption and intentionally choose to subvert it for personal gain. Indeed, within the context of a globalized world, transnational criminal organizations appear to develop and thrive when (1) illegal markets exist for goods and services outside the business scope of a state's jurisdiction or (2) protection vulnerabilities for citizens exist within the geographical scope of a state's jurisdiction.[35]

Looking first at porous borders, market-oriented reforms of the 1990s created incentives to break through—legally or illegally—the traditional government "sealants" restraining undesired cross-border activities.[36] Rapid transportation and communication advances have led to a much greater volume of international transactions, and this growth in trade, investment, and travel has allowed those seeking to move covertly illegal people and products across national boundaries to hide easily within the mass of legitimate travelers and commodities.[37] The increased number and heterogeneity of cross-border migrants[38] facilitate the hiding not only of illicit goods but also of the criminal perpetrators themselves. The international spread of liberal democratic beliefs, including support (especially at the rhetorical level) for free movement of goods and people across boundaries, has greatly lessened border police capacities to detect and restrict surreptitious cross-border flows;[39] in contrast, the Cold War presence of police states with their informants and tight monitoring had made much more difficult such illicit criminal transactions.[40] In particular, "the globalisation of capital from money to electronic transfer or credit, of transactions of wealth from exchange of property to info-technology, and the seemingly limitless expanse of immediate and instantaneous global markets, have enabled the transformation of crime beyond people, places, and even identifiable victims."[41] Transnational criminals now have "no respect for, or loyalty to, nations, boundaries, or sovereignty."[42]

Turning to foreign disruption of local economies, globalization may induce inequalities within and among states that foster unemployment and deprivation conducive to criminal recruitment, as well as short-term economic dislocations that feed the flow of illegal migrants across borders and push people toward participating in the illicit economy.[43] Contributing to the mushrooming of transnational organized crime may have been too little regulation of global markets within the financial sector and too much regulation of global markets in the labor and agricultural sectors.[44] Nonetheless, globalization's ongoing push to loosen restrictions on international transactions could actually reduce the need for illegal cross-border smuggling of goods and services and end up, under some circumstances, inhibiting transnational organized crime.[45]

Proliferating Politically Fragile or Failing States

Second, regarding politically fragile or failing states, transnational organized crime has taken advantage—following a long-standing tradition of preying on those who are poor at protecting themselves[46]—of globally vulnerable areas with weak governments and resurgent ethnic and regional conflicts.[47] Developing states with economies in transition or with internal conflicts appear to be particularly vulnerable in this regard: within these countries, "organized crime poses a real threat to development of reformed institutions, such as police, customs and judiciary, which may turn to criminal and corrupt practices, posing a serious obstacle to achieving stable, more prosperous societies."[48] Often the cultural context in developing areas is highly conducive to the entrance of transnational organized crime: "If society countenances violence, considers personal gain to be more important than equity, and is willing to bend the law in the pursuit of wealth, power and personal gratification, then society itself will always be receptive to illicit enterprise."[49] The proliferation of fragile or failing states can lead to a host of pernicious consequences, including creating breeding grounds for instability and conflict, terrorism, and sinister networks of all kinds; contributing to humanitarian disasters, poverty, starvation, disease, and refugee flows; and fostering human rights violations and genocide.[50] Although this susceptibility to transnational organized crime is by no means unique to fragile or failing states, they certainly are—often inadvertently—highly hospitable.

With respect to weak national government institutions, there are three common types of state failures: (1) illegitimacy, where political leaders lack legitimacy in the eyes of their citizens; (2) incapacity, where political leaders lack the capacity to address national problems; and (3) excessive force, where political leaders overuse repressive coercive force to deal with these problems.[51] Today "a vicious downward spiral" exists in which deteriorating popular and institutional acceptance of and support for weak and ineffective national governments have generated further disorder, violence, and subnational political autonomy demands.[52] Such state weakness seems particularly likely to give rise to transnational organized crime when governments (1) have inefficient premodern institutions, personalized patronage systems, and an inability to compel citizens to obey laws; (2) are too unitary or noncompetitive, with government officials subject to few internal or external checks and balances; or (3) exhibit devalued and unstable domestic currency, inducing access to foreign currencies to be gained through transnational criminal organizations.[53] The end to Cold War superpower aid propping up shaky regimes opened the door to transnational organized crime, which "feeds parasitically"[54] off the body of state governments that fail to provide basic needs and social services or to extend legitimate authority throughout their sovereign territories.[55] Criminal elements seek easy-to-manipulate political regimes to provide safe havens,[56] with the ripest conditions combining official corruption; unfavorable economic conditions; nontransparent financial institutions; poorly guarded national borders; and inadequately formulated, enforced, and respected national laws.[57] When a government collapses, transnational organized crime is usually ready to exploit existing opportunities.[58] Thus a key trigger of global threat has moved paradoxically from Cold War enemy strength to post–Cold War state weakness.[59]

Regarding conflict zones, transnational organized crime appears to "thrive in the chaos of war,"[60] as the locations of violent insurgencies correlate with those of delegitimized government and criminal activity.[61] Often within collapsing, imploding, or "black hole" states, "central authority has largely disintegrated in the face of local warlordism, ethnic groups, crime syndicates, or terrorist groups."[62] Indeed, the spread of all forms of global privatized violence goes hand in hand with this international authority vacuum. After the Cold War, Western states lessened their influence over conflict zones in a manner quite beneficial to criminal elements: transnational organized crime can prosper under political and economic unrest because conflict zones exhibit loosened controls, sizable capital availability due to the need for hard cash, and significant returns on investment due to high risks.[63] Given that a somewhat stable business climate is usually conducive to criminal profits, however, there is probably an upper threshold of warfare severity—such as when no shipment of illicit goods or services can reliably get in or out—beyond which even transnational organized crime is unable to function effectively.

Accelerating Technological Transformation

Third, accelerating technological transformation has facilitated transnational organized crime's ability to expand both the geographical scope of its operations and the range of goods and services transferred (many of which were not previously available).[64] In particular, "the emergence of instantaneous, global and secure forms of communication is the foundation of the global spread of criminal networks that exist simultaneously in multiple countries."[65] Partially spurring this technological impact has been the sluggish adjustment of law enforcement to changing trends and the speed of transnational criminal adjustment to and clever use of emerging technologies.[66] Transnational criminals possess a much greater capacity to take advantage quickly of technological changes than do national governments.

Regarding the expanded scope of operations, the combination of dense global interconnections and low communication and transportation costs has made illicit cross-border activities virtually "impossible to stop,"[67] with criminals now able to penetrate remotely any target area.[68] For example, the relative difficulty in tracing mobile phone communications, the low ability to detect containerized deliveries through private carriers, and the anonymous capacities of the Internet allow criminals to distance themselves from their illicit activities.[69] Electronic communication and data storage systems, in particular, have facilitated an ease and speed of disruption and manipulation previously unprecedented in the history of global criminal activities. In particular, cybercrime—involving illegal hacking into financial accounts and credit card, Internet, and identity fraud—has been facilitated by computerization.

Regarding the range of goods and services, massive cross-border diffusion of proprietary technologies (often dual-use) once under exclusive national government control—including "products ranging from rocket launchers to SCUD missiles and nuclear designs"—has created a tracking and sanctioning nightmare.[70] For expanding both the scope of operations and the range of goods and services, reliance on advanced technology can reduce paperwork and thus eliminate incriminating evidence that could facilitate police action.[71] On the other side of the coin, however, such reliance on technology can open the door to government hacking and jamming to interfere with criminal activities. Moreover, although accelerating technological change can increase criminal opportunities, ironically it can sometimes render large transnational criminal organizations both "uncompetitive and unnecessary"[72] because reliance on electronic forms of disruption can introduce efficiencies that make the participation of large numbers of human criminals in any illicit operation both superfluous and costly.

CLASH OF ANARCHY, SOVEREIGNTY, AND INTERDEPENDENCE

Much of the chaos within the global post–Cold War threat environment, and its susceptibility to disruption by transnational organized crime, is due to the competing pressures of anarchy, sovereignty, and interdependence. These three forces push responses to cross-national phenomena in very different directions. Yet, in analyzing the context of the current global security setting, some sort of balance is necessary for complete paralysis to be avoided.

The state of anarchy reflects the absence of overarching common norms and common meaningful authority structures on the international level, fostering a kind of "every-state-for-itself" mentality. Although formal international institutions and informal international regimes do exist, they generally do not possess sufficient coercive authority to make a difference when it comes to security threats. We live in a world that could hardly be more hospitable to the illicit cross-border transfer of goods and services via the corrupt and violent practices of transnational organized crime. Today's global security setting is full of diffuse transnational coercive nonstate threats, many of which are socioeconomic rather than military, nonterritorial rather than territorial, challenging to the rule of law rather than to the stability of political regimes, and penetrating states through corruption rather than by conquest.[73] Ongoing dangers so resist being pinned down and come from so many different directions that rational allocation of defense resources is difficult. Conventional policy tools for promoting security are ill-equipped to deal with this kind of dispersed intangible threat. The larger the range and severity of unmanaged separate dangers within the international system, the more likely it is for a sense of anarchy to intensify.

Even from the perspective of a great power like the United States, the global anarchic security setting looks ominous. The 2002 *National Security Strategy of the United States of America* notes that although "enemies in the past needed great armies and great industrial capabilities to endanger America, now shadowy networks of individuals can bring great chaos and suffering to our shores for less than it costs to purchase a single tank."[74] The ability of unruly elements within the international system to engage in such low-cost disruption of the status quo appears to be unprecedented since the emergence of the nation-state. Even with high-quality intelligence and advanced technology, both the predictability and the preventability of such under-the-radar havoc appear to be exceedingly low.

The perpetuation of the notion of national sovereignty involves a continuing belief by states that they should be able to have complete jurisdiction over what goes on within their boundaries, and that they should not have to accept significant compromise in these state rights for the common good. National governments do not wish to share sovereignty either with other states or with subnational or transnational groups, out of fear that this sharing might dilute government control or subvert state interests. State sovereignty is thus still viewed as a proxy for overall power to chart one's own course.

Increasingly, subnational separatist and nationalist movements—usually reflecting political, religious, ethnic, or cultural identities—want similar levels of autonomy over their own affairs, complicating jurisdictional issues tremendously. At the same time, transnational groups (including transnational criminal organizations) not only want this autonomy but also feel that they have the power and the right to substitute for the authority of both national governments and intergovernmental organizations because of their widely dispersed constituencies often tightly networked together for cohesive and timely action on matters of common concern: these groups see themselves as more functional and adaptive than what they perceive as a somewhat arbitrary and outmoded state structure. As a result, it is not uncommon to see illegal armed nonstate groups "challenging the nation-state's physical and moral right to govern" and interfering with state authority through their "violent, intimidating, and corrupting activities."[75]

Modern interdependence implies that, because of growing cross-linkages among states, each party's actions will increasingly have international repercussions, and that, as a result, it might make the most sense to approach issues on a broad multilateral basis. When international problems occur that affect multiple states at the same time, or when states import common goods and services (legal or illegal) from similar sources, interdependence can promote joint action while at the same time constraining certain kinds of independent responses. In its ideal form, interdependence promotes tolerance, understanding, and openness, but the skewed nature of most interdependence relationships within today's international system works against this end.

Operating within a globalized international system, interdependence can unwittingly aid the global spread of unruly forces, highlighting Western states' considerable vulnerability to disruption in the current security environment:

> When markets quake in Indonesia or Mexico, they send tremors from Main Street to Wall Street. When political unrest racks Central America, southern California's social services feel the aftershock. When our allies are struggling with economic recession, they are unwilling or unable to pull their weight on the global stage—leaving us to shoulder more of the burdens. When new democracies lack the means or experience to enforce their domestic laws, in-

ternational criminals can set up shop—and stretch their tentacles beyond our doorstep.[76]

An open interdependent world magnifies the impact of any localized disruption and prevents states from being effective in attempts to sanction selectively certain types of dangerous cross-national activities but not others. Interdependence can occur not only among states but also among subnational groups, among transnational groups, and between these two types of groups and states, so the overall impact can create quite a confusing variety of cross-cutting ties that are relatively difficult to isolate and interdict. Interdependence thus readily facilitates the spread of transnational organized crime among interconnected countries.

Major tensions develop when anarchy, sovereignty, and interdependence collide in the contemporary global security setting, with the impact on transnational organized crime summarized in figure 2.1. This kind of collision seems especially likely to occur when authority challenges develop or when unattended vulnerabilities are exposed. If globalized threats emerge, clinging to national sovereignty can lead to a stubborn refusal to confront them cooperatively, recognizing a prevailing sense of anarchy can create a fatalistic expectation that efforts to act jointly are doomed to failure, and constraining interdependence can create an inability to contain these threats while simultaneously allowing desired cross-border transactions to continue. Sovereignty concerns can also provoke an unwillingness to allow foreign officials to track down perpetrators of disruptive activities or to establish common punishments for these threat sources no matter where they operate.

Moreover, the clash among anarchy, sovereignty, and interdependence highlights inconsistencies within the prevailing international value system. For example, seemingly universal global beliefs exist that (1) free-market economics is preferable to centralized protectionist market structures, (2) materialism and the profit motive are acceptable market motivations, (3) capital should be competitive and should promote competition, and (4) transnational commercial priorities should predominate over local cultural preferences; yet a major exception to each of these principles can occur when the international community somewhat arbitrarily identifies transactions as "illegitimate" or associated with "vice," resulting from "crime cultures" or from the proceeds of criminal activity.[77] Because of the potential social turmoil that might ensue, these value inconsistencies are often ones neither government officials nor private citizens want to acknowledge or confront in any significant way,

Figure 2.1. Impact of clashes of anarchy, sovereignty, and globalization on transnational organized crime

Clashes among anarchy, sovereignty, and interdependence seem most likely to occur when authority challenges develop or when unattended vulnerabilities are exposed.

IMPEDES COOPERATION AMONG STATES

Clinging to national sovereignty fosters reluctance to confront threats cooperatively, recognizing anarchy creates fatalism that joint efforts will fail, and constraining interdependence allows in undesired threats as well as desired cross-border transactions.

Sovereignty concerns provoke foreign law enforcement officials' unwillingness to track down perpetrators of disruptive activities or to establish common punishments for these threat sources no matter where they operate.

IMPEDES INTERNATIONAL ORGANIZATION INVOLVEMENT

Transnational criminals' infusion into legitimate businesses and clouding of unacceptable behavior prevents, through the self-determination of peoples principle, international organization interference with misguided popular preferences.

The presence of high interdependence can cause these questionable popular choices—and the associated security fears that prompt them—to spread contagiously to the populations of neighboring states.

IMPEDES CONSENSUS ON VALUES

The clash among anarchy, sovereignty, and interdependence highlights value inconsistencies—Western states trumpet freedom of political expression, yet clamp down on this freedom when perceived as directly endangering state stability.

Awareness of this value inconsistency creates politically disruptive rifts and friction within domestic populations, causing political headaches for national governments.

FACILITATES MOBILITY OF TRANSNATIONAL CRIMINALS

Transnational criminals are adept at exploiting international vulnerabilities and readily locate areas with the most distracted, inept, or corruptible authority structures where politicized violence is most ignored, most tolerated, or least severely prosecuted.

Transnational criminals can then expand globally by overcoming the rigidities of sovereignty, taking advantage of anarchy, and mirroring a kind of interdependent efficiency greater than most status quo Western states or legitimate businesses.

FACILITATES LEGITIMACY OF TRANSNATIONAL CRIMINALS

Transnational criminals are diversifying their activities to demonstrate their unique advantages and their willingness to satisfy the full range of popular desires compared to bloated, sluggish, judgmental, and unwieldy state bureaucracies.

Repeated demonstrations of state incompetence causes tax-paying citizens to question not only the state's right to be the primary authority structure but also the value of state sovereignty itself within a world of anarchic interdependence.

preferring instead to imply to observers that the principles mentioned previously are absolutely universal.

As a result, transnational criminal organizations can move across possible target regions, finding the ones with the most distracted, inept, or corruptible authority structures in which to operate and where violence is most tolerated or least prosecuted. The continued internal and international bickering over sovereign rights needing to be sacrificed for the common global good plays right into the hands of criminals. Transnational criminal organizations can then thrive and expand globally because their ability to overcome the rigidities of sovereignty, take advantage of anarchy, and mirror a kind of interdependent efficiency that may be far greater than that of most status quo Western states. The most important advantage of transnational organized crime in this adaptation thus is its flexibility and fluidity in confronting changing global opportunities to turn an illicit profit.

Because transnational criminals insinuate themselves and their activities within legitimate business operations, in the public mind this behavior can cloud standards for deeming such actions as unacceptable and lead to inadvertent collusion by otherwise law-abiding citizens. The more common such shady activities become, the more acceptable they seem to be. The net result is to make it extremely difficult to eradicate such murky criminal operations within the current international system structure. Respecting sovereignty under anarchy, the widely accepted notion of self-determination of peoples prevents any form of international organization from interfering with the popular preferences of national citizens, no matter how misguided or counterproductive they may be in the long run. A high degree of interdependence can cause these questionable popular choices—and the associated security fears that prompt them—to spread contagiously to the populations of neighboring states.

In the future, transnational criminals seem likely to diversify their methods to demonstrate their unique advantages and their willingness to satisfy the full range of popular desires without any trace of judgmentalism about what constitutes virtue and what constitutes vice. Because of the unique advantages they possess in comparison to bloated, sluggish, and unwieldy state bureaucracies, transnational criminals may convincingly demonstrate that they can be better at quickly and cheaply attending to these cravings than both national governments and legitimate private businesses. Repeated demonstrations of state incompetence and blockage of widespread, if not universal, consumer preferences for black-market goods and services can cause taxpaying citizens to question not only the legitimacy of the state as the primary authority structure but also the value of state sovereignty itself within a world of anarchic interdependence.

SECURITY THREAT EMANATING FROM TRANSNATIONAL ORGANIZED CRIME

Within this problematic global setting, changes in transnational organized crime have resulted in many security threats. Recently, the U.S. Department of Justice voiced a growing concern about these dangers:

> In recent years, international organized crime has expanded considerably in presence, sophistication and significance—and it now threatens many aspects of how Americans live, work and do business. International organized crime promotes corruption, violence and other illegal activities, jeopardizes our border security, and causes human misery. It undermines the integrity of our banking and financial systems, commodities and securities markets, and our cyberspace. In short, international organized crime is a national security problem that demands a strategic, targeted and concerted U.S. Government response.[78]

This kind of enemy is in many ways considerably harder to identify, monitor, target, contain, and destroy than the Cold War Soviets.[79]

Because transnational criminals focus rather exclusively on profit maximization, many of the security threats posed by their global activities may be inadvertent rather than deliberate. One example is the self-images of Chinese human smugglers, who revealed in interviews that they "do not perceive themselves as criminals—they feel they are providing a valuable service to Chinese who want to immigrate but cannot do so legally."[80] Recognizing the possibility of unintentionally generated dangers does not make the security challenge any less severe or easier to manage, but it does provide a stark contrast to other globally unruly groups—particularly terrorists—who seek intentionally to maximize the security disruptions they create. It might even be fair to state that many transnational criminals are blissfully unaware of the true nature of the havoc they wreak within and across societies.

The four particular areas of greatest security threat generated by transnational organized crime appear to be (1) challenging high-quality national governance, (2) complicating identification and prosecution of disruptive societal elements, (3) promoting socioeconomic decay and turmoil, and (4) highlighting international system vulnerabilities. The first area represents a threat to national/state security, the second and third areas represent threats to individual/human security, and the fourth area represents a threat to global security. Modern transnational organized crime can clearly have indirect effects on many other areas as well, but these four realms—summarized in figure 2.2—represent the greatest security dangers.

Looking first at challenging high-quality national governance, transnational organized crime can break down the very foundation of responsive and impartial democratic rule. In particular, transnational criminal activity can reduce a state's ability to maintain control of what goes on within its territory, diminishing its sovereignty from external or internal interference and undermining its domestic laws. Because transnational organized crime and the state are both in the business of providing protection, a natural rivalry exists between the two that can at times promote "unremitting hostility."[81] Although in most cases transnational organized crime does not become the national government, it can play a major role in determining government infrastructure, by controlling elections, key appointments, important public investment decisions, and tax and trade policies.[82] Trust in and deference to authority may then be diminished. As a result, in many countries today, "non-state governance from below" is commonplace, where national government authorities no longer monopolize policing functions, and instead groups without official sanction attempt to identify and guard against emerging risks.[83] In cases where "criminal networks take over law enforcement functions and monopolize violence at the local level, as well as engage in distributive and service-providing activities normally associated with the state, a local dependence on international networks of organized crime can develop, creating serious internal security problems."[84] Furthermore, the intertwining of public and private authority structures induced through transnational organized crime reduces government accountability for actions undertaken.

Moving to complicating identification and prosecution of disruptive societal elements, the nature of transnational criminal activity makes evasion the norm rather than the exception. Frequently operating under the radar makes this activity extremely difficult to isolate, as both individual criminals and criminal goods and services become functionally invisible. Indeed, distinguishing between legitimate and illegitimate business enterprises—globally challenging because of differing value systems—has become nearly

Figure 2.2. Security threats emanating from transnational organized crime

CHALLENGES TO HIGH-QUALITY NATIONAL GOVERNANCE

Breaks down the very foundation of responsive and impartial democratic rule.

Reduces a state's ability to maintain control of what goes on within its territory.

Limits implicit social contract between the rulers and the ruled.

Leads to emergence of nonstate governance from below.

Lessens government accountability for actions undertaken.

Makes the dividing line between narrow law-and-order issues and broader national defense concerns more difficult to delineate.

COMPLICATION OF IDENTIFICATION AND PROSECUTION OF DISRUPTIVE SOCIETAL ELEMENTS

Makes evasion the norm rather than the exception.

Impedes detection of criminal activity, as both individual criminals and criminal goods and services become functionally invisible.

Prevents distinguishing between legitimate and illegitimate business enterprises.

Fosters moral murkiness in condemnation and aggressive prosecution of transnational criminals

PROMOTION OF SOCIOECONOMIC DECAY

Interferes with optimum efficient functioning of domestic financial structure and international trade.

Causes basic social services for those in need to disappear or to become highly unpredictable.

Jeopardizes the security of personal information.

Leads to illicit control of global energy and strategic materials markets vital to national security interests.

Contaminates health and education management.

Endangers safety of individual citizens, as the fiber of community and civilized society begins to disappear.

EXPOSURE OF INTERNATIONAL SYSTEM VULNERABILITIES

Ferrets out those system components that either do not function properly or are most open to disruption.

Demonstrates how porous borders allow virtually anything to pass unnoticed and uninterrupted from country to country.

Facilitates unintended backfire effects—the emergence or expansion of black markets— resulting from standard responses to illicit activities.

Reveals tight and growing linkages among unruly disruptive nonstate forces in international relations.

impossible, with no credible way for paying customers to discriminate even if they were motivated to do so. What this implies is that (1) it is exceedingly difficult for law enforcement to launch a campaign against transnational organized crime because doing so runs the risk of accidentally interfering with and alienating legitimate businesses vital to a national economy; and (2) once transnational criminals are apprehended, it is exceedingly difficult to convict them in courts of law because they can claim that they just sell goods and services requested by legal citizenry and engage in practices common in legitimate global businesses. Finally, because of the benefits reaped by national governments and their citizens, both find condemnation and aggressive prosecution of transnational criminals to be difficult and morally murky.

Turning to promoting socioeconomic decay and turmoil, because of this deteriorating governance and prosecutorial ability, societal conditions begin to unravel. The domestic financial structure and international trade no longer function with optimal efficiency, and basic social services for those in need begin to disappear or to become highly unpredictable. Even safeguarding the integrity of health and education systems can be significantly impaired. Impacts normally peripheral to security, such as road and building construction projects, may become pivotal when reliability dips beneath an acceptable threshold. Transnational criminal organizations—which now "control significant positions in the global energy and strategic materials markets" vital to national security interests—"use an endless variety of cyberspace schemes" to steal money, jeopardizing "the security of personal information, the stability of business and government infrastructures, and the security and solvency of financial investment markets."[85] Furthermore, although transnational organized crime does not usually cause violent conflicts, it can perpetuate social turmoil by supplying weapons to combatants (particularly if an arms embargo is in place); by complicating delicate postwar reconstruction; and by providing "the transportation, distribution, and marketing of products such as narcotics, timber, precious gems, and minerals from conflict zones."[85] The net effect endangers citizens' physical safety, as the fiber of community and civilized society begins to erode.

Finally, concluding with highlighting international system vulnerabilities, transnational criminal activity appears to be more proficient than anything else at ferreting out those dimensions of the current international system that either do not function properly or are most open to disruption. Examples of these dimensions are conflicting or nonexistent national jurisdiction in certain geographical locations; state-to-state disagreements about the acceptability of cross-border transmission of certain goods and services; unintended negative side effects of certain widely approved international sanctions targeting transnational organized crime; and hypocritical gaps between the principled rhetoric of certain states in their international policies combating transnational organized crime and the pragmatic practice of these states in their tolerance or even encouragement of illicit cross-border transfers. Transnational criminal activities place a spotlight on the dark side of globalization, in which porous borders allow virtually anything—even commodities universally considered to be highly dangerous—to pass unnoticed and uninterrupted from country to country. These activities, through their intrusion into authority structures, help to facilitate a clash of values and the previously discussed collision among anarchy, sovereignty, and interdependence. Furthermore, transnational criminal activities reveal tight and growing linkages among unruly disruptive forces in international relations—especially between transnational criminals and transnational terrorists—that magnify the dangers and complicate efforts to restrain any one unruly group.

DEBATE OVER THE DANGER OF TRANSNATIONAL ORGANIZED CRIME

On the surface, from the preceding analysis it appears that transnational organized crime is unambiguously disruptive from individual, state, and international security perspectives. This view is not universally shared, however, and some analysts do not see this phenomenon as particularly threatening, and instead perceive that it generates distinct benefits:

> Many of the activities of transnational criminal organizations are designed to provide illicit goods and services for which there is a large and flourishing demand. Because of this, organized crime is sometimes portrayed as relatively harmless, a form of borderline entrepreneurship that feeds on opportunities provided by various forms of prohibition. The criminals, and those who defend their activities, contend that they are simply meeting the demands of consumers willing to pay for certain kinds of commodities and services that are not regarded as socially acceptable.[87]

In this view, transnational criminal organizations are "not entirely parasitic," as they may provide desired services, introduce "elements of order and dispute resolution," and serve as "a source of social stability and depoliticisation."[88] The many alleged positive payoffs from transnational organized crime include low-cost merchandise, expanded employment opportunities, compliant workers, ready availability of a wider range of services, and nonjudgmental means of escape from the grind of daily life. Because of these presumed benefits, and because of criminals' self-portrayal as profit maximizers who simply want to satisfy public cravings, successful security management of this phenomenon would be exceedingly complex; because "parts of the upperworld need the underworld,"[89] neither national governments nor their citizens have a uniform view of transnational organized crime as an evil enemy that needs to be totally eradicated. In this way, transnational organized crime can be viewed as more responsive to the mass public than either the state or legitimate business.

Moreover, many debt-strapped developing states in particular believe that they benefit from transnational organized crime generating jobs and bringing in hard currency,[90] and some of their citizens even feel that engaging in unlawful activities is the only way to survive.[91] Exemplifying this perceived benefit are illicit drugs and maritime piracy. In terms of illicit drugs, strong global grassroots resistance to coca or opium eradication initiatives reflects the importance of these illegal transfers to local communities,[92] as frequently drug growers claim that it is the only way to generate needed revenues to support themselves.[93] With regard to maritime piracy, there can be a "two-wrongs-make-a-right" mentality where pirates argue that they have had to resort to a life of crime because foreign ships threaten their livelihood by illegally fishing within their territorial waters.[94]

The inherent difficulty with this perspective contending that transnational organized crime is not threatening but instead is beneficial is that it seems to ignore how these benefits are achieved, how the rights and lives of legitimate individuals and groups may end up being trampled, and how crucial stabilizing societal norms may be eroded in the process. Regardless of the truth of the allegations of benefits from transnational organized crime, if those involved believe them, then criminals are the clear winners, and law enforcement systems are the clear losers. An extreme outcome could be a public that sees little difference between transnational criminals and dysfunctional government officials. Furthermore, as a result of a perceived necessity for survival, many debt-ridden states have become increasingly dependent on the illicit global economy for their continued well-being,[95] and this dependence can create many side effects detrimental to these countries' ability to pursue, without distraction, their own national interests.

Besides those who minimize the threat from transnational organized crime because of its alleged benefits, other analysts question whether transnational organized crime directly poses its own distinct security threat to the international community or simply amplifies existing security threats emerging from other sources. Seeing transnational criminal organizations simply as facilitators of other threats—a belief common among some observers[96]—leads to substantially different countermeasures than seeing these organizations and their activities as constituting threats in and of themselves. Moreover, when viewed simply as a threat amplifier, transnational criminal activity might not be given as high priority on national security agendas as the perceived root causes of dangers, reinforcing the belief that this activity is simply an overblown law enforcement concern that pales in comparison to fundamental national security threats.

Because of the multitude of activities transnational organized crime undertakes, however, interpreting it simply as a threat amplifier appears, under close scrutiny, to be much too restrictive to encompass the full range of its security impacts. For example, the criminal initiation of illicit transfers of arms, drugs, and humans can create security, human rights, and economic problems that otherwise might not be present at all. Although transnational organized crime is tightly interconnected with other internationally disruptive forces, it appears to be able to wreak havoc all on its own.

THE ULTIMATE RESULTING SECURITY DISRUPTION

Perhaps the most vivid illustration of the importance of the transnational criminal security challenges was the emergence of "the world's first independent mafia state"—Aruba—in 1993.[97] This event represented an extreme signal of a heightened criminal thrust, involving the desire of transnational criminals to become respectable local power elites, to worm their way into legitimate commercial and governmental activities, so as to secure their survival protection, social status, and business success:[98]

This process of merging reaches its logical conclusion when organized criminals actually seize control of the state, an entire country effectively being run as a criminal enterprise. In parts of Latin America, the Caribbean, Eastern and Southern Europe, South-East Asia and Sub-Saharan Africa this is precisely what has occurred. It has led in some cases to the privatization not just of specific utilities and public companies but of key elements of governance, ranging from the police or military to the presidency itself. In such cases the criminals either operate under unofficial license from the civil authority or are indistinguishable from it. . . . . This entails neutering political obstacles such as an independent judiciary and a free press. It constitutes a model of governance based on the acquisition of power as a means of self enrichment.[99]

This taking over of national government functions—sometimes referred to as "the black hole syndrome"[100]—represents "the dark side of state displacement": combining "socio-economic decay and state retreat," dilapidated major urban areas within advanced industrial societies and devastated parts of the developing world provide comfortable niches where criminal activity can thrive without interference.[101] Within weak states, the organs of government are "eminently purchasable," and when these organs fall into the hands of organized criminals and warlords, the frequent result is that "government and crime become indistinguishable or identical."[102] If this outcome occurs, the principle of the sovereign rights of states is thrown into disarray.

In the future, transnational criminal organizations seem likely to diversify their methods for demonstrating to citizen onlookers their superior abilities to provide protection in comparison to often-crippled state governments. Because of the unique advantages certain transnational nonstate groups possess compared to bloated, sluggish, and unwieldy state bureaucracies, these nongovernmental groups may show that, during times of crisis, they can be better at quickly sizing up the situation and providing basic needs than national governments. Exemplifying this pattern are Hezbollah's provision of reconstruction aid, including "substantial economic resources" and "elaborate welfare and education programmes," in Lebanon during and after the 2006 war with Israel;[103] and the Japanese Yakuza's provision of much-needed assistance to the citizens of Kobe, Japan, after the 1995 earthquake.[104]

Globally, many marginalized populations have their security provided by transnational criminal organizations, to such an extent that such organizations pose the possibility of becoming "proto-states," which replace many of the political, military, and economic functions of the state.[105] In parts of West Africa, for example, transnational organized crime controls many of these critical functions. In this way, transnational organized crime can provide an alternative form of "parallel state" that challenges national government legitimacy and provides, particularly in weak states, many benefits—including social advancement, security, and prohibited goods and services—to needy populations. In those cases where transnational organized crime cannot dominate countries, it is often powerful enough to create its own "states within states," undermining the political integrity of host countries.[106] These high criminal levels of penetration and control challenge both the most basic assumptions of national sovereignty and the functional dynamics of the state system. Repeated state failures can cause tax-paying citizens to question not only the legitimacy of the state as the primary authority structure but also the value of state sovereignty itself within a world of anarchic interdependence.

CONCLUDING THOUGHTS

The current global stew in most ways seems ideal for the continuation and flourishing of transnational organized crime in the future, barring unforeseen and unorthodox intervention interfering with ongoing trends. The ingredients of this facilitating recipe include (1) the post–Cold War changes in transnational organized crime increasing the difficulty of constraining or curtailing it; (2) the growth in globalization, fragile or failing states, and technological innovation stimulating the pervasiveness of this threat; (3) the competing global pressures of anarchy, sovereignty, and interdependence enhancing transnational organized crime's power; (4) transnational organized crime's security threats challenging high-quality national governance, complicating identification and prosecution of disruptive societal elements, promoting socioeconomic decay, and highlighting international system vulnerabilities; and (5) an absence of consensus about the need to address transnational organized crime effectively because of beliefs that its benefits may outweigh its costs or that it may simply be a facilitator of other more fundamental dangers. Because so many of the strong instigations and the weak inhibitions surrounding transnational criminal activity are structural and systemic, without a dramatic shift in policy the current predicament will persist. As one analyst colorfully puts it, "as long as we live in a world where a seventeenth-century philosophy of sovereignty is reinforced with an eighteenth-century judicial model, defended by a nineteenth-century concept of law enforcement that is still trying to come to terms with twentieth-century technology, the twenty-first century will belong to transnational criminals."[107]

Any attempt to formulate a universal globally standardized response to transnational organized crime appears to ignore the reality that transnational criminals do not rely on a single strategic orientation to achieve their illicit goals, do not blindly perpetuate strategies regardless of how states respond, and do not restrict their transactions so as to focus just on one type of activity or on one set of geographical targets. Instead, these criminals attempt to expand operations deftly using corruption and violence as disruptive tactics, subtly eroding both individual/human security and national/state security. This flexibility and adaptability make the need to alter conventional modes of response all the more urgent, with the need for them to be powerful enough to buck the forces that facilitate transnational criminal activities, including (1) the strong positive incentives promoting illicit transfers deriving from the international system and (2) weak negative incentives discouraging illicit transfers deriving from global ambivalence about them.

3 CORRUPTION/VIOLENCE AND INDIVIDUAL/ STATE SECURITY

THIS CHAPTER PROVIDES AN OVERVIEW of the central concepts guiding this study's conditional analysis of transnational organized crime. The focus here is on the disruptive tactics of corruption versus violence and the disruptive security impacts on individual/human security versus national/state security. Incorporated in this discussion are an explanation of their global significance, the means of gauging their severity, their different orientations, and their particular relationship to transnational organized crime.

CORRUPTION VERSUS VIOLENCE

Transnational criminal organizations decidedly do not select their tactics randomly or haphazardly: "One of the answers to the question of how these vast international extra-state networks operate as coherently as they do is that people in these systems generally 'trust' that the transaction will occur as predicted."[1] Criminal groups "approach logistics, personnel, and accounting professionally," hiring experts and acquiring vital information and skills when needed and rationally undertaking cost-benefit analyses to maximize profit just like sound multinational corporations do.[2] These careful calculations of criminal minds, when combined with vast financial resources, facilitate the successful use of both corruption and violence on a significant scale[3] under differing circumstances. Figure 3.1 highlights differences in objectives, underlying motives, targets, and desired reactions in transnational organized crime's use of corruption versus violence tactics.

Transnational criminal organizations often find that corruption and violence go hand in hand in ways that are mutually reinforcing, and so these

Figure 3.1. Contrasting orientation of transnational criminal organizations toward corruption tactics versus violence tactics

---

CRIMINAL ORIENTATION TOWARD CORRUPTION TACTICS

Objectives
Has as main goal undermining the regulatory apparatus.
Looks to blend in invisibly and covertly with status quo transactions.

Underlying motives
Is associated with greed, unscrupulousness, and injustice.
Links to attitudes of openness toward mutual cooperation to achieve common goals.

Facilitators of use
Results from states' attempts to regulate illicit commerce.
Takes advantage of weak law enforcement, cultural norms, and asymmetries of power.

Impacts
Interferes with political stability, legitimacy, accountability, and efficiency of government regimes.
Focuses on countries lacking a tradition of integrity in governance.

Desired reactions
Causes state authorities to turn a blind eye to offenses and to operate on favoritism rather than on justice.
Undercuts public confidence in integrity of government officials.

CRIMINAL ORIENTATION TOWARD VIOLENCE TACTICS

Objectives
Has as main goal enhancing a group's marketplace position and driving away competitors.
Looks for highly overt shock value challenging the status quo.

Underlying motives
Is associated with terror, fear, and intimidation.
Links to "might-makes-right" and "zero-sum" interpretations of the world.

Facilitators of use
Links to dysfunctional governments, human rights abuses, enemy demonization, unemployment, and arms access.
Results from innate human aggressiveness; virulent nationalism; cultural norms; and ethnic, racial, and religious ties.

Impacts
Interferes with the lives of law-abiding citizens.
Focuses on unstable countries lacking civil society, fostering doubts that government can protect citizenry.

Desired reactions
Prevents state authorities from responding to offenses with massive retaliation.
Undercuts public confidence in ability of government to provide protection.

groups frequently mix corruption and violence tactics—such as when bribery offers to government officials convey veiled hints of violent consequences for noncompliance, or, alternatively, violence against citizens serves to reinforce their need to pay extorted tribute for their protection. Given that this is not an either/or choice, however, this study seeks to determine when each constitutes the predominant means criminal groups choose to achieve their illicit ends. This determination is based on the frequency/duration and severity of corrupt and violent behavior in particular situations.

Global Significance

Both corruption and violence tactics involve violation of the established legitimate societal rules in different ways: violence incorporates actual or threatened physical harm to persons or property, kidnapping and hijacking, extortion, and most generally creating an atmosphere of terror or intimidation; and corruption incorporates offering or receiving bribes, money laundering and counterfeiting, industrial espionage, and most generally any form of fraud that sanctions illegal transactions or causes them to be overlooked. Although both tactics attempt to protect a criminal group from state governments and other external agents endangering its ability to continue and expand,[4] violence and corruption can serve distinctive functions for transnational organized crime: the goal of violence is frequently to enhance a group's marketplace position and to drive away competitors, whereas the goal of corruption is often to undermine the regulatory apparatus.[5] Corruption often takes place out of sight[6] and can remain hidden indefinitely, whereas violence is usually quickly in the public spotlight. In some ways, corruption and violence represent two alternative types of relationships between criminals and society: corruption signals a "parasitic" relationship in which a criminal organization seeks to insert itself into society and government to protect its interests; and violence signals a "predatory" relationship in which a criminal organization adopts terrorist tactics to confront society and government to achieve specific objectives.[7]

It is ironic that corruption and violence are thriving worldwide at the same time that democracy has spread among most countries around the globe. Democratic values emphasize (1) civil discourse instead of violence as a means of ensuring fair and smooth resolution of disagreements and (2) checks and balances instead of corruption or nepotism as a means of ensuring fair and representative decision making. So if democratic societies fit the theoretical ideal, corruption and violence would be marginal at best. Through their frequent erosion of this ideal, however, transnational criminal activities serve to highlight hyperbole, hypocrisy, and downright failure in highly touted positive domestic and international response mechanisms for ensuring societal function according to principles of justice and integrity, with the high frequency of dysfunction belying optimism about global civil society.

Means of Gauging Severity

Within and across societies, corruption and violence take place with considerable variance in terms of their severity levels. Complicating the analysis of this variation in severity is that it may be a function of perceived legitimacy in light of prevalent cultural norms and tangible national and international security impact. With criminally induced corruption and violence occurring in transnational criminal organizations' home states, host states, or transshipment states, the value context may differ markedly.

Furthermore, precise determination of the frequency of global corruption and violence—whether or not they are criminally induced—is extremely difficult. The frequency of corruption is the harder of the two to gauge: because "corruption is usually a consensual crime, secrecy and collusion characterize its many forms; even major exposures of corruption may only scratch the surface of much larger conspiracies," as "most corruption goes unreported."[8] Even with violence, however, in many societies incidents go unreported because of fear of retaliation or fatalistic acceptance of its inevitability. In either case, there is no systematic way to determine how representative well-publicized incidents are of the more general picture.

Transnational organized crime tends to operate more at higher levels of corruption and violence, and thus much work explaining petty low-level corruption (such as avoiding payment of parking tickets) and violence (such as road rage) is less relevant. Although sometimes perversely described as functional or necessary within certain cultural contexts, the most severe corruption and violence have decidedly dire consequences, so what is most needed is identification of thresholds of violence and corruption that should trigger restraining intervention. As a first step in this direction, tables 3.1 and 3.2 present the various ways to gauge the severity of criminally induced corruption and violence—the purpose of corruption and violence, the mode of corruption and violence, the scope of corruption and violence, the type of corruption and violence target, and the kind of confrontation.

Table 3.1. Severity of transnational criminal corruption tactics

	Lowest	Lower	Higher	Highest
Purpose of corruption	Gaining access to enter desired region	Reducing surveillance of criminal activity	Lowering penalties for convicted criminals	Establishing collusion with authorities
Mode of corruption	Little money involved in bribes			Lots of money involved in bribes
	Attempts to achieve passive cooperation among targets	Attempts to achieve facilitating action among targets		Attempts to achieve active initiation among targets
Scope of corruption	Low-level officials			High-level officials
	Small number of officials			Large number of officials
	Minor decisions			Major decisions
	Small number of decisions			Large number of decisions
	Low frequency and pervasiveness—sporadic corruption	Medium frequency and pervasiveness—systemic corruption		High frequency and pervasiveness—institutionalized corruption
Type of corruption target	Nonprofit groups	Private corporations	International organizations	Public law enforcement officials and defense authorities
Kind of confrontation	Interaction with strong and resistant targets			Interaction with weak and willing targets

For corruption, a small bribe to a low-level official to exert some influence over a minor decision (sometimes termed "petty corruption"[9]) needs to be conceptually separated from spending massive funds to buy out an entire set of high-ranking officials (sometimes termed "grand corruption"[10]) so that their entire set of key decisions is completely externally controlled. The most severe corruption would appear to occur when "there is active complicity by some governments in permitting organized crime to thrive," where "states will sometimes seek to contain the problem of organized crime by turning a blind eye to some of its activities";[11] or when there is "the capture of the state's policies by criminal groups who are then able to unduly influence law

Table 3.2. Severity of Transnational Criminal Violence Tactics

	Lowest	*Lower*	*Higher*	*Highest*
Purpose of violence	Defensive deterrence of interfering action by others	Offensive intimidation of those wishing to interfere in criminal activities		Extermination of competing criminal or adversarial law enforcement groups
Mode of violence	Threats to use violence			Actual engaging in acts of violence
	Little harm done to persons or property	Significant harm done to persons or property	Numerous targets murdered or destroyed	Gruesome acts of mass carnage (such as beheadings)
	Impulsive unpremeditated aggression			Systematically planned and executed aggression
Scope of violence	Small number of individuals and groups affected			Large number of individuals and groups affected
	Low frequency and pervasiveness of violence within society			High frequency and pervasiveness of violence within society
Type of violence target	Rival criminal groups	Public law enforcement officials and defense authorities		Innocent citizens
Kind of confrontation	Battle with other criminals over sharing of power in a competitive environment			Battle with the state over establishing hegemony and criminal control

making, policy setting, and crucial (appeals court) judicial decisions" (called "state capture" by the World Bank).[12]

More specifically, at the individual level of analysis, a corruption severity scale could move from passive cooperators at the low end to facilitators to initiators of corruption (often drug-dealing police chiefs, generals, or dictators) at the high end; at the structural/institutional level of analysis, such a corruption scale could move from sporadic corruption at the low end to systemic corruption to institutionalized corruption (where there is a single "payoff cone") at the high end.[13] Expressed differently, criminal groups may engage in (1) lower-level narrow instrumental or operational corruption to facilitate cross-border trafficking activities, where criminals target customs and immigration officers charged with border protection; or (2) higher-level broader systemic or institutionalized corruption, where criminals target policy makers, bureaucrats, law enforcement personnel, and members of the judiciary "in order to maintain a low-risk environment from which they can operate with a high level of impunity."[14] As to the purpose of corruption, the severity ranking would appear to go (from low to high) from gaining access to a region of operation, to reducing the monitoring of criminal activities, to lightening criminal penalties, to establishing collusive relationships with those in power. The least severe criminal corruption efforts generally target nonprofit groups, with severity increasing when targeting private corporations, international organizations, and—the most severe level—public law enforcement and defense authorities. Interacting with weak and willing targets usually involves more severe corruption (although less criminal effort may be necessary to induce corruption here) than interaction with strong and resistant targets. Generally, the higher the level of corruption, the more difficult it is to root out.

For violence, threatening or carrying out the roughing up of a single individual is quite different from the systematic massacre of hundreds or thousands of people. The most severe violence would occur when transnational criminal organizations (1) seek to eradicate completely competing criminal forces or restraining law enforcement agents; or (2) engage in gruesome violence, such as the beheadings and mutilation recently witnessed in Mexico, against unarmed and often uninvolved citizens. Often the shock value surrounding violence—which usually gets more media coverage than corruption—depends on the level to which onlookers have been desensitized by recent events. Frequently, however, major severe incidents of violence have resulted in the most organized and effective law enforcement responses.

More specifically, the purpose of criminal violence ranges in severity from the defensive deterrence of interfering action by others to offensive intimidation of those who might interfere in criminal activities to extermination of competing criminal groups and adversarial law enforcement groups. The mode of violence ranges in severity from threats to actual application of violence, from little harm to persons and property to gruesome acts of mass carnage, and from impulsive unpremeditated aggression to systematically planned and executed aggression. The scope of violence ranges in severity from a small to a large number of individuals and groups affected, and from low to high frequency and pervasiveness of violence within societies. Criminal violence is considered least severe when targeting other criminal groups and most severe when targeting innocent citizen bystanders. Finally, in terms of the kind of confrontation involved, lower severity is associated with battles with other criminals over sharing of power in a competitive environment, and higher severity is associated with battles with the state over establishing hegemony and criminal control.

The Criminal Tactic of Corruption

The respected nongovernmental organization Transparency International has created a widely accepted definition of corruption as "the abuse of entrusted power for private gain."[15] Nonetheless, the close connections between corrupt and legitimate politics and business make isolating corruption quite difficult.[16] Corruption can be initiated from either side of a criminal transaction: illegal syndicates can initiate payoffs to police officers, politicians, and judges, or law enforcement authorities can elicit payments from shady businesses in return for overlooking illegal activities or reducing penalties.[17] Transnational criminal organizations often nurture close ties with political leaders and influential businesspeople, helping these individuals maintain or expand their power in return for impunity or a portion of the proceeds from public contracts.[18] Most generally, transnational criminals use corruption either to influence government authorities or to create their own state.

Recently, the occurrence—or at least its detection and exposure—of corruption worldwide has been on the rise. The U.S. Department of Justice has a dim view of the current state of affairs regarding criminal corruption:

> International organized criminals must corrupt public officials to operate and protect their illegal operations, and to increase their sphere of influence. They have been successful in systematically corrupting public officials around the world, including countries of vital strategic importance to the United States. . . .
>
> In some countries, corrupt public figures and organized criminals have attained status, power and wealth far outweighing those of legitimate authorities. In others, corruption occurs as an accepted means of doing business. Corrupt foreign leaders who aid, support and are beholden to organized crime cause substantial harm to their own people and often to U.S. strategic interests. In the most serious instances, the corrupt official him [sic] or herself is for all practical purposes the leader of an organized criminal group.[19]

Before the 1990s, it was common[20] to think of "corruption as something largely confined to the developing countries, where economic hardship means that norms of 'due process' tend to be less deeply rooted than they are in the wealthier liberal democracies"; if scandals did emerge within advanced industrial society governments, this viewpoint would interpret their exposure as evidence that existing due process norms ensured that such corruption would remain "incidental and sporadic." Since that time, however, the spate of prominent political leaders embroiled in scandals across a growing number of democratic states—including, for example, Felipe González in Spain, Neil Hamilton in Great Britain, Bettino Craxi in Italy, Helmut Kohl in Germany, and Edith Cresson of the European Commission—has forced analysts "to consider whether democratic arrangements might not actually harbour institutions whose functioning itself tended to *stimulate* corruption."[21] Perhaps for this reason the first multilateral agreement among states to combat bribery of foreign officials did not occur until May 1994.[22]

Most basically, transnational criminal use of corruption may often be due to states' attempts to interfere with shady cross-border commerce:

> One should not lose sight of the fact that it is the very existence of state controls that makes it necessary for smugglers and other criminalized transnational actors to try to devise such creative and elaborate means to evade and circumvent them. Transnational crimes such as drug trafficking and migrant smuggling are so enormously profitable precisely because states impose and enforce prohibitions. Transnational criminal organizations attempt to bully and buy off state officials, but in most cases this is primarily because they lack the capacity to bypass them. Corruption reflects state weakness, but also state power: most transnational criminals, after all, would prefer to evade state controls entirely rather than have to pay for state protection and nonenforcement of the law.[23]

In this regard, it is noteworthy that corruption is at least as rampant in weak states without meaningful law enforcement mechanisms as in strong states with ironclad law enforcement. Overall, across most countries "official corruption (that is, committed by officers of the state) and organised crime feed off each other, and often work hand in glove."[24]

Criminal corruption conforms nicely with prevailing values in areas in which it occurs: "The symbiosis of corruption and legitimacy is created, sustained and developed by the political configurations that mark out some countries as especially propitious for criminal enterprise."[25] Consensus exists that susceptibility to corruption across countries is a function of both weak law enforcement and supportive cultural norms.[26] As exemplified by Colombia, a defective social order is often critical to susceptibility to corruption, and the government alone—even if unaffected by corruption—is incapable of remedying related social order problems. In particular, the causes of corruption include cultural attitudes not supportive of a country's democratic institutions, beliefs that law and its enforcement are negotiable, insufficient public pressure on politicians to act responsibly, patron-client relationships allowing personal connections to facilitate illicit exchanges, executive autonomy with protection from outside scrutiny and bureaucratic checks, and long-term dominance of a single political party or parties.[27] The use of corruption by transnational criminal organizations thus often reflects asymmetric power: the more societies exhibit privileged inequality rather than merit-based opportunity, or have weak or nonexistent law enforcement, the more likely criminal groups are to pay bribes in order to secure jobs or other favors.[28]

Frequently the personal attitudes of individual government bureaucrats contribute to the susceptibility to corruption:

> Prime locations for criminal groups are those in which the personal interests and loyalties of public officials take precedence over most civic considerations. In such circumstances, relations are based on a system of nearly unchecked power; there is a precarious reliance on persons rather than institutions. Indeed, where so-called leaders constantly jockey for position and control over ever diminishing resources, and when political survival is based more on the dispensation of favors to loyal followers than on any public legitimacy, there is little room for the business of institutional government.[29]

The lure of money to officials is substantial: it is thus not surprising to see incidents occur such as "Vladimir Montesinos's use of office to traffic arms, drugs and cash, and A. Q. Khan's use of office to traffic nuclear goods and services";[30] or the March 2008 revelation that officials in the Bulgarian Chief Directorate for Combating Organized Crime had contacts with businessmen linked to transnational organized crime.[31] The presence of government trappings in such corrupt dealings can make the transactions seem legitimate in the eyes of some participants. One of the unintended consequences of democratization is the long-term weakening of pre-existing formal and informal authoritarian institutions in such a way that the rules of the game become considerably more ambiguous, opening the door to corruption. Especially within new democracies, the increased blurring between legal and illegal activities has led many of the police to have too close relationships with members of criminal organizations, breeding "suspicion for the law and law enforcement agencies, both of which are seen as not impartial and predictable instruments of the state, but as political instruments."[32]

The prevalence of corruption, however, is not simply a function of deficiencies in local cultures or national governments. Transnational organized crime finds the corruption tactic quite in tune with the globally promoted emphasis on material wealth. As more people in more societies measure success through money, the scarcity of legitimate income-generating activities in much of the world makes corruption an easy and logical means to this end.

Some observers make the overly sweeping blanket claim that global corruption "hurts everyone," but realistically it does trap many people in poverty and misery; breed social, economic, and political unrest; undermine democracy and the rule of law; distort international trade; jeopardize sound governance and private sector ethics; endanger the sustainability of natural resources; and threaten domestic and international security.[33] More concretely, corruption may spread contagiously within the organizations affected and may create an arbitrary and unequal distribution of money and other resources, subvert accountability and a sense of trust and collective responsibility within liberal democratic regimes, waste duly collected taxes and trigger a financial drain on the state, promote capital flight and reduced domestic and foreign investment, and perpetuate administrative inefficiency.[34] Criminally induced corruption may decrease the reporting of crimes because of the fear of retaliation, endangering entire communities. Looking at the global picture, "almost half of the world's countries have been brought nearly to economic and political ruin by misguided and corrupt leadership, estimated losses due to corruption exceed some countries' foreign debts," and "corruption and incompetence have degraded state institutions to the point that there is a chronic inability to deal with perceived social injustice and deprivations."[35]

Although transnational criminal organizations often possess more firepower than target state governments, "they cannot sustain direct violence against official bodies," so "they use bribery in order to corrupt the legal system and evade prosecution, with their vast amounts of ready cash affording them considerable flexibility in suborning key government officials."[36] Moreover, the bribery involved in corruption may reflect efforts by transnational criminals to gain legitimacy and to receive special favorable treatment. Given that criminal leaders may wish "to become part of the social elite from which they often feel they have been intentionally excluded," they try to convince both private citizens and government officials that their wealth derives from legitimate sources and activities, and through that ruse criminals attempt to forge strong and lasting bonds facilitating peaceful coexistence and mutual assistance with members of the established political, social, and economic infrastructure.[37]

Although generally "low levels of transparency encourage high levels of corruption,"[38] corruption can in some ways become more subtle as monitoring (or fear of monitoring) increases. For example, in some places the "old-fashioned cash-for-favors exchange" may be in the process of being replaced by "a system that trades political influence for campaign financing, international 'business trips' on corporate jets, and highly-paid post-government employment."[39] These styles of corruption adapt and mutate depending on the opportunities and limitations encountered.

The Criminal Tactic of Violence

Violence is "any act or situation that injures the health and well-being of others, including direct attacks on a person's physical or psychological integrity, as well as destructive actions that do not necessarily involve a direct relationship between the victim and the institution responsible for the harm."[40] Intimidating threats of physical harm are included here. With regard to transnational organized crime, this tactic is sometimes termed "violent entrepreneurship," reflecting the use of force to make money.[41]

Considering violence broadly beyond the domain of transnational organized crime, today there is a staggering scale of global violence, as "murders, kidnappings, and car-jackings are part of daily life in the sprawling megacities of the developing world"[42] and in many advanced industrial societies. Because the scope and severity of violence (outside of formal wars) have become more visible in recent decades, in many states the shock value of witnessing frequent deaths through unnatural means has substantially diminished, leading to a desensitized fatalistic acceptance of continuing escalating carnage.

In this international security context, new kinds of violence have emerged, not "waged by armies but by groups we today call terrorists, guerrillas, bandits, and robbers."[43] Ongoing threats now operate within a system in which states no longer have even close to a monopoly on the use of instruments of violence.[44] Undeclared conflicts within states are increasing at the same time as declared wars between states are decreasing, with death rates seemingly constantly on the rise from unending armed aggression. In that vein, much of the violence occurring in the world today is in the form of "nonstate wars," occurring when a state has limited capacity to impose order or has simply collapsed:[45] in these cases, mass populations suffer tremendously, with campaigns of often brutal violence against civilians carried out by nonstate forces (including transnational criminal organizations). Indeed, 75 percent of those killed in all wars today are civilians.[46]

The global occurrence of subnational and transnational violence has complex psychological, sociological, political, and economic roots. Traditional sources include the aggressive nature of individual humans, sharp divides within states, inequality and rising expectations, detrimental internal characteristics of states (including dysfunctional political systems), and volatile conditions within the global system that are conducive to militarizing disputes. Strong ethnic, racial, or religious identifications within societies, compounded by virulent nationalism, abuse of human rights, relative deprivation, greed, or demonization of enemies, can also lead to bloodshed. High unemployment rates in many countries, combined with high frustration with the status quo and distrust of the state government, provide an ample supply of those ready to commit violence for personal gain. The ready access by subversive societal elements to powerful weaponry—often superior to that of local armies and police forces—is a crucial trigger for violence. Some analysts view violence as a "cultural trait" and identify cultures dependent on the existence of crime,[47] because of a long history of uninterrupted carnage without significant protest or with significant glorification of this activity from within affected societies. Weak law enforcement structures and the absence of civil society eliminate the expected restraints on the violent expression of disagreements. It is commonly assumed that the prevalence of unsanctioned societal violence is a symptom of a state's inherent instability and the absence of civil society.

Turning specifically to the violence associated with transnational organized crime, recent events "have highlighted the continued willingness of organized crime syndicate members to use violently ruthless means to protect and expand their criminal domains."[48] Overall homicide rates correlate with the extent of organized crime activity in countries as diverse as the United States, Colombia, Mexico, and Italy.[49] A classic illustration of criminal violence occurred in August 2007, when, in a dispute between two rival gangs in the 'Ndrangheta crime syndicate (part of the Italian Mafia), six Italian men were killed as they left a pizzeria in Duisburg, Germany, with the killers firing at least seventy shots with automatic weapons, followed by shooting each victim once in the head.[50] The ongoing extreme violence by the Mexican drug lords provides another contemporary example. Transnational criminal acts of violence, typically "carefully planned and executed with professional skills and due caution," are usually difficult for police to solve even without considering the investigative reluctance associated with corruption or fear of retaliation.[51]

Even from the perspective of stable advanced industrial societies, the presence of criminally induced violence can be disruptive. Within the United States, for example, violent transnational criminal activities not only pose "a threat to the physical security of the U.S. public" but also endanger the country's economic well-being and law enforcement officials' ability to investigate violent crimes; outside of the United States, transnational criminals' use of violent tactics "threaten U.S. interests when their violence sustains and increases their power to operate globally."[52] Because any citizen could become a victim of transnational criminal violence, doubts can develop about whether national governments are fulfilling their protection responsibilities: "The proliferation of nonstate violence, a threat to state authority in and of itself, begins to erode civil society as people question the ability of state officials to offer protection, further undermining the authority of the state."[53] Violence can promote a variety of forms of social dysfunction "through the enforcement of deviant authority and order."[54] Sometimes widespread criminal use of violence galvanizes state authorities to respond with massive coercive retaliation against perpetrators perceived to be both unsavory and ruthless,[55] triggering an escalating negative action-reaction cycle.

Transnational criminal organizations play a direct role in promoting global violence in three major ways: armed conflict can result from a violent struggle between a predatory transnational criminal organization and a state government; transnational organized crime can emerge as a by-product of armed conflict and other forms of political violence; and armed conflict or lower-level violence may result from intense competition among transnational criminal groups, particularly those adopting symbiotic or parasitic strategies.[56] Transnational organized crime "is seldom the root cause of armed conflict, but it is a major source of revenue for terrorists, warring factions, insurgencies, and underdeveloped states in conflict"; and "conflict intervention and peace agreements are much more difficult to achieve when opposing forces have the resources to continue fighting."[57] Thus criminal groups both internally use violence to achieve their own illicit ends and externally promote the use of violence by others.

Violent criminals possess different implicit and explicit metrics for gauging the success of this tactic, with many expecting not tangible outright target capitulation for immediate purposes but rather intangible offensive intimidation and defensive deterrence useful for long-term benefits. Because transnational criminals use violence as an instrumental means toward designated ends, the occurrence of violence might be associated with criminal concern that control of a desired area or activity was not secure. Within regions containing highly valuable contested assets or targets, few organizations are likely to feel secure over the long run.

On the surface it might seem logical to assume that the more entrenched and well established a transnational criminal organization becomes, the less it would depend on the violence tactic to achieve its goals. One might specifically expect that, as transnational organized crime moves from the pursuit of monopolistic control—where it "brooks no competition," suppresses rivals, and seeks "exclusive influence" in operational areas[58]—toward mutual cooperation to achieve common goals,[59] there should be a decline in the use of violence normally associated with turf protection. Indeed, there is some evidence that as criminal cartels move through three evolutionary stages—aggressive competitor, subtle co-opter, and criminal state successor—their reliance on violent tactics to achieve their illicit ends may become more limited and carefully calculated.[60] Even well-established transnational criminals, however, continue to employ terror tactics and "selected and calibrated violence" to fulfill certain types of operational aims:[61] most commonly, "it is directed outward to intimidate or eliminate rivals and threats, and it is directed inward to enforce discipline within the organization."[62] Beyond these purposes, violence may serve the purposes of transnational criminal organizations when a state government frontally attacks them or "political elites fail to provide the protection that the criminals have come to expect through the development of symbiotic relationships."[63]

Similarly, on the surface one might readily expect violence to always be a tactic of last resort for transnational criminal organizations because corruption is more widespread and accepted among more countries of the world than is violence, reflected by the substantially greater penalties that most places impose for those convicted for violence than for those convicted for corruption. The desire of many transnational criminal organizations to remain low profile would also seem to reinforce the preference for corruption over violence. Furthermore, it would seem that the presence of criminally induced corruption and criminally induced violence within a society ought to be inversely proportional, with transnational organized crime feeling that widespread corruption successful at achieving its ends makes violence unnecessary. However, the dark logic of transnational criminal organizations is more complicated than this simple hydraulic relationship, and therefore— regardless of state penalties or low-profile desires—transnational criminal organizations do not use violence only as a tactic of last resort.

INDIVIDUAL/HUMAN SECURITY VERSUS NATIONAL/ STATE SECURITY IMPACTS

Transnational criminal activities present grave long-term individual, national, and international security dangers, especially if security encompasses not just safeguarding against incoming military threats but also maintaining an effectively functioning society.[64] Determining which of these distinct levels is subject to the most direct devastating security disruptions from transnational criminal activities is a function of changing circumstances rather than a fixed general formula. Although transnational criminal activities often affect both individual and state security simultaneously, this study's quest is to discover when each security impact is likely to be the primary one with the most devastating ramifications. Figure 3.2 depicts the contrasting orientation of individual security versus state security in response to transnational criminal activities.

Global Significance

Both individual/human and national/state security policies attempt to protect against disruptions to the status quo within states. One focuses on keeping those in power safe and the political regime intact, whereas the other focuses on keeping the mass citizenry safe and keeping societal norms and the way of life intact. Left unchecked, transnational organized crime would significantly alter the status quo in both cases in ways that would be highly disruptive to those affected.

The irony embedded in having threats to individual and state security escalating within today's international relations setting is that there are now an unprecedented number of global governmental institutions, informal multilateral regimes, and transnational nonprofit organizations attempting to bring order and cooperation to the international system and attempting to restrain the disruptive impact of unruly forces such as transnational organized crime. The sorry state of individual and state security in many parts of the world thus reflects poorly on the success of any form of global governance.

Figure 3.2. Contrasting orientation of individual security versus state security in response to transnational criminal activities

---

INDIVIDUAL/HUMAN SECURITY ORIENTATION

Individual security objectives

Provides a safe environment protecting the welfare of ordinary citizens.

Maintains and promotes civil society.

Primary fears

Instills fear of threatened violence and pressured corruption to promote compliance.

Demoralizes citizens, alienates them from the government, and deprives them of basic rights.

Primary targets protected

Affects innocent individual citizens and neighborhood groups.

Interferes with small businesses, private nonprofit organizations, and multinational corporations.

Typical modes of criminal infiltration

Fosters purchases illicitly obtained well below the prevailing market price.

Gets people addicted to consumption of vice-oriented goods and services.

Common means of individual protection

Leads to highly decentralized and well-publicized neighborhood watches.

Stimulates public education about criminal threat.

NATIONAL/STATE SECURITY ORIENTATION

State security objectives

Protects the government regime and its national interests.

Maintains and promotes political stability and regime legitimacy.

Primary fears

Makes government institutions dysfunctional, impeding democracy and the rule of law.

Undermines state sovereign control, drains state funds, and tarnishes image of trust.

Primary targets protected

Affects key political leaders.

Endangers government institutions and buildings.

Typical modes of criminal infiltration

Induces government officials to accept or ignore criminal activities.

Fosters an image of legitimacy for all criminal activities.

Common means of state protection

Leads to centralized and top-secret contingency plans for protecting key government leaders and structures.

Stimulates covert containment of criminal elements to keep them far from administrative structures.

Means of Gauging Severity

An examination of the global security predicament reveals a huge variance in the severity evidenced of insecurity at both the individual/human level and the national/state level, directly affecting when nonstate governance from below is most and least disruptive to the functioning of government and society. Some individuals lack any access to basic survival needs, enjoy few, if any, basic human rights, and are constantly in fear and exposed to life-threatening peril, whereas others live in the lap of luxury with all the rights in the world in heavily fortified and protected areas. Some states are failing, unable to carry out any significant government functions effectively, unable to garner any significant public support, and unable to last more than a short period of time, whereas other states have regimes and leaders that are quite stable and popular and reflect political systems that have functioned well for centuries. Transnational organized crime tends to thrive in areas where individual security and state security are lowest.

Severity scales for individual and state security disruptions have been much more widely discussed than those for corruption and violence. Especially within democracies, severe internal disruptions to individual and state security are often difficult for governments to manage while simultaneously attempting to maintain the civil liberties of the citizenry. As with the severity of corruption and violence, there needs to be much better identification of thresholds of individual and state (and global) security disruption beyond which restraining intervention would be warranted. As an initial move in this direction, tables 3.3 and 3.4 present a summary of the various ways to gauge the severity of the transnational criminal impact on individual/human security and on national/state security.

Examining first the severity of the criminal impact on individual security, the psychological effects seem low when people feel secure and protected and bask in a positive national glow, and seem high when people constantly sense fear and danger and are demoralized and depressed. The economic effects seem low when people live in the lap of luxury and banks are stable, and seem high when people lack basic survival needs and banks collapse. The social effects seem low when social institutions are stable and helpful and community associations flourish, and seem high when social institutions are dysfunctional and community associations wither. The political effects seem low when citizens enjoy full political freedoms and are fully participatory politically, and seem high when citizens lack human rights and are alienated from

Table 3.3. Severity of criminal impact on individual/human security

	Low	High
Psychological effects	People feeling totally secure and protected	People feeling constant sense of fear and danger
	People basking in positive glow	People totally demoralized and depressed
Economic effects	People living in the lap of luxury	People lacking basic survival needs
	Banks stable	Banks collapsing
Social effects	Social institutions stable and helpful	Social institutions dysfunctional
	Community associations flourishing	Community associations withering
Political effects	Citizens enjoying full political freedoms	Citizens lacking human rights
	Citizens fully participatory politically	Citizens alienated from political system
Protection effects	Police fortifying area from harm	Lots of loss of life, personal injury, and property damage
	Violence rare and frowned upon	Violence epidemic and accepted as inevitable
	Law enforcement ironclad	Law enforcement spotty and ineffective
	Order-promoting neighborhood watches	Order-destroying chaos and anarchy

Table 3.4. Severity of criminal impact on national/state security

	Low	High
Effect on regime viability	Government and ideology stable	Government failed or failing
	State functioning coherently and effectively	State unable to carry out vital functions
	Leaders rotating regularly but infrequently	Frequent irregular turnover of leaders
	Rule of law and democratic institutions intact	Eroding democratic institutions and rule of law
Effect on state integrity	Minimal corruption among state officials	Rampant corruption among state officials
	Criminal element kept out of government	Criminal element taking over government
Effect on popular support	Huge public support for government	Little popular support for government
	Citizens feeling government is accountable	Citizens feeling government is not accountable
Effect on opposition movements	No significant domestic opposition	Powerful insurgents capable of regime overthrow
	Little internal grumbling about regime	Massive vocal demands for new political leadership
Effect on outside involvement	Domestic control by legitimate local authorities	Control by foreigners opposing state interests
	International image of trust maintained	International image of trust tarnished

the political system. Finally, protection effects seem low when police fortify an area from harm, violence is rare and frowned upon, law enforcement is ironclad, and order-promoting neighborhood watches proliferate; and these effects seem high when there is considerable loss of life, personal injuries, and property damage, when violence is epidemic and accepted as inevitable, when law enforcement is spotty and ineffective, and when order-destroying chaos and anarchy prevail.

Turning to the severity of the criminal impact on state security, a key dimension is the effect on regime viability: this effect seems low when the government and ideology are stable, the state is able to function coherently and effectively, leaders rotate regularly but infrequently, and the rule of law and democratic institutions remain intact; and this effect seems high when the government has failed or is failing, the state is unable to carry out vital functions, frequent irregular leader turnover occurs, and democratic institutions and the rule of law are eroding. The effect on state integrity seems low when minimal corruption exists among state officials and the criminal element is kept out of government, and seems high when rampant corruption exists among state officials and the criminal element takes over the government. The effect on popular support seems low when huge public support exists for the government and when citizens feel the government is accountable, and seems high when little public support for the government exists and citizens feel that the government is not accountable. The effect on opposition movements is low when there is no significant domestic opposition and little internal grumbling about the regime, and seems high when powerful insurgents emerge capable of overthrowing the regime and massive vocal demands emerge for new political leadership. Finally, the effect on outside involvement seems low when domestic control exists through legitimate local authorities and an international image of trust is maintained, and seems high when foreigners gain control with interests different from those of the state and when the international image of trust is tarnished.

Individual/Human Security Impacts

Looking first at individual security, although there are numerous variations on its definition, most analysts focus on "the welfare of ordinary people."[65] Whereas state security emphasizes protection of the government regime and its national interests, individual or human security emphasizes from a bottom-up perspective "the provision of a relatively safe environment in which citizens do not fear violence or intimidation."[66] Ironically, it is precisely this kind of fear—of both threatened violence and pressured corruption—that criminals often most seek to instill in target populations in order to promote compliance with their illicit global transfers. When transnational criminal organizations become too powerful, people live in constant fear, facing the kind of arbitrary decisions about their fate traditionally encountered in repressive dictatorships. Overall, transnational organized crime "has had a profound impact on human security, imperiling numerous individuals worldwide."[67]

The concerns of individual citizens and state governments often diverge—governments may not care if citizens obtain illicit goods or suffer personal losses because of crime, and citizens may not care if government officials take bribes or in other ways violate fair business practices. Moreover, the security measures for protecting mass populations are quite distinct from those involved in keeping a regime in power: for example, in deterring disruptive activity, the means for protecting a state's citizens from harm may involve highly decentralized and well-publicized "neighborhood watches" or public education about the criminal threat; in contrast, the means for keeping a state regime in power may involve highly centralized and top-secret contingency plans for protecting key government leaders or for keeping criminals away from administrative structures. Furthermore, family, ethnic, or national ties still play some role in transnational organized crime, with distinguishing codes of recognition reducing the chances of hostile penetration,[68] and these ties can be inherently dangerous to social cohesion. Indeed, "ethnic links, with their systems of loyalty, solidarity, and sanctions often superimposed on the legislation of the countries where immigrants live, indirectly facilitate the implantation of organized crime."[69]

More specifically, transnational criminal activities can threaten human security by making people demoralized and socioeconomic institutions dysfunctional, degrading the lives of law-abiding citizens.[70] For example, in West Africa, the effects of drug trafficking on human security have recently been "devastating": because drug traffickers have far more resources than these poor West African states, this illicit activity funds and perpetuates regional insurgencies, scaring away tourists and business investors and making socioeconomic problems "ever more intractable."[71] These criminal activities may undermine human rights and freedoms and transparent justice in domestic affairs. Transnational criminals can disrupt society "by offering incentives to the marginalized segments of the population trying to cope with the adjustment costs of globalization."[72] Citizens may feel disconnected and alienated from a de facto authority structure quite dissimilar from that they were led to expect and depriving them of any real policy-making input. They may become angry and hypercritical of a system that would allow this kind of development to occur, leading to friction among social groups with different opinions about the problem. Aside from government agencies (incorporated in the state security section), the victims of transnational organized crime include innocent individual civilians, neighborhood groups, small businesses, private nonprofit organizations, and multinational corporations.

National/State Security Impacts

Moving to state security, transnational organized crime poses a direct top-down challenge to states' sovereign ability to control what transpires within their boundaries.[73] The entrance of transnational criminal organizations often causes business activities to be directed by foreigners whose interests differ sharply from those of the state. Yet, in comparison to terrorism, transnational organized crime may have a less direct and immediate impact on national security: "The terrorist threat is rather like smallpox—when it erupts it is immediate and devastating in its impact; transnational organized crime, in contrast, is rather more like AIDS—it breaks down the defences of the body politic, using corruption as a selectively targeted instrument to weaken or neutralize law enforcement, the judiciary, and even the government as a whole."[74]

More specifically, transnational organized crime may disrupt state security by impeding the development of democratic institutions and the rule of law (by interfering with law enforcement agencies, police forces, and courts of justice), thus endangering political stability and regime legitimacy. This impact by disruptive transnational forces on state security is not new, as during the nineteenth century in western Europe, "there was also a plethora of political activity by nonstate actors who utilized migration channels and immigrant communities to mobilize transnationally and, at times, employed political violence that challenged state security interests."[75] Criminal activities "can destabilize the internal cohesion of the state and also undermine the components of power so important to realists and security planners": these illicit activities can sap national government power by draining potential tax revenues and inducing the dedication of more resources to border control and law enforcement for violence control, and they can reduce a state's soft power by tarnishing, through rampant corruption, a government's image of trust and authority in the international system.[76] As discussed in the previous chapter, in their most dominant manifestation, transnational criminal organizations may even replace traditional state authority and functions completely. Furthermore, global criminal activity challenges two foundational elements of state authority—the monopoly on violence and border control.[77] Indeed, "in their search for illicit profits, criminals implicitly and explicitly . . . work at cross purposes to the aim of good government, which is to protect the rights, property, welfare, and security of its citizens."[78] Even for nondemocratic authoritarian states, the presence of pervasive and powerful transnational criminal activities within their national boundaries can readily subvert any of the principles and plans pursued by national political leaders. Overall, the greatest national security concern by Western defense officials appears to be the threat of the criminal dissemination of weapons of mass destruction.[79]

International System Impacts

Although this study focuses on contrasting individual/human security and national/state security, the corruption and violence tactics of transnational criminal organizations do affect the international system, working more through disruption to states than to individuals. These global consequences involve changing the rules, creating new players, and reconfiguring power.[80] With an increasing number and power of unruly transnational nonstate groups, including terrorists with whom criminals frequently do business, those facilitating illicit transfers seem bound together by a desire to attack the rule of law "either to destroy it or (as in more recent times) to change it radically."[81] The ensuing challenge to the integrity of Western societies[82] constitutes "one of the most serious security threats to democratic institutions, the rule of law, community welfare, and basic values and norms," for "a corrupt society ravaged by greed, violence, lawlessness and drugs does not allow, let alone support, the flourishing of a democratic, stable civilization and of a peaceful world."[83]

More specifically, transnational criminal activities can interfere with the underlying intent of the enlightened principles behind an open globalized system permitting the unencumbered movement of goods, services, people, and ideas across national boundaries. In terms of goods and services, transnational criminal activities can promote purchases illicitly obtained well below the prevailing market price, purchases of counterfeit merchandise, or, alternatively, purchases reflecting items prevailing societal values associate with vice rather than with virtue; in all cases, the norms of fair market value, integrity of production process, transparency in transactions, or upholding the law are undermined. As to the cross-boundary movement of people, transnational criminal activities can transform the societally desired free choice of those with the capabilities to relocate internationally into a societally undesired "bait-and-switch" operation in which people who cannot legally move pay exorbitant prices only to find themselves in virtual slavery once they arrive at their destinations. With regard to ideas, besides their traditional emphasis on the accumulation of power, resources, and territory, a greater international security threat may now lie in transnational criminal organizations' control of information[84] (including ownership of data, manipulation of data, and dissemination/transmission of data) that is vital to the functioning of global society.

Transnational criminal activities thus can "subvert the norms and institutions that underpin global order"[85] and can undermine progress toward the development a global civil society.[86] Illicit cross-border global transfers can, in effect, set up covert transnational governance systems to replace the existing state-centric world order. The net effect is to weaken dramatically and directly undercut attempts by legitimate political, economic, and social cross-national institutions to formulate and implement transparent international mechanisms incorporating fair market value and following existing laws to promote the smooth orderly functioning of the international system with integrity following the dictates of global civil society.

CONCLUDING THOUGHTS

With regard to the choice of corruption tactics versus violence tactics, this chapter's basic premise is that transnational criminal organizations discriminate carefully between these two distinct ways to achieve their goals, and that this choice reflects two very different orientations. This premise directly challenges the notion that transnational criminals are impulsive mindless irrational thugs who do not engage in serious premeditation—and who do not systematically study what has worked and what has failed in the past—before undertaking their criminal activities. This premise pivotally implies that states possess the capacity to alter the mix of corruption versus violence criminals use by sensitively and selectively altering the economic incentives and disincentives, regulations, enforcement focal points, and penalties applied to various kinds of unruly behavior. To accomplish this end, national governments and international organizations confronting transnational organized crime need to be highly discriminating in recognizing which of these two very different tactics is predominant and in dealing with them in such a way as to reduce their security disruption.

As to individual/human security versus national/state security impacts, transnational criminal activities challenge the traditional state-centric national security emphasis on state governments and call for a rethinking of security priorities. Although some observers still assume that the only prospective danger from transnational organized crime is state failure or violent restructuring of the regime,[87] in reality the human security threat posed to stable civil society is at least as important due not only to the searing trauma it creates within society but also to its upward-moving disruption of political stability. As used by transnational criminal organizations, both corruption and violence have identifiable and relatively predictable ways of gradually eroding critical attitudes of trust and institutions of integrity within any society.

Accepting the notion that transnational criminal activities affect both private and public individuals and institutions means that any protection system must address the vulnerability of both sets of targets. The blurring of military and police functions that results from these two sets of targets' intertwined needs calls out for much more cross-bureau cooperation, information sharing, and flexibility in tackling the ominous global criminal threat. The susceptibility of all those involved in this effort to both corruption and violence call out for more checks and balances, protective measures, and accountability systems to ensure the proper functioning of this anticrime effort.

For full comprehension and effective management, it seems essential to link the tactical choices of transnational criminal organizations to the security impacts of their activities, for there appears to be a tight synergistic relationship between the two. Becoming aware that a particular transnational criminal organization tends to rely more on corruption or violence—and the type and context of the corruption and violence applied—provides an important clue to what kind of security impact its activities are having and thus what kind of protective response might be most effective. Conversely, knowing that a particular transnational criminal activity tends to be associated more with an individual or state security impact provides a crucial hint about what kind of tactic is being used to accomplish illicit ends and thus about what kinds of thwarting countermeasures might be effective. In the current clash between regulators and transnational organized crime, neither the type of criminal tactic nor the type of security impact appears to be a focus of interdiction efforts.

4 MAJOR TRANSNATIONAL CRIMINAL ORGANIZATIONS

THIS CHAPTER FOCUSES ON the traditional "Big Five" transnational criminal organizations—the Chinese triads, the Colombian cartels, the Italian Mafia, the Japanese Yakuza, and the Russian Mob. The analysis is composed of three parts—general organizational background, the choice of criminal tactics of corruption versus violence, and the criminal impact on individual/human security versus national/state security. The discussion intentionally encompasses brief summaries rather than detailed descriptions of the patterns described. This chapter does make a concerted effort to highlight changes in groups over time, differences among them, and prevailing trends and future directions in their development.

Three principal clarifications appear necessary to correct common misconceptions about these five major transnational criminal organizations. First, aside from key differences in the tactics chosen and the security impacts generated, these organizations vary considerably in terms of years of existence, membership size, geographical scope beyond their home base, cultural scope beyond their original nationality/ethnicity, range of activities, government ties, and principles of conduct. Second, none of these five organizations is monolithic, as each contains several discrete elements, and because each criminal group is increasingly fluid, decentralized, and highly adaptive to changing international circumstances, patterns are neither static nor uniform across countries. Third, in recent years transnational organized crime has diversified well beyond these five major players to include other large emerging criminal syndicates—such as Albanian, Mexican, and Nigerian criminal organizations—as well as a proliferation of "mom-and-pop" operations; the lucrative opportunities have been simply too tempting to keep entrants out of illicit trade, and the barriers to entry in most parts of the world are quite low. Indeed, "the fragmentation of organized crime seems to be a worldwide trend," and "this new generation of 'Mafias' does not conform to the hierarchical, static, and semi-bureaucratic structures"—"in many cases, territorially oriented groups have been replaced by criminal organizations that are smaller, less stable, and lighter on their feet."[1] As a consequence of these realities, assigning blame for a particular transnational criminal problem to one particular organization is increasingly difficult, and caution should be exercised when drawing overarching conclusions about transnational organized crime from an analysis of the "Big Five."

These major transnational criminal groups have many interlocking connections with one another. The Chinese triads have long-standing ties to the Italian Mafia, beginning in 1972 when Turkey banned opium production, forcing the Italian Mafia to look for new go-betweens to provide a reliable supply of opium to sell in the United States;[2] the triads and the Japanese Yakuza have recently formed an alliance, as the Chinese spread to Tokyo and other large cities in Japan has necessitated cooperation with the local Yakuza syndicates;[3] the triads are in business with Colombian cartels, specifically introducing the Colombian cocaine barons to the heroin manufacturing process;[4] and, when opening up operations in the United States, the triads cozied up to the Russian Mob, as the Mob and triads cooperate in running illegal immigration circuits.[5] The Colombian cartels and the Russian Mob formed strategic alliances in the early 1990s, and sometimes the Italian Mafia has participated in joint ventures with these two groups; the Colombian cartels have also networked with the Japanese Yakuza, Nigerian organized crime syndicates transporting cocaine to Europe, Mexican organized crime groups, and criminal gangs in the United States.[6] The Russian Mob has colluded with local Chinese gangs in the Russian Far East, the Italian Mafia, and Colombian cartels.[7] Because of this web of interconnections and membership diversification, it is admittedly somewhat anachronistic to identify each of these five groups strictly according to their ethnic membership or cultural/national origins.[8]

Aside from cross-group collusion, these transnational criminal organizations collaborate with governments and multinational corporations. This symbiotic relationship can work to mutual advantage: for example, the Colombian cartels have co-opted elements of the government police and military to help provide transport and protect drug shipments in return for noninterference in legitimate transactions, the Japanese Yakuza has caused government police to "look the other way" during illicit operations in return for information and maintenance of order in an area, and the Russian Mob has made deals with multinational corporations to guarantee their access to natural resources in return for funds sustaining its criminal activities.[9] In some cases, transnational criminals would have difficulty entering or thriving within a country without this cooperation with legitimate government or corporate officials. Because of these manifold ties with other criminal groups, governments, and multinational corporations, it would be misleading to evaluate transnational criminal organizations in a vacuum, as if each operated alone.

CHINESE TRIADS

General Organizational Background

The Chinese triads comprise an ethnically Chinese consortium composed of seven major groups: the Sun Yee On (based in Hong Kong and the largest and most powerful of the triads), the Wo Group, the 14K, the Luen, the Big Circle Gang, the United Bamboo, and the Four Seas Gang. The combined membership is about 300,000.[10] Originating in the seventeenth century as revolutionary political associations, the triads have now grown to become a truly global force. Many elements contributed to this post–Cold War overseas expansion, including the liberal American offer of political asylum after the 1989 Tiananmen Square protests[11] and the changes that followed the Chinese takeover of Hong Kong in 1997. Today, however, much transnational activity by Chinese criminal organizations is based on *guanxi* networks rather than on traditional hierarchical structured organizations like the triads, as they may not have adapted as well as they might have to the criminal opportunities provided by globalization: for example, human smuggling operations in the area have often been controlled by small entrepreneurial groups.[12]

Within China, criminal gangs are most active in Shanghai, Tianjin, Shenyang, Guangzhou, and Hong Kong, and "the number of people involved in organized crime on the mainland has risen from around 100,000 in 1986 to around 1.5 million in 2000."[13] The foreign countries in which the Chinese triads are most active include Australia, Canada, France, Germany, Italy, Japan, Korea, Macao, the Netherlands, New Zealand, the Philippines, Saudi Arabia, Taiwan, Thailand, the United Kingdom, the United States (where they are known as "tongs"), and Vietnam—basically anywhere where there is a substantial Chinese émigré community. Indeed, "no matter where these migrants have established their communities, Triad societies have set themselves up."[14]

The Chinese triads are now involved in illegal gambling, extortion, prostitution, loan sharking, credit card fraud, drug trafficking, counterfeiting, money laundering, and running massage parlors.[15] Showing their capacity to outmaneuver competitors, the Chinese triads have become the dominant illicit trader for most of Asia's narcotics.[16] Since the 1990s, the triads have shown considerable versatility by expanding into both new territories and new illicit activities: over the last decade and a half, the triads have branched out into the home decorating business; the film industry; and restaurant, bar, and dance hall management, as well as into high-tech fraud and human trafficking.[17] Recently, they have become heavily involved in computer software piracy. The illicit sex trade is a very high-profit, low-cost enterprise for the Chinese triads, and they "routinely lure young girls with the promise of jobs, smuggle them into another country, and then sell them to brothels."[18]

Originally characterized by a tight hierarchy, secrecy, and unwavering loyalty, with similar organizational structures and rituals to bind members together and to prevent outside penetration,[19] the triad organizations have recently adopted a more relaxed and fluid cellular structure. During the past century, Chinese secret criminal societies have demonstrated a significant capacity to adapt and currently are more willing to exploit legitimate market mechanisms and more democratic associational forms.[20] Indeed, "compared with the strict hierarchical structure of Italian crime groups, for example, the Triads are 'loose affiliations in the extreme,' offering full autonomy to members in their selection of criminal activities."[21] Those at the top of the Chinese triad structure have often established firm reputations as legitimate business entrepreneurs. The Chinese government has not been very effective at reining in the activities of the triads because it has "looked only for tight-knit organizations with a pyramid-like structure" (including secret societies), whereas Chinese criminal forces often prefer fluid networking arrangements (which can integrate vertically and horizontally).[22]

Corruption versus Violence

Regarding corruption, although they do make a cult out of membership through rituals, passwords, oaths, and specialized dress, Chinese triad members are relatively well integrated into society and tend to prefer business ties embedded with corruption to achieve their goals. In recent years, triad bosses have learned that the best way to ensure cooperation from government institutions is to infiltrate their ranks, and the prevalent corruption in government and the police force have made expansion relatively easy, "reflecting a systemic degradation within China's law-enforcement system."[23] When many high-ranking officials are part of a corruption scheme, it lowers the chance of oversight and exposure, because it is in the self-interest of the people who should be regulating corruption to cover up the wrongdoing.[24] The triads' migrant labor smuggling business, for example, is one realm where they rely heavily on corruption rather than on violence to ensure cooperation, as positive incentives exist for the other party (usually government employees) to engage in collusion. Bribery specifically and corruption more generally seem to be more often used when the exchange is noncompetitive, where there are positive material gains for each party involved (in other words, corruption seems more likely than violence in situations perceived as non-zero-sum).

Nevertheless, "violence . . . or the threat of violence is implicit in every single transaction" the Chinese triads undertake.[25] They engage in heinous violence abroad, so as both to keep members of their own syndicate in line and to resolve business disputes,[26] but the violence has usually been limited to their own ethnic communities and has rarely affected citizens of other nationalities. Turf wars between different triads over gambling and prostitution are frequent, with the signature instrument of torture, punishment, and execution being the kitchen meat cleaver (triad victims are often horribly mutilated).[27] The triads' violent reputation is instrumental to their success, for they "thrive on public fear through their mystery and intimidation,"[28] and for this reason a reputation for violent retaliation is a highly valuable commodity that these gangs seek concertedly to acquire and nurture. The triads' modus operandi in the business world is systemized takeover of a specific area, which the triads then monopolize by either excluding all other competitors or allowing them to operate in the vicinity for a percentage of their profits. Either way, an ultimatum is presented in a menacing fashion and enforced with exacting and merciless violence if need be. The triads resort to violence especially when attempts to recruit new members fail. Recent incidents indicate increasing use of violence and movement beyond the Chinese community by the triads, with new younger triad members tending to be more opportunistic and driven ruthlessly by a desire for profits.[29]

Individual/Human Security versus National/State Security

The Chinese triads pose mainly an individual/human security threat for the citizens of the states in which they operate. Triad terror tactics negatively affect individual security—sometimes of the triads' patrons, sometimes of their targets, and sometimes of the triads' "employees" (prostitutes and indentured servants). For example, the Chinese triads' involvement in the drug trade and sex trafficking has dramatically aggravated the HIV/AIDS problem—and that of other infectious diseases such as tuberculosis—in areas in which they operate.[30] More generally, the nonreporting of crimes committed by triad members due to corruption of local officials has spread beyond China to places like Los Angeles County, California, directly endangering the safety of uninvolved citizens living within affected areas.[31]

The majority of the triads' illicit activities do not directly endanger state security. For example, the smuggling of heroin from the Golden Triangle to North America and the smuggling of Chinese aliens from China into the United States have not yet directly threatened national government stability. The Chinese triads, however, often work with local warlords and rebels in Southeast Asia, and these insurgents use the proceeds from criminal activities (often involving illicit drugs) to finance their regime-destabilizing agendas; more generally, eroding sound governance is the criminally induced corruption of government officials, police, and judges, to the point where this has become "the major source of discontent among the Chinese population."[32] The triads have become "extremely efficient" in exploiting law enforcement weaknesses within individual countries.[33] Tarnishing of a state image—such as in Macao—occurs when societal reputation degenerates to the point that it negatively affects tourism. Moreover, the triads make over $500 billion from the production, transport, and distribution of arms,[34] which can undermine political stability within recipient states. Thus the Chinese triads pose a major indirect threat to the political, economic, and social stability of East Asian states.[35]

COLOMBIAN CARTELS

General Organizational Background

Since their emergence in the 1970s when the global drug trade began booming, the Colombian cartels have been a dynamic consortium of mega-cartels that have played a pivotal role in the global narcotics industry.[36] The two most well known are the Medellín and Cali cartels, but because of the arrests and deaths of dominant cartel leaders, these two organizations declined in the mid-1990s and are now defunct, with activity having been diversified in recent years. The Norte del Valle Cartel, formed in the mid-1990s as a loose confederation of various drug-trafficking families, became one of Colombia's most powerful cartels: it used front companies to cover the illicit transfer of goods and money laundering and exported an estimated 550 tons of cocaine worth $10 billion from Colombia between 1990 and 2004.[37] In January 2007, however, authorities caught one of the main Norte del Valle Cartel leaders, Eugenio Montoya, and in February 2008, Norte del Valle drug lord Wilber Varela was found dead. A smaller and more decentralized organization, the North Coast Cartel, runs a profitable and intimidating drug business.

Colombia's gradual emergence as Latin America's pre-eminent drug supplier was a result of its geopolitical position, its vast central forests that effectively hide secret processing laboratories and airstrips facilitating the flow of drugs, the strong entrepreneurial skills of the Colombian people, and the willingness of the Colombian community in the United States to function as a distribution network.[38] Colombian traffickers control the manufacture of the vast majority of cocaine in South America (Nigeria, Mexico, and Myanmar are also major suppliers of illicit drugs). Today "the drugs still flow" despite massive American investment in the global "war on drugs," "the decapitation of the Medellín and Cali Cartels, and scores of arrests, extraditions, and convictions resulting in long sentences in U.S. jails."[39] The Colombian cartels have become so powerful that many call the Colombian government a "narcodemocracy," with drug traffickers having purchased the compliance of key personnel in every key government institution.[40] The cartel leaders (called *narcos*) are primarily engaged in drug trafficking and kidnapping for profit in order to sustain their operations and to obtain political collateral that they can exchange for prisoners held in Colombian prisons.

During the 1980s, the domestic drug industry skyrocketed in Colombia, and its reach grew internationally. During that same time period, when Colombian cocaine began to flood the American market, the Colombian cartels used the routes and services of Mexican marijuana dealers, which, in turn, caused a huge increase in the number of Mexican drug traffickers (and can be linked directly to the recent widespread criminal violence in Mexico).[41] Colombian cartels have bases in Barcelona and Madrid in Spain, and much of the cocaine produced in Colombia is shipped through Venezuela, with most of it bound for the United States (the primary international consumer of illicit drugs), Great Britain, Italy, and Spain.[42] Indeed, within the region, Colombian cartels now have links not only to Venezuela but to Mexico and Panama as well.

In recent years, the Colombian cartels have weakened, but they are still involved in a continuing war against the state. The more rapid turnover in leaders and alliances among narco-traffickers has caused major problems for those responsible for curtailing this activity, and victories in the war on drugs in Colombia often seem simply to push the illicit drug activity elsewhere (such as to Mexico). The Colombian cartels are now seeing growing fragmentation in organizational structure, so much so that it is common to describe the trend as moving from cartels to "cartelitos": Colombia's drug cartels are now relying on smaller and more dispersed and compartmentalized operational units because they realize that large, expansive organizations like the old Medellín and Cali cartels are more vulnerable to detection and disruption by American and Colombian security services; the Colombian National Police and the U.S. Drug Enforcement Administration estimate that there are more than 300 active drug-smuggling organizations in Colombia today.[43] Whereas within Colombia drug lords display a total lack of respect for government law enforcement, abroad they act more conservatively and engage in more cooperative behavior,[44] in part because they realize they cannot as easily buy off law enforcement officers or judges. Although Colombian cartels have operated in collusion with guerrilla groups and paramilitary armies, since 2006—when the Colombian state outlawed paramilitary groups—reliance has increased on less centralized and hierarchical drug gangs: there are now at least twenty-three "emerging gangs" numbering 2,200 fighters, a fraction of the demobilized paramilitary groups.[45]

Corruption versus Violence

Regarding corruption, the Colombian cartels tend to use corruption tactics, or deal making, primarily when they lack a preponderance of power: drug producers often engage in rent paying when they are operating in a territory that is controlled by a more powerful guerrilla or paramilitary group. They tend to use bribery specifically to buy safety and the right to operate in a competitor's territory, reflecting the importance of territorial dominance. Colombian drug runners possess remarkably effective abilities to collaborate with officials in influencing government policy, the law enforcement environment, and the entire political system, as these criminals engage in the promotion of favorable legislation, election, and prosecution outcomes and thus in many ways make the threat to the country's political order greater than the threat to its economic structure.[46] Exemplifying the role of bribery was the significant funding of the 1994 Colombian presidential campaign by drug lords.[47] A tight connection has frequently existed between the use of corruption and violence, as "the choice was often put starkly: *plata o plomo*, that is, accept a bribe or face death."[48] A recent illustration of the link between corruption and violence was the Jamundi massacre, when the cartels used corruption—paying members of the Colombian military—to massacre an entire team of elite antinarcotics agents.[49] With judicial institutions so fragile, and effective government oversight largely nonexistent, corruption seems much more dangerous from a security standpoint than similar tactics would be within more solvent societies because any disruption within such a vulnerable system is likely to spread unchecked.

Regarding violence, the Medellín Cartel under the notorious Pablo Escobar relied on the use of extreme violence until police gunned him down in December 1993 and the cartel's power waned; in contrast, the Cali Cartel preferred to rely on the more low key bribery and corruption of Colombian government officials.[50] Nonetheless, both used a mix of approaches in which corruption and violence were mutually reinforcing. After the era of these two prominent cartels, and after the Colombian drug business was dominated by violent insurgents and former paramilitary forces, violence diminished, as a few large organizations were replaced by many smaller groups. The Norte del Valle Cartel, however, has been especially known for its brutality and violence. The violence in Colombia usually serves to assert dominance (violence generally seems more likely than corruption in situations perceived as zero-sum). Over time, Colombian drug dealers have created elaborate transnational trade networks and, when challenged, have engaged in assassination and even full-scale military assaults.[51] The cartels' use of violence in Colombia differs from much of that used by criminals elsewhere because the Colombian cartels have been looking not just to operate outside of the law but rather to establish themselves through violence as the law in the area. This type of behavior is practical only in a state in which the government is largely insolvent, as in Colombia, with a corrupt judicial system, a volatile economy, and pervasive crime and corruption. Although such problems are common in many developing countries, the difference is the level to which they handicap the government—these deficiencies are deeply entrenched in Colombia, which does not have the means to combat effectively its criminal element. Consequently, the groups in Colombia that wield the most power—measured by manpower, violent reputation, and economic means—have often been the de facto rule makers. The effect of this free-for-all regime is to make violence a useful tool, not just to acquire protection from investigation for illicit activity, or to dominate a sector of the underground market, but also to gain control of the state and consequently the means of production for the one of the world's most profitable industries—drug production.

More specifically, for the Colombian cartels violence has served intimidation purposes—"to intimidate and often eliminate persecutors and to drive home to legislators, government officials, and the general public that they would violently resist any interference with their criminal activities."[52] Both drug traffickers and guerrilla groups in Colombia use violence to exert territorial control and establish a menacing reputation, and their modus operandi has been converging: the guerrillas have traditionally used violence to undermine the state, but over time have become less politically oriented and more involved in drug trafficking for profit;[53] meanwhile drug traffickers have started to take on the characteristics of guerrilla groups by using violence and bribery to influence politics. Cartel bosses use violence when dealing with high-profile victims who are an embarrassment and a hindrance to their business, for these highly visible homicides are intended to make a statement as much as to remove a problem; the difference between figures that the cartel bosses try first to bribe and the highly visible ones that the cartel bosses kill first is the target victim's ability or desire to assist them in some way combined with the victim's general attitude toward the cartel.[54]

Individual/Human Security versus National/State Security

Looking first at individual/human security, the modern era of "narco-guerrilleros-paramilitary warfare" (fighting among cartels, insurgent armies, and paramilitary groups) has led to hundreds of thousands of displaced persons and massive numbers of kidnappings and deaths. As a result, "the amount of human suffering inflicted on civilians during the Colombian internal conflict has been enormous," with terrible atrocities committed against innocent civilians, fighters from rival groups, and the cartels' own members.[55] Reflecting on this narcotics scourge's impact on individual citizens, throughout much of Colombia citizens have not enjoyed the level of security they have the right to expect, and "those few who had the courage to stand openly and call for governmental action became the targets of assassination."[56]

Turning to state/national security, in stark contrast to the Chinese triads, the Colombian cartels have a more direct effect here. The disruption of government security seems particularly acute in a developing state like Colombia where the semblance of democracy is already riddled with corruption and controlled mostly by oligarchic interests. American and European citizens' insatiable "appetite for narcotics Colombia produces has been central in undermining Colombia's law and order, economy, and democratic institutions," with the net result being that governance in Colombia today is "tattered and dysfunctional."[57] Colombian cartel activity has most disrupted the government justice system; the impact on government stability has been especially devastating in instances where judges have been killed or swayed by the threat of violence. Cartel activity has even led to the elimination of entire political groups, undermining democracy and the balanced functioning of the state's political institutions. The Colombian government cannot function effectively if violence and terror tactics are used to ensure that the government is really just a puppet bowing to the demands of the drug cartels. Colombia's drug trafficking also links up with the free flow of regime-destabilizing small arms into the country, as much of the money used for illicit weapons purchases is derived from illicit drug smuggling.[58] The overall psychological effect of the massacres committed by the cartels and paramilitary guerrilla groups has been to undermine both the public's confidence in government institutions and its willingness to participate in governance processes. Although the American war on drugs has achieved some success in Colombia in advancing protection goals, there is certainly a long way to go.

Indeed, drug trafficking undermines not only Colombian state security but also state security in other poor states enmeshed in the expanding drug web. In this regard, the Heritage Foundation has argued that "the threat to U.S. and hemispheric security posed by Colombia's narco-democracy cannot be overestimated."[59] A "drug-insurgency nexus" has emerged, one that has led some analysts to make the seemingly outlandish claim that leftist guerrillas work hand in hand with drug dealers to help undermine the U.S. government through the influx of illicit narcotics, thereby weakening the "dependent-capitalist state" in Colombia and accelerating the pace of revolutionary change there.[60] States neighboring Colombia have become extremely concerned over time about the export of chaotic disorder from that country affecting their own governments' political stability. Recently, however, the key drug-trafficking organizations in the region may have transformed into Mexican rather than Colombian crime syndicates.

ITALIAN MAFIA

General Organizational Background

The Italian Mafia, a group of individual gangs loosely connected to each other, includes three main factions: the Camorra based in Naples, La Cosa Nostra based in Sicily, and the 'Ndrangheta based in Calabria. La Cosa Nostra (formally started in the 1950s) and the 'Ndrangheta (formally started in the

1990s) are the dominant groups, with membership estimated at 3,500 and 5,000 males, respectively.[61] The Italian Mafia is a deeply ingrained cultural and social institution that evolved organically in the late 1800s from bands of common criminals: during a transitional period when the feudal ruling order was collapsing, the affluent classes viewed the Mafia as necessary "to quell disturbances and fill the gap of power."[62] The traditional Sicilian Mafia "remains the classic model of violent non-state governance of territory and population": "Sicily enabled the Mafia, without ceasing in any way to engage in criminality and brutal violence, to substitute for a weak, distant legal authority and appropriate the roles of punishment, dispute mediation, the protection of powerful economic interests and the pacification of the poor."[63] The Italian Mafia has pursued money and power "by organizing itself in a unique way that combines the attributes of a shadow state, an illegal business, and a sworn secret society."[64] Nonetheless, key differences exist among the gangs associated with the Italian Mafia: for example, both the 'Ndrangheta and the Camorra appear to have adapted much better to the opportunities of globalization than has the Sicilian Mafia.

Unlike many other modern transnational criminal organizations, the Italian Mafia has operated internationally for many decades. The Italian Mafia's transnational expansion during the 1990s was characterized more by increased collusion with other criminal groups than by a physical global spread: before the 1990s, the Mafia had been a hierarchical familial organization that dominated markets and was largely exclusive in its operations; during the 1990s, however, the emergence of new markets abroad, a crackdown on business operations within Italy that weakened Mafia organization, and the increasing prominence of rival groups all made the Italian Mafia more open to various kinds of collusion.[65] From the early 1990s onward, the Italian government began a campaign against the Mafia that ultimately caused it to regroup and to take on less overt tactics so as to fly beneath the radar: by the mid-1990s, the most violent part of the Mafia was eliminated, and after that time an "entrepreneurial criminal class" emerged that smoothly mixed legal and illegal activities without engaging in "unnecessary bloodshed."[66]

The Italian Mafia has been escalating activities in its native Italy and elsewhere: the three main factions have been earning an estimated $110 billion a year just from cocaine and heroin trafficking in Argentina, Australia, Bolivia, Brazil, Canada, the Caribbean islands, Peru, Venezuela, and most of Western Europe.[67] The 'Ndrangheta has developed a presence in the United States,

Canada, and Australia as well as parts of Latin America as a result of successive waves of Italian migration; although the 'Ndrangheta has also developed cooperative linkages with Mexican and Colombian drug-trafficking organizations, in part this was facilitated by the presence of Italian immigrants. Overall, the Mafia's primary operations are now in Europe (both Western and Eastern), North America, and Central and South America.[68] Although the American operations of the Italian Mafia had been temporarily weakened, they have shown recent signs of resurgence,[69] and the Mafia still controls the construction industry in some parts of the United States. The most common Mafia activities include drug trafficking, money laundering, loan sharking, counterfeiting, and extortion. Its trademark tactics include excising a tax on goods produced within its territory, political assassinations, robbery and theft, extortion, and manipulating public works contracts especially in the construction industry.

The Italian Mafia has been thriving in recent years, with revenue for 2008 ($167 billion) 40 percent larger than that of the previous year, and drug trafficking remaining the primary source of revenue (59 billion euros) and with arms smuggling remaining a significant venture (5.8 billion euros).[70] Of great concern to crime-fighting officials is that the Italian Mafia violence has been spreading to the rest of Europe, whereas once it was mostly restricted on the continent to Italy.[71] Within the past twenty years, the Italian Mafia has not only internationalized but also become more multiethnic,[72] and its openness in this dimension is perhaps best signaled by its recent willingness to accept the presence of Albanian organized crime—a formerly hated archrival—within Italy. During the last decade and a half, the Mafia has used overt and exacting violence to elicit fear of its power and used corruption to entice business owners into cooperation, or at least force them into complicity: the use of extreme and visible violence is largely limited to the Mafia's bases in Italy, whereas the use of corruption predominates in the United States.[73]

One notable difference between the Italian Mafia and most other transnational criminal organizations is its traditional code of morality, which historically limited its expansion of operations into prostitution, the sex industry, or illicit human trafficking in general: the Italian Mafia has been invested in preserving a reputation of honor and remaining a principled organization at the same time as other transnational criminals have been willing to undertake any activity that makes money.[74] This notion of "honor among thieves" may seem anachronistic and dysfunctional in the transnational criminal context but can ironically sometimes be associated with an image of respect and restraint among onlookers. The record of the Italian Mafia, however, is by no means spotless in this regard; for example, several years ago a major law enforcement effort called Operation Girasole led to the arrest of members of the Italian Mafia—along with Russian, Ukrainian, Serb, and Albanian criminals—involved in the sex trafficking of women.

Corruption versus Violence

Regarding corruption, on the whole the Italian mafiosi first use political corruption, including bribery of the police, as a means to create and secure industrial monopolies. Despite the recent targeting through judicial inquiries of the Mafia's complex web of political and institutional ties, today in Italy "a considerable number of politicians and state officials are still ready to advocate Mafia interests," as "the risk of coming to terms with the Mafia still appears lower than the potential monetary and electoral rewards, and their moral restraints are not high enough to prevent them from entering into such deals."[75] Thus, despite using violence, the Mafia generally seeks to be left alone and to blend in with the status quo—"wishing to pursue its illegal affairs without disruption from the police or judicial system, it needs the protective umbrella of the parties."[76] The Italian government, considered to be more corrupt than any other Western regime,[77] provides an ideal target for bribery by transnational organized crime.

In terms of specific corruption targets, the Italian Mafia uses most of the revenues from its ever-present protection rackets to buy lawyers, judges, police officers, journalists, politicians, and even casual laborers.[78] Because the mafiosi are interested in carrying out business in a normalized economic sphere, and invest in so many legitimate businesses, they use corruption predominantly to ensure they get public service contracts, obtain favorable legislation, and acquire the needed protection from law enforcement. Extortion is one of most common Mafia tactics used to prey upon the legitimate business sector. Through efficient use of corruption, the Italian Mafia has usually been able to achieve "efficient social control which guarantees their members virtual immunity from punishment," as Mafia followers are present in the legislatures, regional governments, and courts and can use their positions to influence police officers, building inspectors, and even health care providers.[79] Infiltrating parties and controlling votes are simply means to achieve the desired end of establishing control over territories so as to ensure judicial indemnity, freedom from uncomfortable oversight, and control over its enterprises and illicit operations; parallel to the force used by the Italian Mafia to control its territory, this transnational criminal organization uses similar tactics to restrain the entry of competitors in activities it chooses to undertake.[80]

Regarding violence, the Italian Mafia uses violence at home and abroad, but—as mentioned earlier—Mafia members do so more frequently and less reservedly in Italy: the domestic Italian Mafia uses violence to invoke fear of reprisal and to demonstrate its power, whereas foreign Mafia syndicates tend to use violence only when necessary to facilitate their illicit activities.[81] Generally the mafiosi use violence to defend their territory, both tangibly to safeguard their property and families (the protection of which the mafiosi emphasize with a machismo-type mentality) and less tangibly to defend their markets. Indeed, the Mafia perceives the use of violence as absolutely crucial to establish its reputation as a reliable protection provider by showing that it is readily capable of fulfilling its promises by punishing misbehavior.[82]

Given that the Italian Mafia claims the right of violence, it resorts to secrecy to avoid repressive retaliation from the state; once secrecy is adopted, violence becomes "an indispensable resource."[83] Although the Mafia has been trying to downplay its use of violence after the blowback from the increased vigilance and anti-Mafia legislation of the early 1990s, for the group found that it was in its own best interest to avoid the statewide attention associated with high-profile carnage, this criminal group has not ceased to use any of its more subversive violence and threatening tactics.[84] Indeed, the mafiosi often end up using violence when compromise fails.[85] Overall, "the more treacherous, violent, and profitable a market is—the obvious case is narcotics trafficking and dealing—the more Mafiosi who enter that market benefit from having a world-renowned and utterly reliable brand of blood-curdling intimidation behind them."[86] A recent example of violence by the Italian Mafia occurred in June 2008, when mafiosi in Naples gunned down a "super-witness" due to testify on the connections between government politicians and Mafia mobsters (the fourth victim in a month of shootings directed against witnesses who had turned state's evidence), highlighting "the Italian state's inability to protect people prepared to give evidence against organised crime."[87]

Individual/Human Security versus National/State Security

The primary impact of the Italian Mafia appears to be on individual security rather than on state security. Although the mafiosi certainly routinely menace ordinary citizens and in exceptional circumstances commit high-profile murders to control or eliminate political opposition and annoying police interference, most Mafia violence is intraorganizational, with retaliatory murders for breaking the code or targeted assassinations of competing gangs posing little, if any, direct threat to the state or to uninvolved citizens.[88] Outside of threats of loss of life, it is largely because of the Italian Mafia that "in almost every Italian city there is a hardcore of drug addicts for whom the use and procurement of drugs represent two of their most important daily activities"; the proportion of people in Italy who shoot up on heroin and other hard drugs is higher than the European average.[89] A relatively unnoticed human security threat is that, because Italy is "almost legendary for its organized crime groups," foreign criminal groups (such as Albanian heroin traffickers) have been attracted to the country and have begun illicit operations,[90] further endangering the lives and property of innocent citizens.

An indirect negative impact on state security occurs, however, when the Mafia undermines the national economy, usurps state policing power, and gains the reputation as a functioning government: legitimate business entrepreneurs may feel forced to submit to the Mafia and pay a form of tax to it, thereby transferring key state privileges to the Mafia and reducing public confidence in state power.[91] In this sense, the basis for existence of the Mafia is "by infiltrating the legal state and twisting it to its own purposes."[92] Besides discrediting the state's political reputation, the Mafia's insidious corruption of Italy's law enforcement agencies has hindered the state's abilities to protect its citizens and administer justice: within Italy, the mafiosi have attained a high level of virtual control; infiltrated legislatures, regional governments, court systems, and law enforcement agencies; bought numerous high-placed officials to ensure their own protection and favorable treatment; and, consequently, have been able to act more brashly than they would elsewhere.[93]

JAPANESE YAKUZA

General Organizational Background

The Japanese Yakuza encompasses three primary organizations (composed of thousands of smaller gangs): the Yamaguchi-gumi, the Inagawa-kai, and the Sumiyoshi-kai. There are more than 86,000 members operating under this Japanese criminal umbrella[94] This venerable criminal nexus dates back to 1612, though it was not until the nineteenth century that many of the currently prominent factions emerged. During the 1960s and 1970s, the Yakuza began to delve into the illicit drug trade; more recently, it has become involved in arms and contraband smuggling. By 1989, the Yakuza received one-third of its income from the sale of drugs; one-third from gambling, protection payments, and intervention in civil disputes; and one-third from indeterminate sources.[95] Like other transnational criminal organizations, the Yakuza began to accelerate its overseas expansion in the 1990s. Aside from loosening borders, globalizing trade, and opening markets abroad offering enticing profitable opportunities, during this period the Japanese government began to toughen its stance on illegal activity, making countries with less oversight more attractive to the Yakuza.

The Yakuza originates from and has its primary operations in Japan, and its secondary stronghold is Korea, with operations recently expanding to Brazil, Costa Rica, the Netherlands, the United Kingdom, and the United States.[96] Unlike in Japan, in foreign countries the Yakuza—like the Chinese triads—generally confines its use of violence to its ethnic communities, and it is a bit handicapped because it lacks access to foreign corrupt government organizations or complicit police allowing it to run its extortion schemes smoothly.[97] In addition to drug running and the sex trade, Yakuza criminal operations include skimming a percentage of laborers' wages, smuggling weapons, engaging in loan-shark activities, running underground legal services, acquiring coercively valuable real estate, forcing kickbacks in the construction industry, pirating in the entertainment industry, gambling, and extortion (with annual profits from protection rackets alone estimated at nearly $1 billion).[98] Sparking the pattern of expansion across geographical areas and illicit activities was the normalization of relations between Japan and Korea and the growing popular appeal of the methamphetamine trade and the sex industry.[99] Within Japan, one special advantage possessed by the Japanese Yakuza is that Japanese citizens rarely use the legal system to adjudicate disputes: "the failure of the state to afford a system by which citizens can seek to protect their interests and redress grievances" provides a natural market niche to the Yakuza.[100]

Recently, specifically since 2000, the Yakuza has begun to operate in the global financial industry, moving illicit funds in and out of countries with ease.[101] In 2007, Yakuza black-market business earnings alone were estimated at over $10 billion.[102] The Yakuza's investment and enterprises in the financial and technology industry (including film, computer software, and pornographic material piracy) are now much more sophisticated than those of most other criminal groups. Although the relationship between the Yakuza and the Japanese authorities is becoming more hostile[103]—leading to a recent government crackdown prompting "the upper elites of Yakuza gangs to evolve into socially acceptable, less overtly criminal individuals"—the Yakuza leadership now supports covertly unrestrained street-level criminal gangs that allow its supply of illicit profits to continue unabated.[104] Regardless, the new Japanese government initiatives have so far evidenced limited effectiveness.

Corruption versus Violence

Corruption is the routine and dominant tactic of the Yakuza, which uses this approach as the primary means for both political and economic coercion. The Yakuza operates in Japan through a relatively closed social network, making it hard for outsiders to penetrate.[105] By slipping bribes to police officers, the Yakuza can ensure that it will be informed about up-and-coming police raids. The relationships between the police and the Yakuza are symbiotic, with reciprocity an ingrained part of the system in Japan, allowing each to survive in its own sphere: for example, occasionally the Yakuza will allow the raiding police to confiscate some of its weapons or illicit goods so that the police appear to be accomplishing their given task.[106] Police may also ignore Yakuza activities or accept bribes to drop charges.[107] This close relationship exists not just for profit but also because "there is a great deal of personal rapport between the Yakuza and the police; local cops know local gangsters by name, and there is an easy familiarity between them."[108] In addition, many Japanese law enforcement officers have right-wing political views, making them sympathetic to the Yakuza members who "are ultra-nationalistic and conservative on matters of foreign policy" and "vigorously anti-communist."[109] Private institutions, including Japan's largest stock brokerage firms, also cooperate with the Yakuza.

Although the Yakuza has adopted corruption as its primary means of attaining its ends, criminal corruption in Japan is difficult to isolate "largely due to the deep-rooted culture of gift-giving, reciprocity, and obligation in which all major social occasions are marked by presentations of envelopes filled with cash."[110] Today the Japanese Yakuza seems "to be somewhat accepted as a part of everyday life" in Japan because of the tight interpenetration of political, economic, and social institutions—this pervasiveness of corruption in the political sphere is difficult to manage because conflicts of interest exist among politicians, bureaucrats, and other ruling elite and because "many are hesitant to confront Yakuza involvement because of heavy reliance on them for campaign funding and for getting rid of rivals."[111] Indeed, before the Boryokudan Countermeasures Law was enacted in 1992, Yakuza membership was perfectly legal. Illustrating the depth of this corruption, a Japanese scandal involved former prime minister Noboru Takeshita, who resigned his position in June 1989 after accusations of corruption involving the Yakuza and various prominent businessmen and politicians surfaced.[112]

As to violence, Japanese Yakuza members are "known for their prevalent use of violence," with law enforcement officials calling them *boryokudan* (violent ones).[113] The Yakuza is the predominant player in Japan's credit industry, where it uses strong-armed tactics to extort money; ruthless real estate criminals are also known to use threatening and violent coercion, including phone harassment, death threats, and abduction of tenants, to achieve their ends.[114] The Yakuza adeptly uses terror tactics in its operations in the banking industry, often applying starkly violent means to achieve its ends: there has been a rash of killings among members of the banking industry since the 1990s, most of them directly linked to the credit industry. The Yakuza does not always go directly for the kill; it also uses circuitous terror such as through targeting family members, in many ways a more menacing approach.[115] The Yakuza seems to resort to murder more frequently when dealing with high-profile bankers and industry executives, as well as high-ranking investigators, officials, and journalists who deal with debt recovery; when the Yakuza targets these high-profile victims, the economic incentives are much higher, usually involving millions of dollars in bank loans that need to be repaid or financial ruin if the repayments are not made.

Individual/Human Security versus National/State Security

Considering individual/human security, the Yakuza threatens the security of Japan's citizens primarily through its extortion activities.[116] This criminal group victimizes many average citizens through its loan-shark activities; engages in the destruction of personal property through home invasion robberies; and perpetuates addictive and abusive habits through the gambling, sex, and drug industries. The Yakuza's extensive involvement in drug trafficking and sex trafficking, in particular, endangers the individual safety and well-being of both buyers and sellers involved in these activities. In addition, the extortion and intimidation practiced by the Yakuza during the economic expansion of Japan in the 1980s contributed to a huge state financial crisis and regional economic instability.[117] More recently, the Yakuza has hampered Japan's economic development because banks cannot easily recover nonperforming loans extended to Yakuza-affiliated organizations.[118]

Regarding national/state security, the Yakuza seems alone among transnational criminal organizations in possessing considerable home state legitimacy. Armed with "the unique advantage of relative acceptance within Japanese culture,"[119] "what differentiates the Yakuza from other organized crime groups is the societal acceptance of its members": "Membership is respected and these 'businessmen' carry business cards and conduct operations out of offices alongside legitimate businesses"; people even hire the Yakuza for protection against small criminal groups.[120] The illicit corrupt reciprocity in Japan is born out of a sense of mutual respect rather than economic gain, and the Yakuza has become so entrenched in the Japanese government and the economy that it is considered as almost an operative part.[121] As a result, the net threat to state security may be perceived in Japan as lower than it would be otherwise.

Nonetheless, members of the Yakuza pose a serious threat to the state of Japan because, unlike some transnational criminal organizations, "they do not content themselves with producing and selling illegal goods and services" and instead seek exacting control over their members, territory, and reputation, in sum "the exercise of political dominion."[122] Furthermore, the Yakuza is undermining its government's legitimacy and devaluing the regime's international reputation: for example, "the public exposure of close corrupt ties between the Japanese Liberal Democrat Party and the domestic Yakuza led to the fall of a government which had lasted more than forty-five years and discredited democracy itself in the eyes of a good part of the population."[123] According to one Japanese politician, "there isn't a single Japanese politician who doesn't know his local Yakuza boss," and "ties between corporate Japan and the Japanese underworld are so extensive it's impossible to even get a grip on where and how they're joined together."[124] The subtle ways in which the Yakuza has attached itself to the state's very existence has made it virtually impossible to purge Yakuza members from government ranks.

RUSSIAN MOB

General Organizational Background

The Russian Mob (also widely known as the Russian Mafiya) is an amorphous collection of loosely interconnected gangs, largely devoid of a coherent hierarchy, a central leadership, or a common bloodline or uniform ethnic base. Organized crime in Russia is rooted in the revolutionary era of the early 1900s, and the Russian Mob is a direct descendant of the culture of corruption that characterized Soviet rule during the Cold War. In stimulating illicit activity, the fall of the Soviet Union made the impact of economic liberalization and globalization much more profound than in other countries, leaving a political vacuum, a vulnerable economy, and a lapse in both formal market regulations and enforcement capacity.[125] After the Cold War ended in 1989, the Russian Mob coalesced around an unprecedented era of free markets and a free-for-all sale of state capital,[126] with the lawlessness, the abundance of dirt-cheap raw materials, and the weak ruble being incredibly attractive to transnational criminal organizations:

> After the Soviet system collapsed, organized crime exploded, filling every state and nonstate void. Since laws concerning property and asset control were not enforced following the collapse, those who took advantage of the situation acted with impunity. Organized criminals' internal and external connections from their days of operating under the Soviets ensured they gobbled up the oil, gas, mineral and telecommunications industries; their smuggling routes (later to become supply chains) let them exploit these assets for financial gain.[127]

According to the Russian Interior Ministry, the increase in Russian crime was especially significant between 1989 and 1992, when most registered offenses rose by 20 to 25 percent a year.[128] By all accounts, this set of criminals "is the world's largest, busiest, and possibly meanest collection of organized hoods," with five thousand gangs and three million helpers operating in all fifteen of the former Soviet republics.[129] From a global security standpoint, the Russian Mob is especially concerning because of deficient Russian government law enforcement and "the huge flow of dirty money through Russian banks."[130]

Over time, "it becomes harder and harder to distinguish parts of the Russian government from the Russian Mob," composed of increasingly organized "once-disconnected gangs of thugs, thieves, and ex-intelligence officers" involved in the "hijacking of a nation's entire economy."[131] One analyst even claims that "organized criminal groups are the only effective government in Russia—they control 40 percent of all private businesses, 60 percent of state-owned businesses, and 80 to 90 percent of the banks" in Russia.[132] It is thus no coincidence that the Russian Mob has recruited numerous ex-KGB and former Spetsnaz (Russian Special Forces) operatives.[133]

In comparing the Russian Mob's illicit transnational activities in the twenty-first century to those of the early 1990s, these activities have become bolder, more sophisticated, and more far-flung than during the early years following the collapse of the Soviet Union. Organized crime in Russia today "is highly diverse and fractured, with ethnic divisions, divisions based on territorial and sectoral control, and generational splits."[134] Since coming to power in 1999, however, the Russian president Vladimir Putin (and his hand-picked successor Dmitry Medvedev) has been "wary of organized crime's threat to the sovereignty of the state," and as a result he has been "eager to consolidate power and resources under his own control" and "has reined in some aspects of Russian organized crime."[135] Nonetheless, this attempt to reduce the impact of the Mob on Russian government and society has not at least as yet been totally successful.

The geographical scope of Russian Mob activity now extends into Austria, Cyprus, France, Germany, Great Britain, Hungary, Israel, Jordan, Monaco, the Netherlands, Poland, Turkey, the United States, and the former Yugoslavia (especially Serbia).[136] A special feature of current organized crime activities in Russia is that they tend to concentrate in and around large cities and industrial centers.[137] The range of activities conducted by the Russian Mob is wide and growing, including racketeering, stealing cars, distributing illicit drugs, trafficking of weapons and radioactive materials, promoting prostitution, and infiltrating and buying Russian banks.[138] In the area of covert arms transfers, Russian criminal organizations are active not only within Russia itself but also in volatile areas such as Chechnya, Armenia, and Azerbaijan.[139]

The Russian Mob is not a hierarchical monolithic transnational organization,[140] and instead is divided into networks organized along regional or ethnic lines.[141] So members of the Russian Mob do not follow any form of uniform code when operating overseas: for example, the Mob appears to be the most violent in Eastern European countries, where "the embryonic law and weak institutional structures create a ripe climate, while it tends to be less aggressive in North America, carrying out criminal activities in the region with a relatively low profile, to avoid detection by authorities, and to reduce their risk of arrest, infiltration, and loss of profits."[142] The level of central coordination of what takes place in various settings is quite low.

Corruption versus Violence

Regarding corruption, the Russian Mob is particularly well stationed to bribe, extort, and blackmail government officials because it has almost completely infiltrated the most important government institutions, including the Ministry of Internal Affairs, the procurator, the Federal Counterintelligence Service (formerly the KGB), and the court system.[143] Corruption within Russia has progressed over time to the point that isolated criminal activities have begun to coalesce into well-organized and coordinated corruption networks intended to protect crime syndicates from prosecution and to provide a secure home base from which they can mastermind expanding corruption networks.[144] Corruption has been threatening to absorb the Russian government: "Russia has become a state where anarchy is continuous, where people, radioactive materials, weapons, and narcotics are easily bought and sold," with "coldblooded organized crime groups and corrupt government executives who are working together to generate not so much a new market economy as a truly new criminal state."[145]

After the end of the Cold War, corruption within the Russian government became more widespread (though under communism it was already quite prevalent), and since that time the benefits from illicit transactions have "grown immeasurably" while "at the same time the risks of being punished and the degree of negative consequences have decreased substantially."[146] Russian criminal organizations now spend between 30 and 60 percent of their income on bribery and various forms of political lobbying.[147] After the Soviet system collapsed, "the problems of corruption were rampant and provided fertile soil for the further development of organized crime," as Russian citizens had to provide bribes even to receive the most basic government services.[148] Corruption is deeply embedded within the Russian government, where the system of administrative bargaining has opened the door to seeking and receiving bribes.[149] Stimulating the rise in Russian government corruption were vulnerabilities associated with the poorly regulated property rights system, economic instability, and nonrestrictive business ethics. Today "corruption in Russia is interwoven into societal relations and the problem is that with removal of corruption the economy could collapse," as "corrupt networks between state authorities and businesses exist at every level throughout the society, from garbage cleaning to school textbook supply."[150] After the dramatic transformation in 1989, the new Russian state was unable to protect either its own citizens' lives (evidenced by a huge increase in the crime rate during subsequent years) or private property rights (evidenced by widespread citizen fears of fraud and property loss); as a result, for many citizens it became necessary to buy private protection, causing protection suppliers like the Russian Mob to thrive and to become "the new arm of order."[151] Indeed, the Russian Mob has become heavily involved in privatized protection rackets,[152] and this activity has become a particular irritation and target for change for the Putin (and Medvedev) regime.[153]

Turning to violence, the most common reasons the Russian Mob engages in violence are (1) to assert power and reinforce its reputation, (2) to intimidate victims into compliance, and (3) to protect itself: despite their veneer of respectability, Mob members "have never shrunk from the use of violence as a means of establishing themselves in a new area and maintaining control."[154] A distinguishing characteristic of the Russian Mob compared to other transnational criminal organizations is its more indiscriminate application of violent tactics, often based on "greed or personal vendetta."[155] Indeed, the Mob has indulged in "uninhibited use of intimidation and violence, epitomized by an increased prevalence of contract killings," employing violence generally in power struggles with other groups and contract killings specifically in infiltrating a particular industry or in eliminating individuals—including journalists, law enforcement officials, and politicians—willing to confront them directly.[156] When the Mob targets local businesses, it usually employs violence first only tacitly, as a condition contingent upon satisfactory cooperation, and carries out the threat of violence only when extortion targets do not meet specified demands. Although many Mob exchanges with business owners profit both parties, both business executives and celebrities have been killed if they attempt to resist extortion pressures.[157]

In recent years, contradictory pressures have been evident with respect to Russian Mob violence. On the one hand, pressures for increased Mob violence have accelerated in response to intensified competition with other criminal groups.[158] On the other hand, at the same time the emergence of a more legitimate, regulated Russian economy has created counterpressures that have caused some observers to conclude that "violent organized crime is declining."[159] In this regard, as a result of reforms in the Russian economic system, the Russian Mob may be shifting from violent crime toward economic crime and toward a consolidation and interregional integration among criminal groups.[160] Nonetheless, the Russian Mob continues to employ violent tactics: for example, in February 2008, a dramatic surge in contract killings occurred that directly threatened to damage then president Vladimir Putin's legacy of stability, and even Russia's prosecutor general Yuri Chaika had to admit at the time that assassinations linked to the Russian Mob "were again on the rise."[161]

Individual/Human Security versus National/State Security

Regarding individual/human security, Russian Mob violence poses a direct bodily threat to both intended targets and innocent bystanders: a survey indicated that three out of four Muscovites were afraid to walk the streets at night, and 49 percent of Russians rated crime higher on their list of concerns than unemployment.[162] The economic havoc the Mob has wreaked on the state's finances since the fall of the Soviet Union has indirectly caused the impoverishment, suffering, and death of untold number of Russian citizens, with at least $100 billion having been illegally exported.[163] Indeed, because of the Russian Mob, "for the average Russian, life is harder now than it ever was under the old system," as "beggars crowd the subway stops in Moscow," "famine stalks the once productive mill cities of Siberia and the Urals," and "street crime is everywhere," whereas "news of murders, muggings, and robberies dominate the newspapers and television reports."[164]

Turning to state security, Russian Mob activities seem potentially even more calamitous. The Mob's potential involvement in cross-border smuggling of nuclear components[165] quickly became a grave global security concern, with a key threat element being criminal sales of nuclear technology to terrorists. The attraction for unscrupulous individuals within Russia to steal nuclear technology is a direct result of the fall of the Soviet government, resulting in lax control of nuclear weapons and growing economic deprivation.[166]

Outside of this potential leakage of nuclear technology, Russian Mob activities threaten Russian state security by undermining its reputation and fostering societal chaos. Most commonly, Russian criminal organizations "not only threaten government authority" but also have a mass public image of being "alternatives to state authority"; if left unrestrained, "Russian organized crime groups will ignite a lethal mix of social and economic turmoil in Russia in which the persistent greed and opportunism of Russian organized crime could precipitate a political crisis that would destroy the reform processes and prevent Russia from joining the community of liberal democratic nations."[167] More than under the Soviet communist political system, ongoing corruption in Russia has significantly interfered with government security,[168] for "organized crime has been able to penetrate Russian business and state enterprises to a degree that is inconceivable in most other countries of the world."[169]

5 MAJOR TRANSNATIONAL CRIMINAL ACTIVITIES

IN PARALLEL FASHION, this chapter closely inspects transnational organized crime's three major illicit global activities—illicit arms transfers, illicit drug transfers, and illicit human transfers. This discussion focuses on those segments of these three illegal transactions controlled by transnational organized crime. The evidence presented for the illicit cross-border activities incorporates the general scope and nature of each activity, the roots of and responses to each activity, the key subcategories of each activity, the choice of tactics of corruption versus violence, and the impact on individual/human security versus national/state security.

Like the major transnational criminal organizations, these three illicit transfers are tightly interconnected, with growing ties developing among illicit human transfers, illicit drug transfers, and illicit arms transfers.[1] The myriad possibilities involved in these interconnected relationships among the three types of illicit transfers include that the profits made from the sale of illicit drugs have often fueled the purchase of covert arms to be used in insurgency or terrorist activities;[2] that, since 2002, nuclear trafficking incidents have come to light showing the involvement of drug dealers and traffickers;[3] that illegal aliens entering a country may serve as vehicles for transporting illicit drugs across borders undetected;[4] and that drug traffickers have used immigrants as slave labor in their drug business within their country of destination.[5] As a specific example of one of these general patterns, it was reported in the early 1990s that the Italian Mafia used much of its profit in drug trafficking to purchase arms, which were later exported through a Syrian government connection to various Arab countries.[6]

The logic behind this intertwining of different criminal activities is readily apparent:

> The people who are involved in moving drugs are very often the same people who will use the same infrastructure to move human beings as illegal migrants, traffic in weapons, and smuggle any other high-value items. It's like being a good trucker. You don't want to travel the return leg with an empty truck. If you use that sort of analogy, you have drugs coming out one way and that produces money and that buys the weapons and then the weapons go back in.[7]

Conditions favorable to each of these illicit transfers tend to be favorable to the others,[8] partially explaining why these activities are becoming even more intertwined over time.

What is perhaps most disconcerting is that, as the web of linkages among these illicit cross-national flows and their perpetrators become both tighter and more multifaceted, it becomes increasingly difficult to detect who is doing what and to decide where to begin in managing these transactions. This difficulty is compounded by the reality that, within each of the three areas of activity, legitimate cross-border activity occurs at the same time as the illicit criminal activity: states regularly transfer and sell arms to each other, multinational corporations in the pharmaceutical industry regularly market drugs internationally approved by the states in which they are sold, and permanent immigrants and temporary tourists regularly move from country to country facilitated by official state-sanctioned documentation. So if illicit arms transfers, illicit drug transfers, or illicit human transfers are to be properly addressed, the first hurdle is not apprehending the perpetrators or interdicting the activity but rather finding a way cleanly to differentiate illicit activities from legal movement of arms, drugs, or people across national boundaries.

Furthermore, special complications specific to each of the three criminal activities impede coherent interdiction policies. For illicit drug transfers and illicit arms transfers, criminal cross-border transfers may consist of components—potentially dual-use weapons parts that could be assembled later and drug paraphernalia that could be used to create designer drugs or to imbibe drugs—rather than finished products. For illicit arms transfers exclusively, determining legality or illegality may necessitate examining not the weapons themselves but rather the ultimate recipients of the weapons, because what is illegal for a private citizen to obtain may be perfectly legal for a government military or police officer to obtain. For illicit human transfers, ambiguities surround to what extent people are moving across borders on their own volition versus criminal coercive pressure, to what extent these people are considered illegal migrants versus legitimate refugees, to what extent legitimate citizens of the destination country are complicit in this illegal border crossing, and to what extent the people can stay in the destination country with some basic rights versus the need to be returned home if they make it to their destination. Together such complexities make it considerably easier for transnational criminal organizations engaged in illicit arms transfers, illicit drug transfers, and illicit human transfers to shield their shady activities from scrutiny and to evade efforts to curtail these operations.

ILLICIT ARMS TRANSFERS

General Scope and Nature of the Activity

The clandestine transfer of arms across national boundaries usually reflects either (1) pent-up fear and feelings of insecurity that the status quo is in danger or (2) pent-up hostility and desire to change the status quo. This area of global smuggling incorporates both nuclear and conventional weapons systems (encompassing trade in both components and finished weapons systems). Transnational criminal organizations are in a prime position illicitly to buy and sell these arms and arms components, and this capability has for some time permitted criminal networks "to mount successful challenges to the monopoly on coercive force conventionally claimed by governments."[9] This global weapons traffic allows transnational organized crime to maintain its disruptive power through illegitimate possession of instruments of violent force: just the demand for illicit arms within a society attracts opportunistic criminal groups and almost inevitably causes an increase in violence within the region.[10] Because most illicit arms transfers do not end up in state hands, and because officially sanctioned sources of arms would usually not provide arms to eager nonstate recipients, the transactions that occur are often secret.

Because it is unusual for criminal organizations, paramilitary and insurgent groups, or "repressive" national governments to produce their own armaments, most customers rely on illicit black-market transnational arms smuggling for their nefarious ends.[11] In this way, illicit arms transfers are similar to illicit human transfers (but not to illicit drug transfers) in that (1) transnational criminals are usually simply transfer agents rather than manufacturers of the illicit commodities from which they derive huge profits, and (2) the commodities transferred are usually not themselves intrinsically illegal. Nonetheless, an increasing number of countries, and companies within these countries, are producing small arms, expanding the possibilities for diversion into the illegal global market.[12]

Roots of and Responses to the Activity

After the end of the Cold War, false hopes were present among those opposed to arms proliferation—"many observers breathed a sigh of relief that the winding down of the bipolar ideological rivalry would finally curtail the widespread development and exchange of potentially lethal weapons systems."[13] On the surface, the diminishing global demand for legitimately traded arms since the end of the Cold War,[14] with levels in the 1990s significantly lower than those in the 1970s and 1980s, seemed to fulfill these hopes. Much to these observers' chagrin, however, excess supply of arms and excess capacity in arms production, combined with greater visibility of subnational turmoil, have fostered intensified competition by arms producers to enter foreign markets. It appears that the robust international weapons infrastructure stimulated by the boom of the 1980s refused to wither in the face of what might be perceived as a temporary downturn in arms demand. Specifically, in recent years "the demand for weapons of all kinds is boundless," as the huge surplus capacity has fostered "an explosion in intrastate conflicts, insurgencies, civil wars, and armed criminal enterprises of every kind."[15] Most recent international arms smuggling appears to be economically motivated rather than politically motivated.[16] Nuclear smuggling has had special post–Cold War precipitants:[17] on the supply side, "the disintegration of the USSR and its 'guards, guns, gates, and gulags' machinery of totalitarian control made privatized nuclear deals both thinkable and possible"; on the demand side, although the market for nuclear weapons components is "narrow and rarefied," "a handful of anti-Western states with nuclear weapons programs and a few relatively well-heeled terrorist organizations appear to have joined the nuclear procurement game."

International efforts to regulate the illicit arms trade began in the early 1990s, but, up to this point, "the process of establishing uniform laws has been slow and uneven."[18] Domestic gun control efforts, which are inextricably linked to international arms smuggling because "the same distribution networks that serve warring factions also supply organized criminals,"[19] have also floundered to a certain extent. Different countries are most concerned about different types of criminally induced arms transfers. Notably, the legal and illicit networks that manufacture and distribute arms and ammunition are intertwined, sharing many of the same resources, customers, and modes of operation.[20] In parallel fashion, the arms trade takes place using similar routes and routines regardless of whether the transactions are legal or illicit and whether they rely on corruption or deception.[21] Thus legal sanctions targeting just illicit transfers are quite difficult, with laws prohibiting illicit arms smuggling full of holes, in some cases deliberately created by governments.[22] Furthermore, arms embargoes are relatively futile as means of restricting this activity, for criminal groups can simply transship weapons via a third state (1) with no embargo on the arms in question or (2) whose government officials can be bribed for export licenses.[23] A consistent problem in stopping illicit arms smuggling is that "if gun-runners get caught, they are easy to replace."[24] In the end, because so many states engage in legal open arms transfers, and because exchanging weapons systems is globally seen to be much more legitimate than illicit drugs or sex trafficking, governments may be reluctant to clamp down hard in this area.

Nuclear Weapons/Components

With respect to smuggling nuclear weapons components, the impact could be monumental, but the frequency of such activity still appears to be relatively low. Transnational criminals are involved in the smuggling of nuclear technology, but it is "not the primary or secondary source of business today" for them, according to former director of the Central Intelligence Agency, James Woolsey; transnational criminal organizations have little interest in making the nuclear trade a dominant activity because it involves high risks and opportunity costs with low returns.[25] Indeed, "the nuclear black market, such as it is, does not follow the pattern of conventional criminal businesses: the market as a whole is populated by amateur criminals, scam artists, and (on the demand side) undercover police and police decoys."[26]

After the end of the Cold War, when publicity exploded about the breakdown of the Russian military, the thousands of Russian scientists going for months without pay, and missing fissile material from formerly top-secret Russian installations, Western fears escalated concerning the possibility that rogue states and transnational terrorists might obtain nuclear weapons capabilities through the illicit cross-border transfer of nuclear expertise, materials, and technology.[27] Since that time, nuclear smuggling has indeed occurred throughout the world (including the United States).[28] The International Atomic

Energy Agency Illicit Trafficking Database indicates that, although trafficking in nuclear material has been fairly stable over the last decade and a half, major increases have occurred in the illicit transfer of other radioactive materials.[29] Examples of the criminal transfer of nuclear components include the Italian Mafia exchanging counterfeit merchandise with the Russian Mob for highly sophisticated military equipment, heavy and light weapons, and uranium; in 1995, a Murmansk–Saint Petersburg criminal ring smuggling nuclear materials offering members of the Russian navy $400,000 to $1,000,000 for each kilogram of highly enriched uranium they were able to deliver; and in 1999, a criminal group from Saint Petersburg offering a crew member of a nuclear-powered icebreaker in Murmansk $100,000 for five grams of californium-252, used to start up nuclear reactors.[30] Because of the difficulty of smuggling a complete nuclear bomb, most illicit nuclear transactions have focused on nuclear raw materials, including uranium and plutonium.[31]

Conventional Weapons/Components

The vast majority of criminally induced illicit arms transfers involve small arms and light weapons. Transnational organized crime's involvement in the international black market in conventional arms frequently entails "the barter of weapons for natural resources, animal products, drugs, and other commodities."[32] Organized crime syndicates often let petty criminals control parts of the illicit arms exchanges or outsource the business; these syndicates will sometimes require a payoff, or take the majority of the profits while paying the petty criminals only an employer's wage for their roles.[33]

Although major weapons systems "dwarf the capacities" of small arms, hundreds of millions of low-tech weapons are responsible for most of the killing—as much as 90 percent of the deaths—in ongoing conflicts around the globe.[34] The global market for illicit weapons systems is growing:[35] pistols and revolvers, assault rifles, hand grenades, machine guns, missile launchers, light mortars, light antitank weapons, and antipersonnel landmines constitute the bulk of the of goods trafficked. The weapons' portability makes them easy to transport across borders and difficult to detect. Virtually all of the weapons in the black market were at one time legal, with illegally manufactured guns accounting for a very small percentage of those trafficked. Both black-market transactions and gray-market transactions occur here: black-market transfers directly violate relevant laws and usually involve weapons improperly obtained from government arsenals or legitimate arms dealers, whereas gray-market transfers are more legally ambiguous and may involve "dual-use" products shipped to recipients ineligible for military arms, goods sold from the licit to the illicit sector of the economy, or government-sponsored transfers that violate existing prohibitions.[36]

With respect to dual-use technologies that can be used in weapons systems, transnational criminals delight in smuggling these across national boundaries because they can, in yet another way, help them maintain the false image that they are part of completely legitimate enterprises trading legal items to meet the demands of conventional consumers. Deception and disguise are often involved in the many cases of defense technologies that originate from civilian breakthroughs or are interconnected with nonmilitary commercial products: "Commodities being smuggled are sometimes kept in plain sight and simply presented as legitimate in declarations to customs authorities; this approach is particularly effective in the case of dual use items where it is difficult to distinguish a weapon or component from something innocuous."[37] Aside from oft-discussed dual-use strategic metals used to facilitate nuclear capabilities, many transferred commodities fall into this dual-use category because they could be creatively adapted for use in conventional weapons systems, such as machinery that can be modified to manufacture armaments; vehicles that, with slight modifications, can be used as military units; and computerized navigation systems and communications systems that could be used for weapons guidance. Although regulatory bodies (including the U.S. Department of Commerce) are increasingly vigilant about such unsanctioned cross-border shipments, these dual-use items are in many ways even harder to forestall than single-use weapons systems.

Although the exact dollar amount of these covert flows of small arms is unknown, "guesses range from $1 billion–$2 billion for the average year's skullduggery (mostly by governments that do not want their neighbors to know what weapons they are buying or selling), to $5 billion–$10 billion if there is a good war or two to drive demand."[38] These figures are, of course, substantially lower than those for the public international transfers of large conventional weapons systems (the value of the legal global arms trade in 2002 was between $26.3 and $34 billion), but the clandestine traffic is more likely to involve the kind of small arms actually used in ongoing conflicts and shows no signs of abating.[39] With about 500 million arms on the world's weapons market,[40] the illicit trade in small arms probably constitutes between 10 and 20 percent of the total.[41] The United States is the top supplier of small arms to the Caribbean, linking illicit arms and illicit drugs together. Elsewhere in the world, Eastern Europe and the former Soviet Union—particularly Russia, Ukraine, Belarus, and Kazakhstan—constitute major points of origin for criminal arms smuggling.[42] For example, two of the major global arms smugglers, Leonid Minin and Viktor Bout, emerged out of the former Soviet Union.

Corruption versus Violence

Corruption is widespread in global arms smuggling. Considering specifically smuggling of conventional weapons, the fundamental logistics of arms smuggling are driven by corruption.[43] There are generally three forms of corruption payments involved in these illicit transactions: direct cash transfers, brokers' commissions, or subcontracts or consultancy arrangements.[44] Because law enforcement against arms smugglers is often "entirely reliant" on police initiatives and conducted in secrecy without transparent accountability, guns and other illicit commodities foster corruption.[45] Nonetheless, many illegal weapons are smuggled out of states with lax controls and then sold without the proper registration or in violation of restrictions, none of which requires any explicit use of corruption (or violence) tactics;[46] indeed, in many states with lax law enforcement, it is easy to forge needed documents, which are rarely checked and almost always accepted unconditionally.[47] Theft is also a common source of weapons sold illegally, often with corrupt government officials committing the crimes. To get arms across borders, smugglers may misreport the number of transferred weapons, use false documentation, and conceal the weapons from authorities.[48] Obtaining this false documentation— government-issued certificates ensuring a legitimate destination for weapons shipments—usually entails corruption, as in many states government bureaucrats, police, or border officials are all too ready to sell these papers (with prospects low of being caught or punished). Given global porous borders and free trade, this tactic is highly effective because of the sheer number of requests for approval that most licensing bodies receive annually, as well as to the difficulty in checking information and ensuring that the thousands of shipments passing through ports each month have made their scheduled stops and have been delivered to the specified parties.

For the cross-national smuggling of nuclear components specifically, corruption is the primary tool that transnational organized crime uses to solicit help from officials. Government authorities suspect that nuclear goods are smuggled through established drug-trafficking routes often controlled by organized crime, and the trade in nuclear materials often relies on "corrupt networks of active or former members of the state bureaucracy, state-controlled enterprises, and the military and security apparatus."[49] Within Russia, for example, corruption is pervasive at all levels in the nuclear industry, making it difficult to discriminate between criminal behavior and state policy.[50] Banks that launder the money pertaining to nuclear arms transfers are also motivated by corruption; for example, Russian banks have willingly collaborated in laundering $400 million earned from illicit Russian armaments and military equipment.[51] Because nuclear transfers largely focus on components and raw materials rather than on finished weapons systems, keeping the veil of secrecy around existing corruption may be easier than with conventional arms.

With respect to violence, given that arms often facilitate violence within and across states, it is deeply ironic that criminally induced cross-border arms smugglers rarely rely on violent tactics to achieve their desired ends. The explanation may lie in the relatively greater acceptability, legitimacy, and normalcy of the presence of armaments within many societies in comparison to illicit drugs and unsanctioned migrants. Unlike unsanctioned human beings or nonmedicinal drugs, transferring weapons across national boundaries is not inherently illegal, and so transnational criminal organizations involved in this activity compete with states and multinational corporations and thus find niche markets such as insurgents and terrorists with whom legitimate arms merchants may not deal.[52] As a consequence, arms can be treated much more as a commodity, and the dynamics of the illicit arms trade may be understood more readily through scrutinizing conventional international business practices. Usually, the implications are that arms can be delivered to foreign buyers using fewer intermediaries than with trafficked drugs or people, and thus there is less need to use any form of coercion to promote compliance. Moreover, unlike illicit drug transfers and illicit human transfers, transnational criminal groups would not usually want to coerce anyone to purchase arms from them, as this could facilitate a speedy lethal backlash from resentful parties. The greatest potential for violent tactics to be part of criminal illicit arms transfers—not substantially different between conventional and nuclear arms—appears to be in situations where criminals anticipate coercive interference from government authorities in delivering their cargo, such as when the regime in power suspects that the weapons being transferred are headed to antigovernment insurgent forces.

Individual/Human Security versus National/State Security

Illicit arms smuggling directly affects security. The global arms distribution system tends to move firepower quickly to the most volatile areas of the world, increasing the likelihood that sparks of turmoil will ignite into flames of violent war, conflicts will last longer and will involve more casualties, and stable long-term resolution of the tensions will be more remote. Global arms dealers such as Monzer al-Kassar, Viktor Bout, Leonid Minin, and Jacques Monsieur have frequently provided violent nonstate groups "with weapons capabilities that allow them to challenge government forces."[53] Illicit arms smuggling creates power asymmetries and challenges state legitimacy because of (1) the ability of smugglers to arm one's adversaries and (2) the destabilizing effects of violent conflicts fueled by these smuggled weapons.[54] The high demand for arms from separatist movements, insurgents, terrorists, and extremist religious and political factions makes the trade highly profitable and therefore attractive to criminal dealers. Because illicit arms transfers involving neighboring states may affect the internal politics of recipients, the potential exists for disrupting regional stability.[55]

For nuclear weapons smuggling, the discovery in 2003–2004 of Pakistani nuclear scientist A. Q. Khan's supplying of nuclear technologies and fissile material to several countries (including Libya, North Korea, and Iran) vividly illustrates how such criminal activity can undermine global nonproliferation regimes. Moreover, states have been quick to recognize the ominous specter of global annihilation: "A strong theoretical possibility exists—and has existed for some time—that nuclear material and even complete weapons could be removed from insecure stockpiles, trafficked abroad, and sold to virulently anti-Western states and groups."[56] Although this threat has not as yet materialized, if it did the security disruption would be huge.

For smuggling of small arms and light weapons, national governments have been somewhat slower to acknowledge the full scope of the security impacts. Because of the efforts of concerned grassroots groups, however, policy makers are beginning to pay more attention to the costs of these unsanctioned transactions involving loss of life and property, disruption of economic development, erosion of democratic governance, and spread of fear and instability.[57] Controversy surrounds the expectations of benefits by illicit arms transfer recipients. Whereas weapons transactions have traditionally been perceived as ways for new states, subnational ethnic separatists, or other somewhat disenfranchised groups to "assert their sovereignty,"[58] in practice the global arms trade today remains dependency generating.[59] Recipients of weapons often exaggerate their benefits; for example, "states that wish to assume a higher regional or global profile often assume that military prowess is the means of advancement, irrespective of whether or not the weapons are acquired to meet a definable threat in a militarily appropriate fashion."[60]

The covert nature of a significant proportion of the global arms traffic dramatically increases the security threat. Given that immediate conflict needs are likely to spur acquisition of illicit arms, these weapons appear more likely to be used in battle than legally obtained arms; such illicit deals challenge legitimate policy making "because they generally occur without full official consideration or public debate and because they increase the chances and severity of further fighting."[61] It is certainly difficult to calculate the military balance between two warring sides if a substantial portion of their arsenals was obtained illicitly. Beyond ordinary soldiers battling in the many ongoing low-level shooting conflicts, terrorists and drug traffickers seem to be the most security-challenging recipients of illicit arms, with the black market in armaments appearing to be more important to drug cartels than to any other nonstate group.[62] Illicit arms smuggling undermines both the credibility of arms control initiatives and the moral authority of major power suppliers.[63] Overall, the illegal global arms trade can expand the number and power of disruptive parties, complicate intelligence on their military capabilities, frustrate efforts to contain conflicts, impede the readiness of national military forces, and damage international relationships.[64]

Looking specifically at the influence of arms smuggling on individual/human security, the arms trade endangers civilians by exacerbating intrastate and regional violence as well as increasing domestic crime rates. Advances in technology and economies of scale efficiencies have increased access among members of the mass public to highly lethal weapons systems.[65] Arms trafficking makes such access even easier and thereby fuels violence,[66] especially in volatile areas such as those that are home to strong ethnic or regional conflicts or disputes over scarce resources. The International Committee of the Red Cross has linked illicit arms smuggling to an alarming rise in civilian casualties globally.[67] In addition to loss of life, this atmosphere of violence may cause individuals to have to leave their dwellings and prevent their return, diminishing their overall welfare. Small arms and light weapons have aggravated communal conflicts, helped to sustain sectionalist conflicts, and contributed to the deaths of thousands of people, mostly civilians.[68] The spread of coercive "might-makes-right" instruments among the mass population can also rip apart the fabric of civil society, increasing the chances that disagreements will be settled outside of normal channels, internal strife will not be resolved peacefully, economic costs to society will escalate, and fear and distrust will rise. The illicit spread of nuclear arms could spread social fears of mass annihilation on a global scale. All of these trends may end up undermining existing social and economic institutions.

Turning to the impact of arms smuggling on national/state security, criminally induced arms transfers have a much larger impact here than on individual security. Illicit arms transfers threaten state security by increasing the capabilities of terrorists and insurgents vis-à-vis the state: antigovernment groups, which are the prominent recipients of contraband arms traffic,[69] threaten the survival of status quo political regimes, for although arms do not cause revolutions, they certainly do empower the discontent. The indirect funding of terrorist groups, insurgencies, civil wars, and ethnonationalistic wars is a primary danger posed by arms trafficking, and if a terrorist cell or insurgent group obtained a preponderance of firepower and influence, it could plausibly overwhelm the government regime. Whereas most large states have enough legitimacy, firepower, and international clout to resist the destabilizing effects of free-flowing weapons, small states with weak regimes are much more vulnerable. Transnational arms transfers often serve to highlight recipient national governments' inadequate regulatory codes and lax law enforcement, allowing arms to spread freely both internally and externally. Because criminally induced cross-border arms smuggling frequently involves legitimate groups and institutions—such as national defense ministries, national security agencies, financial institutions, and political groups involved in internal power struggles within states—these illicit transfers can substantially weaken authority structures within affected states.[70] Nuclear weapons transfers could even more directly affect state security than conventional arms transfers, for, even if they are never used, the mere acquisition of them—particularly if criminals have a role in this acquisition—could alter the existing balance of power and heighten the sense of global instability. Indeed, arms smuggling may trigger more paranoia among observing states, which may assume sinister external sources for the weapons and sinister motives for the arms acquisition, than would internal development of the same armaments.[71] Moreover, states close to illicit arms recipients often have to tolerate disquieting smuggling operations within their borders.[72] Reliance on one's own arms usually sacrifices capability, whereas reliance on arms transfers from abroad usually sacrifices control.[73]

ILLICIT DRUG TRANSFERS

General Scope and Nature of the Activity

Illicit global drug running serves two very different purposes—it caters to addicted pleasure seekers or cynical and disillusioned people wanting escape from the harsh realities that surround them, and it affords transnational criminals a ready way to make lots of money. The net result is simultaneously to neutralize potential opponents, to incapacitate substantial numbers of people, and to drag recipients of narcotics into a complex web of crime. The illicit cross-border drug transfer involves both soft drugs such as marijuana (cannabis) and hard drugs such as heroin (opium) and cocaine. Consolidating drug cultivation, production, and distribution under the control of an organized crime syndicate necessitates a global network of operatives, including local farmers to grow the crops, local traffickers, international distributors, and compliant government and transportation officials.

The global distribution of illicit drugs has a long history. The Turkish and Persian opium trade has been going on for centuries in the Middle East and East and South Asia, with large-scale global distribution of opiates beginning in the second half of the eighteenth century.[74] Reflecting on this history of international drug trafficking, one quickly discovers that "the desire of individuals to alter their state of consciousness is one of the few constants of civilized human history," with a variety of psychoactive substances used for thousands of years for medicinal, ritual, and recreational purposes.[75] Whereas the major powers often initially turned a blind eye to this drug running, during the early twentieth century significant global agreements curtailed government involvement in the illicit drug trade, and these agreements had the unfortunate consequence of opening the door to dominance by transnational organized crime.[76] One relatively recent development that has complicated the management of transnational drug flows has been the growth in the production of "designer drugs" and synthetic narcotics, allowing their creators to enjoy a brief "window of legality" before the regulatory system catches up to them.[77] Like illicit arms transfers but unlike illicit human transfers, global illicit drug transfers are constantly in a state of flux, as new fads and illegal substances ebb and flow in their popularity.

The global illicit drug trade nets between $420 billion and $1 trillion a year, making illicit drugs the largest sector of the global black market and the single best selling product in the world.[78] The United Nations estimates that the global drug trade is worth between $320 billion and $500 billion annually, a staggering 2 percent of the world economy, with the global trade in heroin—the most dangerous drug—valued at $57 billion.[79] Worldwide, there are 200 million users of illicit drugs,[80] and the United States is by far the largest consumer, with 30 million American users spending annually about $28 billion on cocaine, $68 billion on marijuana, and $10 to $12 billion on heroin.[81] Colombia and Afghanistan are the largest sources of supply for cocaine and heroin, with Myanmar, Afghanistan, and Laos together accounting for over 90 percent of the world's heroin production.[82] Most states of the world play a part in the global market for prohibited drugs, "a market almost as large as those for the major permitted drugs—nicotine and alcohol."[83] Indeed, "the global explosion of demand and supply has shattered the illusion of invulnerability that governments—or, for that matter, public opinion—harbored in many countries; now, no country is isolated enough to delude itself or its critics into imagining that it has no part in the world drug trade."[84] The major international sites for laundering drug money include countries as diverse as the Cayman Islands, Colombia, Germany, Hong Kong, Italy, Mexico, the Netherlands, Nigeria, Panama, Singapore, Switzerland, Thailand, the United Kingdom, the United States, and Venezuela.[85]

Roots of and Responses to the Activity

A common explanation for the spread of illicit drug production is inadequate success within source states in growing and marketing traditional agricultural goods. Because farmers in major drug-exporting states face major challenges in selling food crops on the globalized international market for reasonable prices, they feel that "they often have little choice but to grow coca and other illegal drugs."[86] More specifically, "the foreign demand for illicit drugs has represented a principal source of foreign exchange," "a significant proportion of the gross national product," and "an important source of employment for hundreds of thousands of mostly poor people" in drug-exporting states.[87] Because of the large number of coca farmers, exporters, and smugglers, the supply of cocaine is difficult to eliminate, and the rewards from selling it are great because the price rises roughly 200 times between the coca farm and the street.[88] Drug traders generally view globalization as their "greatest growth opportunity,"[89] and given the reluctance of either drug-consuming or drug-producing states to take direct responsibility for the problem, these criminal drug traffickers feel justifiably that they can consistently evade local authorities.[90]

The global "war on drugs" began in the United States in 1985–1986 when President Ronald Reagan identified illicit drug trafficking as a national security threat and authorized the Defense Department to engage in antidrug operations, leading to interdiction expenditures that grew from $400 million in 1987 to $1.2 billion in 1991,[91] but widespread consensus exists that this effort has largely failed to make a major long-term dent in illicit drug running.[92] Although "the global antidrug campaign has been a driving force in forging cooperative links among criminal justice systems," it "has also generated extraordinary levels of crime, violence, corruption, disease, and other ills."[93] Any attempt to interdict global drug smuggling faces nearly insurmountable obstacles, including (1) the eagerness of users/victims to imbibe, making them unlikely to press for prosecution of distributors; (2) reduced government monitoring of domestic activities as a result of economic liberalization and deregulation; (3) the proliferation of weak states with remote areas conducive to drug growing; and (4) the scarcity of alternative sources of income for impoverished workers involved in the production of drugs.[94] Presently, with the widely reported increases in the production of illicit drugs, in the amount of drugs moving across borders, and in the number of countries involved in the drug trade, prospects for effective international interdiction appear to be quite low.

Soft Drugs

When dealing with soft drugs, considerable ambivalence and disagreement persists within and across countries about the appropriateness of the complete prohibition of drug use and drug trade and about the degree of difference between these prohibited substances and legal substances such as nicotine in cigarettes, alcohol in liquor, and even caffeine in coffee and tea. All of these provide physical release or stimulation that many people find to be pleasurable, even though all are dangerous or even lethal when taken in very high concentrations, imbibed inappropriately, or consumed over a very long period of time. This issue becomes even more complicated when considering the medical use of marijuana, already sanctioned in some areas. Possible legalization of the marketing of these substances (which has already occurred in Amsterdam in the Netherlands) comes up with a frequency and intensity unmatched by other disruptive transnational activities, with the underlying motive of many advocates being elimination of the criminally controlled drug trade.

Criminal trafficking of soft drugs, apparently in decline for a couple of decades, usually is not accompanied by as much violence as hard-drug transfers: for example, the market for marijuana and the people who traffic it are often from a subculture disapproving of violence, making its use both uncharacteristic and infrequent.[95] The relative ease of growing one's own marijuana in many places may also contribute to this pattern. Exceptions to this general rule may exist, however, as a recent American government report indicated that violent Mexican drug-trafficking organizations derive the lion's share of their profits from the exportation and sale of marijuana.[96]

Hard Drugs

Hard drugs generally involve more incapacitating addiction, more drastic physical effects on users, more chance of lethal overdose, and more difficulty with withdrawal than do soft drugs. As a result, they usually produce more desperation among those hooked, leading to a willingness to pay higher prices and take greater risks in procurement. This plays right into the hands of transnational criminals, making the threat of an interrupted supply of a hard drug even more of an incentive for compliance than the threat of coercion.

The monetary costs of global hard-drug operations are staggering, but they are more than offset by the monetary benefits. For example, a leading drug baron boasted that he authorized payments of $1 million a day to keep himself out of jail, and a Colombian cocaine cartel is reputed to pay between 17 and 20 percent of its proceeds for money-laundering services that transfer drug profits into cash-intensive travel agencies, exchange houses, casinos, international trading firms, and building construction operations.[97] For young traffickers with few alternative options, on a superficial level the risks sure appear to be attractive.

Corruption versus Violence

For drug traffickers, when a possibility exists of a cozy relationship with local authorities, corruption is generally preferable to violence, resulting in a gradual shift toward the primacy of bribery to maximize profits and to minimize law enforcement intrusion.[98] The huge illicit drug revenues facilitate corruption and intimidation of politicians, judges, bureaucrats, and law enforcement officials "whose active cooperation or passive acquiescence is necessary for the enterprise to succeed."[99] These illicit drug revenues literally make it possible to corrupt government officials at every level;[100] regardless of location, however, most drug runners attempt to bribe low-ranking officials, such as airline employees, truckers, ordinary citizens, and bank workers.

The narcotics industry is often run like a business with a high level of professionalism, and many drug traffickers have prior entrepreneurial experience and use ties to the legitimate business world for links to customers and for access to front companies and transportation.[101] This professional attitude permeates not just the labor relations within the ranks of organized crime but also the interactions among suppliers, distributors, and customers. One dealer explains the unremarkable industry dynamics: "It's all market value," he said. "It's product, price, reputation, and service"; and "with the people I dealt with, there are no guns and no intimidation."[102] Drug runners sometimes prefer corruption because in the long run it may be less costly than violence—because corruption seems less likely to attract an outcry from government officials or the public, traffickers may encounter fewer security problems or inconvenient regulations.

Transnational organized crime relies on corruption in drug running,[103] particularly in areas where the state is weak, law enforcement agencies are unscrupulous, and criminal drug runners can operate with impunity. In Afghanistan, Colombia, and Myanmar, for example, crime syndicates use both corruption and violence, but increasingly rely on corruption to prey upon weak state institutions. Moreover, corruption appears most useful during the transportation stage of drug trafficking, to garner help from legitimate companies to shepherd their shipments of drugs into more tightly regulated destination countries: for example, many drug traffickers use bribes to airline employees, truckers, and average citizens in order to finesse their way through checkpoints in source countries, but do so less frequently in destination counties—which tend to be advanced industrial societies—because most traffickers view officials in destination countries to be more "difficult and dangerous" to bribe.[104] Generally, drug traffickers turn to corruption when they perceive the risk of having their bribe rebuffed or of being betrayed and turned in as being less than the risk of having hidden shipments of drugs discovered.

Nonetheless, especially when facing an antagonistic national government, drug smugglers still employ violent means to protect their territory and profits, to settle disputes, and to intimidate or eliminate high-ranking officials or journalists interfering with their endeavors.[105] According to Peter Phillips, the former minister of national security of Jamaica (a country beset by drug trafficking), "the *modus operandi* of the drug lords internationally is a particularly violent one—it relies on its own enforcement by intimidation, fear and brutality."[106] Illustrating this tendency is the recent resurgence of high-profile

violence by Mexican drug traffickers that is increasingly flagrant, killing innocent bystanders as well as designated human targets. Drug traffickers react
violently when they are threatened by anti-drug-trafficking and extradition
policies, law enforcement officers, or a significant loss of profits; and this violence can serve to settle disputes or to intimidate or eliminate government
officials, judges, journalists, or rival gang members.[107] It is unusual for traffickers to direct violence primarily toward civilian consumers.[108] The security
impacts of drug-related violence are not just on those directly physically in-
jured: "Even though the majority of those killed are people involved in the
drug trade, the violence has come to affect the lives of both ordinary people
who do not dare venture out of their houses at night (or even during the day)
for fear of getting caught in the cross-fire, and of elites who have become targets of extortion."[109]

The modern global market in narcotics is unusual in that it entails a "high
level of violence"[110] yet is also highly professionalized. When transnational
drug traffickers do make use of violence, rather than senseless violence, they
employ "violent behavior with low-profile strategies."[111] Although drug traffickers who conceptualize their trade as an entrepreneurial business normatively prefer business-like transactions to violence, they find its use necessary
in order to protect their territory, collect debts, cultivate a reputation of respect and fear within the industry, and deter betrayal within the ranks of their
network.[112] Although corruption is frequently used to smuggle the drugs from
their source to their destination, it is within the underground economy of
dealers and suppliers, as well as between rival gangs and cartels, that the levels of violence rise: the highest levels of drug violence occur within countries
where the drugs are cultivated or manufactured, or within transit countries
in the smuggling route, in part because these tend to be developing states.

Some retaliatory killings are motivated not just by a desire to collect debts
or recover lost goods but also by a need to enforce norms. Often killers who
commit drug-related homicides do so because they feel that the victims have
"violated rules essential to the proper conduct of the drug-trafficking business."[113] The lengths that drug traffickers go to exact revenge can be extensive
and gruesome, dispelling any doubts that the drug-trafficking business is violent. The higher-ups—cartel heads or mafia bosses—are typically more violent than the autonomous traffickers that they pay to ferry the goods across
borders, at least in part because it serves the long-term interests of organized
criminals to enforce normative codes of behavior.[114] Threats, intimidation, as-

sault, and homicide are "functionally essential for the maintenance and expansion of profit-taking in many heroin, cocaine, and marijuana-trafficking systems."[115] To maintain territorial dominance and deference within their sphere, organized criminals often use violence as a punishment for noncompliance, especially within the ranks of their own syndicate or in the course of intergang disputes. Because the interactions between drug cartels are very violent in nature, the narcotics industry is stigmatized as a bloody, unforgiving one.

Individual/Human Security versus National/State Security

The impact of global illicit drug transfers on security is more indirect than that of global illicit arms transfers. Exemplifying this security influence are revenues that have been pivotal to funding paramilitary forces around the world and opiates that have degraded the political economies of many Southeast and Southwest Asian countries, including Afghanistan, Cambodia, Iran, Myanmar, Pakistan, Thailand, and Vietnam.[116] Drug-related corruption (termed "narco-corruption") is spreading across regimes in both producing and consuming societies and, in the process, posing a major global security threat. With both the police and key government officials directly caught in the lucrative drug web, corrupted individuals tend to lose their sense of dignity and integrity, and corrupted governments tend to lose whatever sense of confidence and legitimacy they possess in the eyes of their citizenry and fellow states.[117] A survey of antidrug enforcement bodies (including the police, customs officials, and the judiciary) tainted by drug money shows that corruption exists at the most senior levels in Afghanistan, Argentina, Armenia, Azerbaijan, Bolivia, Colombia, the Dominican Republic, Ecuador, Guatemala, Honduras, India, Iran, Italy, Kenya, Laos, Mexico, Morocco, Nicaragua, Niger, Nigeria, Pakistan, Panama, Paraguay, Peru, the Philippines, Romania, Senegal, Spain, Suriname, Syria, Tajikistan, Thailand, Turkey, Venezuela, and Zambia.[118] The sizable criminal influence over the governments of key source countries, fueled by illicit drug sales, is a major source of instability.

A couple of explanations exist for why the security impact from global drug running has been so pervasive. One major roadblock to managing illicit drugs is the difficulty surrounding effective international collaboration, whose productive outcomes are specifically hampered by "a combination of political rivalries, jealously guarded national legal systems, official corruption and sheer incompetence" taken advantage of by transnational drug runners who are "cosmopolitan businessmen, well-educated, well-spoken, who know how to move among politicians and officials and transfer money from Wall Street to London to Paris and beyond"; "privileged people with plenty of opportunities"; and those "just more than usually greedy as businessmen and so tempted to take the criminal route."[119] A second obstacle to managing this drug-related security threat is the insistence of policy makers in industrialized nations on attacking only the supply end of the problem: the supply-side approach is deficient because illicit drug revenues are so vast that successes in supply-side enforcement "only marginally offset" economic incentives for further unsanctioned activity;[120] and, as a result, the Central Intelligence Agency concluded that these supply-side efforts have largely failed.[121]

Underlying these problems is the steadfast refusal of anyone to take responsibility for the huge traffic in illicit drugs. Drug-consuming and drug-producing nations continually engage in futile finger-pointing, with each blaming the other for the pernicious consequences of these shady transactions.[122] A classic example here is the relationship between the United States and Mexico: on the drug issue, "each blames the other for its woes," and "each largely ignores its own flaws"; "Americans are preoccupied with addiction and crime, Mexicans with violence and corruption, yet the problems of one are rapidly becoming a menace in the other."[123] During the escalating violence by Mexican drug lords in 2008–2009, Mexicans blamed Americans for their drug demand and the weapons purchased by drug runners, and Americans blamed Mexicans for their corrupt government and ineffective security system.[124] In reality, the threats posed by the illicit traffic in drugs to export and import states are quite different: export states are more concerned with government corruption, domestic economy distortions through misallocation of agricultural land, and a tarnished international image that could lead to negative international sanctions; import states are more concerned with the distraction and degeneration of their citizens who become hooked on illicit drugs and the resulting empowerment of transnational organized crime controlling their distribution.

Regarding the specific impact on individual/human security, this is where drug running has its greatest influence (as compared to that on state security). Because a prevailing view of these unsanctioned substances is that they cause severe physical harm to individuals who use them but generate little direct damage to the state, it is quite common for authorities tacitly to ignore this activity. The cold logic behind this decision is often officials' implicit calculation that those sufficiently shortsighted not to realize the dangers from drug use deserve whatever negative consequences ensue.

Most broadly, illicit drug trafficking is associated with a gradual decline in social cohesion and a rise in societal decay within consuming states, reflected by rapid increases in drug-related violent crimes in inner cities and escalating health care problems, including the accelerated spread of disease via drug users.[125] In particular, the consequences of illicit narcotics on American life include 14,000 drug-related deaths each year, a soaring prison population, and indirect costs estimated at $67 billion a year.[126] The corrosive effects of global narco-trafficking on society include rising "neighborhood crime and transmissible diseases, particularly HIV/AIDS and hepatitis."[127] Growing drug use, especially among youth and minority ethnic populations, "accentuates social cleavages already fueled by the pain and dislocations connected with modernization and post-communist and postindustrial societal transitions."[128] If invidious enough, drug-related corruption may "engender chaos created by injustice and social disorder":[129]

> The drug market is more than just some unsavoury characters making a lot of money: the same people can actually destroy society. As West Africa has recently demonstrated, the effects of drug trafficking on human security are devastating. Drug traffickers use their war-chests to attack vulnerable countries, through business acquisitions, corruption and violence. These processes inevitably converge, as at stake is more than just money-laundering and intimidation: drug cartels buy more than real estate, banks and business. They buy elections, candidates and parties. In a word, they buy power. Here is where the drug business becomes a security threat.[130]

More subtly than any other transnational criminal activity, illicit narcotics transactions eat away at the core of what makes a civil community function properly, drastically skewing the flow of revenues, enhancing the power of organized crime, and hooking individuals into a life of eternal craving devoid of any stable long-term fulfillment.

As with cigarette smoking, it is not just those who take drugs who suffer the debilitating consequences of the illicit drug trade. Innocent bystanders may end up being robbed or killed because of the desperate and unending search for drug money by those addicted to these substances. Communities may have to devote scarce public funds to protect against this threat, depriving areas of money for social services. Long-term drug dependency can break up close-knit families and ruin public educational systems. Distrust may develop among neighbors over suspicions of illicit drug use, eliminating possible positive joint steps toward collective community problem solving. If illegal drug use becomes too rampant, then social friction can ensue between those who attempt to stamp out drug use and those who imbibe and resent the feeling of being inappropriately judged, condemned, and held responsible for all societal problems.

Regarding global drug running's impact on national/state security, this effect is more indirect than that on individual security but can undermine political stability. Manipulative drug terror tactics can lead to the devolution of effectively functioning democracy, as extreme and endemic violence can leave citizens fearful of challenging the criminal perpetrators and disillusioned about the value of government. Furthermore, the use of military force to fight drug trafficking can lead to undue strengthening of coercive tactics within the fragile democracies in some drug-producing states.[131] While attempting to promote political stability, using heavily armed government antidrug forces to settle disputes can inadvertently undercut the proper functioning of democratic governance. Given the public's conflicted feelings about illicit drug use, mass tolerance for this militarization may be low, undercutting the effectiveness of coercive antidrug initiatives and ultimately providing drug traffickers options to gain a secure foothold. On the economic front, despite drug revenues, the economies in drug-producing or drug-consuming states may take a severe hit, as surging illicit profits can weaken financial institutions in a way that directly undermines state infrastructure. Overall, major political and economic costs surround being a drug transport country, including escalating conflict in regions already prone to internal violence and weakened government and financial institutions contributing to suffering within drug-riddled countries.[132]

The state security implications of global drug smuggling revolve heavily around the use of illicit drug revenues:

> Criminal competition for the drug markets is fierce, resulting in real wars on the streets of many cities, worldwide. Profits are ploughed back into increasing the capacity for violence and into corrupting public officials. Together, violence and corruption drive away investment and undermine governance to the point that the rule of law itself becomes questionable. A vicious circle is thus triggered, with lawlessness allowing even greater drug trafficking, with ever higher proceeds abrading the social contract between society and its elected leaders.[133]

Government officials' receipt of illicit drug revenues fundamentally erodes the legitimacy of political and judicial institutions.[134]

The illicit narcotics industry's direct support of terrorist activities threatening to states is well established.[135] For example, individuals and groups in Afghanistan, Russia, and Southeast Asia "tax the growth, processing, transport, and sale of illicit drugs to finance terror, criminal, and other covert activities," and they use the profits "to purchase weapons, safe houses, transportation, and information."[136] During a July 2008 fact-finding trip to Afghanistan, Democratic presidential candidate Barack Obama noted that the drug trade gave terrorists the money to carry out such attacks in the area. Today "the narcotics industry remains the most common and lucrative source of revenue to terrorists groups."[137] Drug traffickers provide substantial financial resources to dangerous radical groups and enemies of the state: for example, al-Qaeda's attacks on the United States, though not the direct result of drug running, resulted partly from the wealth that the poppy trade brought to the otherwise underdeveloped state of Afghanistan.[138] Large-scale drug traffickers have used their exorbitant profits to invest in real estate, modernize their trafficking operations, pay off politicians, and corrupt officials, all of which give drug traffickers considerable political clout and, in some instances, threaten the solvency of the state. Profits from cross-border drug smuggling have helped to fund expanding military operations of stability-threatening insurgencies, with the huge accrued revenues impeding insurgents' acceptance of any war-ending peace agreement when it necessitates forgoing access to this illicit income.[139]

Within weak developing countries, the invidious role of drug traffickers can make them "a veritable state within a state."[140] In these states illicit drug revenues may allow warlords to obtain arms to overthrow or co-opt a national government and ignore international censure.[141] This political control results from drug runners having a lot more money than poor weak states. Areas infested with illicit drug trafficking usually find that this activity scares away tourists, multinational corporations, and foreign investment, "making existing socio-economic problems even more intractable."[142]

ILLICIT HUMAN TRANSFERS

General Scope and Nature of the Activity
Illicit human transfers, involving all forms of criminally facilitated illegal cross-border migration, represent the second largest transnational criminal activity[143] behind illicit drug transfers. These illicit human transfers have two

distinct but interconnected dimensions: (1) migrant labor smuggling, usually facilitating the cross-border movement of eager workers of all types who find themselves unable to enter legally; and (2) human sex trafficking, usually taking primarily women and children by force or deception across an international border.[144] The analysis of each of the two disruptive transnational flows needs to be much more carefully separated than either (1) soft drugs versus hard drugs within the illicit drug transfers discussion or (2) nuclear weapons versus conventional weapons within the illicit arms transfers discussion.

The importance of this partitioning was reinforced in October 2000, when the United Nations completed its Convention against Transnational Organized Crime and supplemented it with two important separate protocols relevant to illicit human transfers: (1) the Protocol against the Smuggling of Migrants by Land, Sea and Air and (2) the Protocol to Prevent, Suppress and Punish Trafficking in Persons, Especially Women and Children. Security-oriented motivations prompted these initiatives: "While human rights concerns may have provided some impetus (or cover) for collective action, it is the sovereignty/security issues surrounding trafficking and migrant smuggling which are the true driving force behind such efforts; wealthy states are increasingly concerned that the actions of traffickers and migrant smugglers interfere with orderly migration and facilitate the circumvention of national immigration restrictions."[145] Despite the clear language in these protocols, however, "implementation of the new distinction between trafficked persons and smuggled migrants is likely to be both difficult and controversial."[146]

General agreement exists that together migrant labor smuggling and human sex trafficking constitute "the most morally repugnant of all the illicit trades that flourish today."[147] Portraying such activity as "a victimless crime" providing a means of circumventing arbitrary national immigration restrictions ignores "the unpleasant realities of a business that reduces people to the level of commodities."[148] Although human sex trafficking garners more international outrage, a 2005 study by the International Labour Organization found that worldwide less than half of all illicit human transfers involve human sex trafficking rather than migrant labor smuggling.[149]

Transnational organized crime controls only a part of the illicit human transfers market, with the Chinese "snakeheads" being among the most prominent criminals involved, for much of this illicit activity remains in the hands of small ad hoc local groups, "mom-and-pop" operations, and individuals.[150] Nonetheless, in recent years, the size and sophistication of illicit human transfer operations have escalated dramatically, with transnational criminal organizations involved in this activity operating "with near impunity" because of corruption in both source and transit states.[151] These criminal operations engaged in moving people across borders take full advantage of the latest technologies, including night vision goggles, cell phones equipped with network cards, and other high-tech gear.[152] The net result is a familiar security paradox: "State aggressiveness in combating human smuggling, in the form of tighter border controls and asylum policies, has prompted more people to seek smugglers and others to enter the migrant smuggling business, including ongoing transnational criminal enterprises attracted by the high profits and low risks of this activity."[153] Criminals involved in illicit human transfers, whether a part of small or large operations, favor countries for finding victims that are either rife with economic and political turmoil (such as states of the former Soviet Union) or have lax regulations regarding trafficking, prostitution, and labor (such as most countries in the Middle East and North Africa).[154]

Estimates for the annual profits from worldwide illicit human transfers range from $7 billion to $10 billion to almost $32 billion.[155] The U.S. Department of State estimates that between 600,000 and 800,000 people are trafficked each year, with the United States and Western Europe being the largest destinations for trafficking syndicates.[156] The profits are substantial, as "smugglers command high prices for their services, ranging from $500 for passage from Morocco to Spain to as much as $70,000 per person from some countries in Asia to the United States."[157] In 2004, there were about 175 million documented international migrants compared to about 262 million undocumented international migrants, with about 4 million people trafficked across borders annually.[158] Illegal migration to the entire industrialized world has sharply increased in recent years:[159] for example, Western Europe has over three million illegal migrants, largely from Eastern Europe and Africa; and Japan now faces increased illegal migration from mainland China, the Philippines, and other parts of Southeast Asia. About 10 to 15 percent of the immigrants in advanced industrial societies are unauthorized, and although most enter illegally, a minority enters legally but fails to depart when visas expire.[160]

Roots of and Responses to the Activity

The reasons for this burgeoning of illicit human transfers include the increased restrictions on legal migration by both developed and developing nations since the 1970s; the growth in global markets, stimulating emerging migration networks; the removal of obstacles to migration because of the breakdown of authoritarian regimes; and, most directly, the emergence of transnational criminal groups—"migration mafia"—that exact exorbitant fees to arrange transportation, documentation, and sometimes employment from those desperate to move abroad.[161] In general, transnational organized crime enters the international migration picture when the supply-demand ratio is a favorable one—"when the demand for opportunities to immigrate outstrips the supply provided by official channels in state migration policies."[162] More specifically, criminal facilitation of illicit human transfers of all kinds is flourishing because start-up costs are small, the people being transported are "durable" and can be used and reused, and the risks are low because the legal penalties for trafficking are minimal and the enforcement is lax.[163] The increased state restrictions in recent decades on the number of legal immigrants have played right into the hands of criminals.

Devising effective responses to illegal migration is difficult in today's world because of deep moral confusion surrounding the issue that national government officials are loath to discuss among themselves or with the public. Indeed, these illegal migrants may be aided—or even enticed and facilitated—by private citizens, often relatives and friends eager to unite with loved ones or businesspeople eager to hire willing or not-so-willing workers. For both migrant labor smuggling and human sex trafficking, "most unauthorized immigrants concentrate in jobs that have long been abandoned by the country's legal work force."[164] As a result, many legitimate businesses—particularly those in agriculture, construction, domestic service, food service, hospitality, and prostitution—have encouraged (even when aware of criminal facilitation of people across borders) lax law enforcement toward illegal immigrants, who provide cheap labor and thus keep profits high and prices low. Furthermore, attempts to restrict illicit human transfers have often backfired: for example, tightened American and European immigration restrictions have caused human traffickers to engage in riskier cross-border tactics, leading to the deaths of hundreds of migrants annually.[165] More generally, reining in illicit human transfers presents a "terrible paradox": the more strictly states enforce national laws against this illicit activity, the more criminals involved in illicit human transfers choose to use extreme tactics to overcome existing barriers so as to make a profit.[166]

Migrant Labor Smuggling

Looking first at migrant labor smuggling, it incorporates both those pushed out by horrendous conditions at home and those pulled in by attractive conditions abroad, in both cases expressly violating the national immigration laws of the receiving states. Although many illegal aliens make and execute their own decisions to move (often with help from relatives and friends in the countries of origin and destination), an increasing proportion of illegal immigration is facilitated by transnational criminal organizations, which find that smuggling human contraband across borders is highly lucrative.[167] This trafficking appears to be a "low-risk, high-gain" proposition: porous global borders and high-volume international human traffic make detection difficult, and the penalties for human smuggling in the United States and Western Europe are relatively lenient compared to those for smuggling narcotics, with the penalties in the rest of the world for human smuggling even lighter.[168] Thus many transnational criminals see illegal transport of people across boundaries as both more profitable and less risky than other criminal activities.[169] For these reasons, the field of smugglers is getting crowded: for example, small "mom-and-pop" organizations in migrant labor smuggling from mainland China now vigorously compete with the Chinese triads,[170] to the point where many of the operations are in the hands of small to medium-sized local groups that do not fit the traditional concept of organized crime.[171]

Despite efforts by law enforcement and immigration authorities, it is relatively easy now to forge immigration documents or obtain genuine ones illegally.[172] In addition, improved information about opportunities abroad and encouragement from foreign friends and relatives may stimulate the desire to migrate illegally.[173] Perhaps the most widely analyzed illegal migrant flow is from Mexico to the United States along their long shared border, driven not only by poverty, unemployment, income disparities, and the linkages between the Mexican and American economies but also by the web of social and family connections and by the cultural experience Mexicans have in the United States.[174] Illegal migrants are motivated not just by a desperate attempt to escape from disadvantaged situations but also by high hopes about improving their lives: despite greater awareness of international conditions, there is still sometimes a "revolution of rising expectations" and "the draw of bright lights and big cities,"[175] accompanied by the optimistic misconception that their destinations have "streets paved with gold."

Because illegal migrants lack international legitimacy, they have no rights, so they are often abused and mistreated by others without fear of notice or retribution. Furthermore, because they are vulnerable, they often become dependent on the services provided by the networks of criminals who illegally facilitated their cross-border transport, and, as a result, they often "become absorbed into these networks," "participating in whatever protection rackets, turf wars, collaborative activities, and other forms of criminality are on offer at the time."[176] At the same time, however, illegal migrants often feel that they do not need to play by established global rules and norms, and many are ignorant of what these rules and norms actually are. Migrant labor smuggling can be positive in "enabling asylum seekers—including some genuine refugees—to escape persecution"; it can also be negative in exposing "the already vulnerable to even greater vulnerability."[177] What complicates the situation further is that (1) those people who sneak illicitly into countries may be aided, or even enticed and facilitated, by legitimate citizens of a receiving state, and (2) law enforcement authorities may turn a blind eye toward these intruders because they end up performing menial tasks receiving societies find useful.

Both developed and developing states are very concerned about migrant labor smuggling, with few countries untouched by this illicit activity and its associated violence and corruption.[178] The United States receives the greatest number of smuggled migrant laborers,[179] with about 400,000 annual illegal immigrants from Mexico alone; the illegal segment of the American population increased from around three million people in 1986 to around eleven million to twelve million people in 2006.[180] Less widely noticed are the annual flows of about 100,000 illegal Chinese migrants into the United States, smuggled in by criminal groups for huge fees and then forced to work in menial jobs in vain attempts to repay their debt under circumstances that can only be described as "virtual slavery."[181] The developing world's rising smuggled migrant labor moves from Indonesia to Malaysia, Bangladesh to India, Nepal to Bhutan, China to Hong Kong and Taiwan, and parts of Africa to Ivory Coast, South Africa, and Nigeria.[182]

Human Sex Trafficking

Turning to human sex trafficking, this activity has a long and sordid history—"until just a few centuries ago, slavery and slave trading were legal and commonplace features of society and commerce throughout the world."[183] However, long after most countries of the world declared the slave trade to be both morally and legally unacceptable, transnational organized crime has revitalized this repugnant illicit cross-border activity: "At the end of the last century, the world witnessed the growth of a modern form of slavery," one that treats "women, men, and children as commodities to abuse, sell, and move across borders like illegal drugs or stolen weapons."[184] Indeed, far more women and girls have been shipped to brothels each year in the early twenty-first century than the number of slaves transferred during the peak transatlantic slave trade during the eighteenth and nineteenth centuries; in 2009, an estimated three million women and girls (along with a smaller number of boys) worldwide were enslaved in the sex trade.[185] This serves to compound an already existing problem of an estimated 27 to 200 million people already living under modern forms of slavery.[186]

The criminal human sex-trafficking business "feeds on poverty, despair, war, crisis, and ignorance," as "traffickers are known to exploit wars, turmoil, and natural disasters to target and enslave victims, especially women and children."[187] Children are often snatched at a very young age (sometimes with the complicity of their parents because of their need or desire for money) and forced into this sordid lifestyle. Over time, the sex trade has become more organized and appealing to criminals. Indeed, human sex trafficking from places such as Laos, Myanmar, Nepal, the Philippines, and Ukraine "is so profitable that criminal business people invest in involuntary brothels much as they would in a mining operation."[188]

Currently, human sex trafficking is booming all over the world, with estimated annual global profits of around $31.7 billion.[189] The top countries from which the victims of human sex trafficking originate are largely in the developing world, including Albania, Belarus, Brazil, Bulgaria, China, Colombia, the Dominican Republic, Guatemala, Lithuania, Mexico, Moldova, Nigeria, Romania, Russia, Thailand, and Ukraine; the top ten destination countries for human sex trafficking include more advanced industrial societies—Belgium, Germany, Greece, Israel, Italy, Japan, the Netherlands, Thailand, Turkey, and the United States.[190] A key focal point for human sex trafficking is Southeast Asia,[191] with Thailand a hub for this undercover activity.

Corruption versus Violence

Looking first at corruption in illicit human transfers, in many ways "the entire illegal migration network is about corruption":[192] illicit human transfers of all varieties would not be so vast and lucrative were it not for corrupt government officials—especially those in customs, the police, and the military—colluding with transnational criminal organizations to circumvent relevant laws.[193] Successful illicit human transfer "requires highly paid facilitators in destination countries, employers prepared to house exploited labour, and the collusion, if not corruption, of the private sector."[194] Complicit immigration officials may passively do nothing as a matter of informal policy as illegal migrants cross borders, receive payoffs from criminal traffickers for turning a blind eye to the illicit activity, or provide false passports and visas to illegal migrants.[195] Criminally induced illegal immigrants frequently travel through an intermediary country to draw attention away from their place of origin, and in order to get through these transit countries—often developing states— the use of bribes and corruption is commonplace. Moreover, human smugglers need to use bribes to get past the police, border guards, and other officials that they encounter during the journey.

With specific regard to corruption in migrant labor smuggling, corruption can occur in terms of (1) payments from both would-be migrants and criminal facilitators to local authorities to overlook the illicit activity and (2) payments to and from unscrupulous employers to bring in more illegal employees. Often the beneficiaries, facilitators, and law enforcement authorities all engage in different kinds of corruption as a part of this process, which in a way works to the advantage of transnational criminals because nobody's hands are clean and thus nobody would be tempted to blow the whistle on anyone else's corrupt activity. However, for illegal migrant laborers who sneak into a destination country with no documentation at all—in contrast to trafficking victims who often are furnished with illegal documents—corruption may not be involved.[196]

In contrast, with specific regard to corruption in human sex trafficking, payoffs to local police ensure that the police give brothel owners and recruiters indemnity; this law enforcement corruption has, in many places, spread to the point where it has become an institutional reality tolerated throughout the chain of command. Criminal human traffickers use highly organized networks that have large-scale operations connected to corrupt officials. Within the sex trade, help from legitimate authorities seems especially important, for "it would be difficult, if not impossible, to move so many women across borders and abuse and exploit them in so many public establishments without the cooperation of the police and/or officials."[197]

Turning to violence in illicit human transfers, transnational criminal organizations sometimes use violence and threats of physical abuse because the inherent disequilibrium of power between the victimizer and the victim makes coercion an effective tool. Because those brought in illegally by criminals have no legal recourse within the country in which they are now located, a facilitating criminal organization feels that it can do whatever it wants to them physically to maximize its profitability as long as it does not damage them so severely that they no longer are of economic value. The purpose of violence and threats of violence in this regard is to induce complete compliance.

With specific regard to violence in migrant labor smuggling, though not as overtly distasteful as in sex trafficking, high levels of violence and abuse are still rampant. Beatings; forced labor without pay; physical abuse; substandard housing; and food, water, and sleep deprivation have been commonplace in treatment of criminally smuggled migrant laborers.[198] Illegal agricultural workers, in particular, often have to live and work for years in subhuman conditions without any form of freedom.

In contrast, with specific regard to violence in human sex trafficking, the sex industry is demonstrably violent because it enslaves women and children and requires the use of coercion to keep them captive. The traffickers consider the women and children disposable and therefore do not lament the loss of a victim. Moreover, the sex industry relies not just on bypassing the legal system but also on creating a long-term master-slave relationship. The power disequilibrium may be a function of the victim's poverty, lack of education, and poor upbringing or loss of parents, combined with a desperate longing for a better life. Illicit sex traffickers usually operate in developing states where there is an abundance of poor vulnerable girls and younger children willing to entrust themselves to strangers for the promise of employment or of a bright future. Some traffickers tell the women that they will be domestic maids or restaurant servers, concealing the true nature of their destiny (children abducted are often so young that they are not given an explanation). In some cases, women voluntarily go with the organized criminals, knowing they are bound for prostitution, but these circumstances may still be highly coercive, as the traffickers make false promises about the benevolence of the prostitution industry and obscure the objectifying and abusive conditions that really prevail.[199] Once brought into their lair, the traffickers generally exercise control over their victims through "confiscation of travel and identity documents, debt bondages, threats, and violence."[200] Often victims are beaten and raped repeatedly to achieve desired ends. Aside from violence toward the women and children themselves, traffickers use violence against competitors in order to gain a stake in profitable sex markets.[201] Colluding officials are often complicit not only in the human rights violations inherent in the condition of slavery but also specifically in the violent treatment of victims.

Individual/Human Security versus National/State Security

Security concerns regarding illicit human transfers reflect considerable international disagreement both within and across states. When illegal migration is facilitated by transnational organized crime, these security impacts become more devastating. As with illicit drug transfers, the tremors from this illicit cross-border activity appear to be largely bottom-up in nature.

Exploring the influence of global illicit human transfers specifically on individual/human security, this human security impact warrants greater emphasis[202] than the impact on state security because illicit human transfers have a much more onerous effect on their victims than on the national governments of the countries where they take place. The emerging transnational criminal networks that use migration strategically can have a major impact on the human security of trafficking victims, including those who die or are abused in transit or when they disembark and those otherwise affected by the violence and corruption associated with criminal illicit human transfers.[203]

With specific regard to individual/human security impacts of migrant labor smuggling, "nearly every week has brought stories of the deaths of clandestine migrants somewhere in the world, deaths resulting from horrendous acts of violence or simple miscalculations on the part of smugglers or the migrants themselves as they attempt to evade the authorities."[204] The significant human rights violations embedded in this re-emerging form of slavery encompass "all too many cases of would be migrants being drowned on substandard ships, suffocated in containers, of left stranded by traffickers who take their money and fail to deliver them to the promised destination."[205] Overall, illicit human transfers challenge the foundation of civil society as a whole, creating a social stratum of second-class inhabitants who simultaneously are completely unaccountable for their actions and are completely vulnerable to every form of exploitation.

The international community's hostility toward open borders has mushroomed in recent years. Long gone is the humanitarian sentiment of Emma Lazarus's famous poem "The New Colossus" inviting in the tired, poor, "huddled masses yearning to breathe free"; under globalization, the free movement of people across borders is viewed in a radically different—and more restrictive— way than free movement of goods and services.[206] Unlike flows of transitory tourists, "the specter of the long term mass transfer of desperate (and frequently undesired) humans across state boundaries associates with a uniquely acute sense of peacetime threat to sovereignty in the current international system."[207]

Within the United States, the anti–illegal immigration upsurge is "fueled by economic frustrations and national-security phobias, and inflamed by voices of hatred"; this increasingly militant grassroots movement believes that private citizens must do "what the federal government refuses to do" to prevent illegal aliens from entering the country.[208] The depth of the widespread American terror of being overwhelmed from abroad is perhaps best illustrated by President Bill Clinton's announcement in September 1994 that the United States intended to invade Haiti unless its military regime relinquished power, with his statement being a direct response to the overwhelming domestic outrage about the flood of Haitian illegal migrants (and refugees) fleeing from both poverty and political oppression.

Within Western Europe, illegal migrants and refugees appear to trigger deep-seated fears by both governments and citizens, sometimes bandied about by politicians to inflame debate about more restrictive immigration laws. This fear revolves around the specter of hordes of unsanctioned aliens from the developing world pouring into these advanced industrialized nations to escape the utter misery experienced in the deprived places from which these desperate travelers flee.[209] For example, this deep Western European concern was reflected in the way the bombings in Madrid in 2004 and in London in 2005 "reinforced already existing fears regarding the links between migration and terrorism in Europe" and, more generally, the potentially dangerous relationship among globalization, migration, and security.[210]

For onlookers within receiving societies, when migrant labor smuggling occurs with sufficient frequency, perceived increasing burdens, risks, and disruptions often translate into attributing threat to the presence of illegal migrants. Natives usually view those who have taken advantage of criminal circumvention of immigration restrictions as the dregs of society, even when they have undergone many heart-rending sacrifices and dangers to make a successful voyage and even when their living conditions upon arrival are decidedly substandard. Amplified by the immediate exposure to the distinctive needs and practices of these unauthorized newcomers, the citizenry may feel both scarcity and divisiveness within their society and a loss of control over preservation of its traditional distinctive features. As a result, illegal migrants are typically held responsible for any problems that emerge within countries they enter:[211] unemployment, overpopulation, land degradation, low wages, deteriorating public education and health care (including both soaring hospital costs and the spread of infectious diseases), overcrowded highways and prisons, official language erosion, public official corruption, foreign relations damage, or any downturn in the cherished lifestyles of the indigenous population. Much of this sense of threat originates at the grassroots level, as illegal migrants send bottom-up shock waves through affected societies, with national governments often bearing the brunt of popular fears.

Nativism[212] may be at the root of this receiving society unrest, and migrants criminally smuggled into countries may cause the greatest socioeconomic turmoil when they differ racially, ethnically, or religiously from the existing citizenry. The presence of undocumented aliens can inadvertently end up (at least in the short term) turning members of one's own society against each other, causing troublesome questions to be raised about basic national values. When overburdening domestic social service systems and raising the crime rate, illegal aliens can cause increasingly putative laws to go into effect in receiving societies aimed at all immigrants.[213] Ultimately, consequences may include (1) growing public xenophobia within receiving states, with pressure on governments to send illegal migrants home and close the borders; and (2) intensifying competition for goods and services within receiving states, with pressure to protect the advantages of the native population.

With specific regard to individual/human security impacts of human sex trafficking, willing or unwilling participants in the global sex trade sacrifice even a base level of human dignity or government protection. Human rights violations are much more profound than with migrant labor smuggling, to the point where any sense of personal value or identity may be irredeemably obliterated. The magnitude of the consequent loss of constructive creative energy to the society as a whole is impossible to estimate. The overall ripple effects on the entire society deriving from allowing this kind of persistent degrading exploitation promote an image of hypocrisy and prevent any movement in other areas toward values of mutual respect, tolerance, and protection of personal dignity.

Even those who may be coerced to migrate and perform demeaning services are frequently viewed without compassion by receiving states as undesirables who require deportation. Ironically, although it is often members of advanced industrial societies who take advantage of the global sex trade, they do not recognize the hypocrisy of doing so while communicating through established policies that those who are victims of this kind of criminal operation do not merit any rights or protection under the law. Whereas many legitimate citizens consort with, encourage the migration of, and even take advantage of criminally induced migrants, it is rare for those smuggled in ever to be totally accepted within recipient societies.

Turning to the influence of illicit human transfers on national/state security, the impact appears to be both more indirect and more long term. In a bottom-up manner, the criminally induced entrance of illegal migrants can undermine state control and ultimately destabilize the government regime. The degree of disruption may depend as much on the treatment and integration of the victims as it does on the ability to stop this illicit influx of people.

With specific regard to national/state impacts of migrant labor smuggling, this activity challenges the state's basic prerogative as a sovereign entity to control its borders[214] and its establishment of a uniform national migration policy, including the determination of asylum and displaced persons. Indeed, it is common now to see references to the dangers posed by illegal migrant flows (in a manner similar to Machiavelli) as comparable to those posed by invading armies.[215] Illicit human transfers on a large scale can also erode democratic governance by cheapening the rights and responsibilities of those who live within a state. Especially when illicit human transfers occurs within weak or failing states, the influx of resources to transnational organized crime can directly and indirectly challenge and corrupt the ability of states to maintain sovereign control over their territory.[216]

Disgruntled citizens within receiving states may turn their anger about the flood of illegal immigrants toward their own governments, claiming these regimes have not adequately protected their native rights and way of life. Indeed, illegal migration can disrupt the relationship between state and society—"many citizens feel that their governments have lost control of their borders, and governments are in turn alarmed by the growing hostility of their citizens to the foreigners living and working in their midst."[217] Often the net result is confrontation, involving expanding internal battles between citizens and their government or external battles between the sending state and the receiving state of the migrants, inflaming historic tensions and creating pressures to resolve or eliminate differences by force.

Although most of the concern about the security implications of illegal migration focuses on the threat to receiving states, sending states also can suffer. Buoyed by messages from friends and relatives who have managed to make a successful illegal crossing into another country, the citizenry of sending states may become simultaneously attracted by external opportunities in receiving states and frustrated and intolerant of internal conditions within their own countries. A common result is that sending state governments become the targets of accusations of incompetence, corruption, or even secret encouragement of the illegal migration, undermining both the legitimacy and the stability of the regimes. The dangers embedded in these accusations may only worsen if disgruntled illegal migrants are apprehended by receiving states and forced to return home.

With specific regard to the national/state security impacts of human sex trafficking, these are even less common and more indirect than those associated with migrant labor smuggling. The presence within enlightened societies of individuals who not only have no rights but are exploited and degraded on a regular basis in inconceivable ways undermines its very core of morality and common values surrounding mutual respect. If national leaders are found to indulge in reaping the benefits of sex trafficking, then the stain on national integrity becomes even more profound. At its most extreme, proliferation of illicit human sex trafficking within a society can inhibit its political regime's ability to govern the society because of a lack of moral compass on which to base national norms and a lack of respected authority from which to instill any form of restraint. The "anything-goes" mentality does not serve the state mandate to occasionally request sacrifices from its citizenry.

6 ANALYSIS OF CASE PATTERNS

THE DETAILED EXAMINATION of the five major transnational criminal organizations and the three major transnational criminal activities reveals patterns that increase understanding of the modus operandi of transnational organized crime in today's world and its potential disruptive security effects. Based on this case examination, this chapter first presents a spectrum of preferred tactics for these organizations and a spectrum of primary security impacts for these activities, and then identifies the conditions under which transnational criminal organizations choose to use corruption versus violence and under which transnational criminal activities produce a major impact on individual/human security versus national/state security. This chapter's insights form the core of this book's contribution enhancing understanding of the dark logic of transnational organized crime.

Although highly tentative and lacking universal applicability, the persistence of these patterns across the different groups and activities lends credence to their validity. Nonetheless, the highlighted patterns are clearly changeable over time and thus most applicable to the contemporary global security environment. If, for example, policy makers transformed the kinds of international laws pertaining to certain kinds of cross-border transactions, changed the kinds of coercive countermeasures used to constrain transnational organized crime, or developed dramatic technological advances essential to illicit global transmission of goods and services, then transnational criminals would probably adjust their choice of tactics, altering the security impacts substantially. The findings from this chapter's conditional analysis of transnational organized crime, however, provide important clues facilitating efforts to comprehend ongoing patterns so as to be able to formulate responses to future criminal behavior before it occurs.

PREFERRED TACTICS OF TRANSNATIONAL CRIMINAL ORGANIZATIONS

Despite significant difficulties in making overall comparisons among criminal groups, figure 6.1 depicts the spectrum of preferred tactics by transnational criminal organizations. Although all five groups use both corruption and violence to some degree, the overall pattern indicates that the Japanese Yakuza and the Chinese triads tend to be more status quo low-profile corruption-oriented groups, the Colombian cartels and Russian Mob tend to be more non–status quo high-profile violence-oriented groups, and the Italian Mafia finds itself somewhere in the middle between these two extremes. As mentioned earlier, because these groups are adept and swift at adapting to changing regulatory environments and to changing societal vulnerabilities and opportunities, and because their fluid networking may continue to mutate in the future, this study's confidence is relatively low in the enduring quality of this particular spectrum of transnational criminal organizations' propensity to use corruption versus violence tactics. Nonetheless, identifying criminal groups' relative tactical propensities at a given point in time seems worthwhile to help pinpoint the kind of strategic threat each type of group poses and thus the kind of constraining responses that might work best.

From a policy standpoint, classifying the major transnational criminal organizations in terms of their proclivity toward corruption or violence tactics as predominant preferences seems highly useful because it is impossible to treat all of these organizations as equally important and address them all simultaneously with equal effectiveness. In many cases, different societal sectors and government branches complain vociferously about different kinds of criminal organizations and tactics. Especially when combined with the severity metrics for corruption and violence presented in chapter 3, this classification spectrum affords a state—independent of prevailing passions—to prioritize these organizations and their tactics specifically relative to its own values and national interests.

A key implication of this analysis is that not all criminal groups operating in more than one country pose a major global security threat. For example, affecting primarily economic well-being but not security would be criminal organizations that are small and local; groups with a behavioral focus on petty offenses or misdemeanors such as criminal libel, criminal tampering,

Figure 6.1. Spectrum of predominant tactics preferred by major transnational criminal organizations

Groups primarily oriented toward status quo low-profile corruption			*Groups primarily oriented toward non–status quo high-profile violence*

Japanese Yakuza	Chinese triads	Italian Mafia	Colombian cartels	Russian Mob

> *Types of Criminal Organizations Posing a Minor Global Security Threat*
>
> Small and local criminal organizations
>
> Criminal organizations with a behavioral focus on petty offenses or misdemeanors:
> Criminal libel
> Criminal tampering
> Disorderly conduct
> Income tax evasion
> Motor vehicle theft
> Traffic violations
> Vagrancy
>
> Organizations committing sporadic and infrequent criminal acts

disorderly conduct, income tax evasion, motor vehicle theft, traffic violations, or vagrancy; and groups committing sporadic and infrequent criminal acts. Although these non-security-threatening criminal groups may wreak considerable economic damage within and across societies, they would clearly not be the focus of national security agencies' countermeasures.

Moreover, no general linkage emerges from the case studies between the type of transnational criminal organization and the type of generated security impact—individual/human versus national/state. Indeed, considering the Chinese triads, Colombian cartels, Italian Mafia, Japanese Yakuza, and Russian Mob, each produces significantly differing combinations of individual and state security disruptions. These patterns have become even more diverse given many criminal groups' recent fragmentation and movement away from hierarchy toward decentralized networks. Some of these groups (such as the Italian Mafia), however, have a distinct well-established public image—often embellished by the media—about the type of security threat generated.

An important security question emerges from the findings about transnational criminal organizations' choice of tactics: Does the prevailing greater national security concern about groups that are non–status quo and violence oriented make sense? The answer to this question appears to be qualified, for what each society cares most about appears to determine which end of the spectrum is more ominous and dangerous. Certainly, the disruption wrought by non–status quo violent groups is more visible and dramatic, but the more invisible corruption-oriented groups slowly and secretly erode basic government and societal institutions in ways that could prove in the long run to be more dangerous. Two important lessons emerge in this regard: (1) the most visible and panic-inducing security concerns resulting from transnational organized crime may not always be the most important ones from a broader security vantage point, and (2) one should not necessarily assume that the most severe security impacts from transnational criminal activity are those that involve direct physical harm to persons or property (whether to government officials and institutions or, alternatively, to private citizens and their personal property). However, attempting to focus popular attention or government policy within democracies on status quo corruption-oriented transnational criminal organizations, without the commission of any visibly egregious wrongs, may prove to be considerably more difficult than getting them to focus on non–status quo violence-oriented groups.

PRIMARY SECURITY IMPACTS OF TRANSNATIONAL CRIMINAL ACTIVITIES

Despite difficulties in evaluating the relative social costs of illicit global transactions, figure 6.2 displays the security impact spectrum for transnational criminal activities, differentiating among those that have (1) a primary impact on national/state security, (2) a primary impact on individual/human security, and (3) relatively equal impacts on individual and state security. The cases indicate that illicit arms transfers impact primarily state security, with nuclear arms and components smuggling having a potentially greater security impact than conventional arms and components smuggling (in actuality today, because of the infrequency of nuclear smuggling, conventional transfers have a larger impact); illicit drug transfers impact relatively equally both individual and state security, with hard drug transfers having a more devastating security impact than soft drug transfers; and illicit human transfers impact primarily individual security, with migrant labor smuggling having a more severe aggregate security impact than human sex trafficking. These findings support the notion that the security impacts of transnational criminal activities can work in both a bottom-up and a top-down manner.

From a policy perspective, categorizing transnational criminal activities in terms of their type of security impact seems important because it would be

Figure 6.2. Spectrum of primary security impacts generated by major transnational criminal activities

Illicit arms transfers | Illicit drug transfers | Illicit human transfers

Nuclear weapons/components smuggling—higher-security priority | *Hard-drugs trafficking such as heroin (opium) and cocaine— higher-security priority* | *Migrant labor smuggling— higher-security priority*

Conventional weapons/ components smuggling— lower-security priority | *Soft-drugs trafficking such as marijuana (cannabis)—lower- security priority* | *Human sex trafficking—lower- security priority*

Impact primarily on national/ state security   ⟵————————⟶   Impact primarily on individual/ human security

---

Types of Criminal Activities Posing a Minor Global Security Threat

Illegal international transmission of legitimate commodities:

Art

Automobiles and automobile parts

Electronics (games, movies, music, computer software, entertainment equipment)

Endangered species

Human organs

Tobacco

Toxic waste/hazardous materials

Counterfeiting

Copying and distributing intellectual property/proprietary technology

---

highly difficult to treat all of these activities as equally significant and manage them all at the same time with equal success. As with transnational criminal organizations and their tactics, different parts of societies and of governments raise a clamor about different kinds of illicit cross-border activities. Independent of prevailing emotions, when combined with the severity considerations presented in chapter 3, this study's classification spectrum allows a state to prioritize the threats embedded in these activities based on its own values and national interests. Improving the prioritization of transnational criminal activities and their security impacts seems especially vital because of the highly skewed nature of public concerns about criminal disruptions within Western societies, where there seems to be little relationship between what people are most angry or excited about and what is really most dangerous: for example, when scrutinizing mass public reactions to transnational criminal activities, in some circles drug running is identified as the most pressing concern, when, in the end, it may not pose the greatest aggregate threat to either individual security or state security.

One implication from this analysis of the three major transnational criminal activities is that not all global criminal behavior poses a significant threat to individual or state security. Most popular anxieties about crime revolve around "common crimes" such as burglaries, car theft, robberies, domestic sexual offenses, kidnapping, and homicide; these are quite different from the cross-border "nonconventional crimes"—illicit arms transfers, illicit drug transfers, and illicit human transfers—associated with transnational organized crime.[1] Some illustrations of instances where cross-border activities might be more likely to endanger economic well-being than national security include illegal international transmission of legitimate commodities such as art, automobiles and automobile parts, electronics (games, movies, music, computer software, and entertainment equipment), endangered species, human organs, tobacco, and toxic waste or hazardous materials; counterfeiting; and copying and distributing intellectual property or proprietary technology.[2] From an international business standpoint, these criminal activities certainly pose major economic problems—as they can bankrupt legitimate firms, promote the occurrence or continuation of recessions, have a devastating effect on profits, and stifle innovation and the search for societally sanctioned substitutes—but they do not belong high on the security agenda.

Furthermore, no general link is evident from the case studies between the type of transnational criminal activity and the type of applied tactic—corruption versus violence. Indeed, in reflecting on illicit arms transfers, illicit drug transfers, and illicit human transfers, each involves widely varying combinations of corruption and violence in pursuit of profit maximization. Although considerable publicity has emerged associating certain criminal tactics with certain illicit activities, such as that linking unrestrained violence to drug lords involved in cross-border trafficking operations, in reality the patterns are not that simple.

One irony in the spectrum of primary security impacts of transnational criminal activities is that illicit arms transfers are most associated with top-down national/state security threats, even though, by their very nature, smuggled weapons can directly facilitate the threat and occurrence of societal violence. The explanation for this perplexing finding lies in the reality that, although some states buy arms from transnational criminals, the majority of illicit weapons purchases appear to be by subversive groups to be used directly or indirectly as coercive tools challenging state control. Thus arms smuggling represents the greatest danger to state security because the commodity transferred in a violent confrontational way often undermines national governmental sovereignty.

CONDITIONS PROMOTING CORRUPTION TACTICS VERSUS VIOLENCE TACTICS

This study's case findings reveal key patterns, summarized in figure 6.3, about the conditions surrounding transnational criminal organizations' choice of corruption versus violence tactics as their predominant strategy. Background

Figure 6.3. Conditions promoting transnational criminal organizations' use of corruption versus violence

CONDITIONS WHEN CRIMINAL ORGANIZATIONS ARE MOST LIKELY
TO USE CORRUPTION

Power Limitations of Criminal Groups or State Governments

Criminal power limitations
When seeing the risk of rebuff or betrayal and prosecution as less than the risk of discovery of a hidden shipment
When lacking a preponderance of power and wanting to gain the right to operate in a competitor's territory
When accepting of sharing business sector with other criminal groups

State power limitations
When operating within weak or failing states with unscrupulous officials and lax law enforcement and monitoring
When dealing with states, given open borders, overwhelmed by the difficulty in checking tons of cross-national shipments
When transporting commodities that many within a receiving state find acceptable (such as soft drugs)

Special Tactical Advantages

Benefits deriving from criminal-state relationship
When possessing a long-standing symbiotic reciprocal relationship with the government and desiring its protection
When having infiltrated all important government agencies
When wanting to avoid attracting the attention of officials or public outcry that could result in inconvenient regulations

Benefits deriving from particular predicament
When enmeshed in a non-zero-sum situation where positive gains seem possible for every party
When involved in the transportation phase of smuggling before arrival at destinations where officials seem harder to bribe
When needing to focus on vulnerable low-ranking officials, such as airline employees, dock workers, or truckers

(continued)

Figure 6.3. *(continued)*

CONDITIONS WHEN CRIMINAL ORGANIZATIONS ARE MOST LIKELY
TO USE VIOLENCE

Offensive and Defensive Exercise of Power

Offensive demonstration of dominance

When attaining a reputation of respect and fear through violent retaliation is crucial

When insisting on asserting control and on being the authority (rather than
compromising) in a zero-sum situation

When experiencing an inherently beneficial disequilibrium of power (making coercion
effective) vis-à-vis a target

Defensive fight for survival

When protecting themselves and defending their territory—their property and families—
as well as their markets

When failing in compromise efforts, extortion demands, or attempts to recruit new members

When operating during a chaotic time of transition during which no effective ruling
authority exists

Deterrence of Internal and External Opposition

Punishment of internal disloyalty/noncompliance

When forestalling betrayal within the ranks of their own criminal network
or disciplining traitors

When needing to enforce norms against targets who have violated rules essential to the
proper conduct of the business

When making a statement by addressing high-profile targets who are embarrassments and
hindrances to one's business

Warding off of external competitors and government regulators

When engaging in a power struggle with another group and using contract killing
to eliminate anyone willing to confront them

When being threatened by anticrime policies, law enforcement officers, competitor
encroachment, or massive loss of profits

When wanting to intimidate prosecutors into compliance to demonstrate staunch
resistance against any government interference

---

influences on this choice include whether designated targets are clean and ethical, whether killing is commonly perceived as necessary from time to time just to send a message, whether a competitive control environment exists, whether coherent state authority exists, and whether crime bosses generally have tight control over their subordinates. The distinctive calculus involved thus reflects both the characteristics of the criminal group and the characteristics of the external environment in which they operate.

Four clusters of conditions emerge concerning when these organizations are most prone to use corruption. First, criminals choose this tactic when they face significant power limitations, such as when a group sees the risk of rebuff and betrayal as less than the risk of discovery of a hidden shipment; lacks preponderance of power and wants to operate within a competitor's territory; or, more generally, accepts sharing of business with other criminal groups. Second, corruption is selected when criminals perceive severe state power limitations, such as when a group operates within weak or failing states with unscrupulous officials and lax law enforcement and monitoring; deals with states—given open porous borders—overwhelmed by the difficulty of checking tons of cross-national shipments; or transports commodities that many within a receiving state find to be acceptable (such as soft drugs). Third, this is the tactic of choice when special benefits derive from the criminal-state relationship, such as when a group possesses a long-standing symbiotic reciprocal relationship with a national government and desires its protection; infiltrates all-important government agencies; or wants to avoid attracting the attention of officials or public outcry that could lead to undesired regulations. Finally, these groups prefer this tactic when benefits derive from a particularly propitious predicament, such as when a group is enmeshed in a non-zero-sum situation where positive gains are possible for every party (for instance where criminal and state interests coincide); is involved in the transportation phase of smuggling before arriving at destinations (particularly Western states) where officials may be more dangerous to bribe; or targets highly vulnerable low-ranking officials such as airline employees, dock workers, or truckers. Thus corruption seems to flourish when there are power limitations of criminal groups or state governments and when special tactical advantages are present.

In contrast, four rather different clusters of conditions indicate when transnational criminal organizations are most prone to use violence. First, they select this tactic when they need an offensive demonstration of dominance, such as when a group feels that attaining a reputation of respect and fear through violent retaliation is crucial; insists on asserting control and on being the authority (rather than compromising) in a zero-sum situation; or experiences an inherently beneficial disequilibrium of power (one making coercion effective) vis-à-vis a target. Second, a preference for this tactic exists when engaging in a defensive fight for one's survival, such as when a group protects itself and defends its territory—its property and families—as well as its markets; fails in compromise efforts, extortion demands, or attempts to recruit new members; or operates during a chaotic time of transition during which no effective ruling authority exists. Third, this is the tactic of choice when they feel compelled to exercise punishment of internal disloyalty or noncompliance, such as when a group forestalls betrayal within the ranks of its own criminal network or disciplines traitors; needs to enforce norms against targets who have violated rules essential to the proper conduct of business; or makes a statement by addressing high-profile targets who are embarrassments and hindrances to its business. Finally, violence is chosen when criminals are worried about warding off external competitors and government regulators, such as when a group engages in a power struggle with other groups and uses contract killing to eliminate those willing to confront them; is threatened by anticrime policies, law enforcement officers, competitor encroachment, or massive loss of profits; or wants to intimidate prosecutors into compliance to demonstrate staunch resistance to any existing or impending government interference in its criminal activities. So violence seems common among transnational criminal organizations when they feel the need for an offensive or defensive exercise of power and deterrence of internal or external opposition.

When reflecting on the identified conditions, two starkly opposing syndromes—summarized in table 6.1—emerge promoting the use of corruption versus violence tactics. Transnational criminal organizations prefer (1) violence over corruption in zero-sum competitive situations, and corruption over violence in non-zero-sum cooperative situations; (2) violence over corruption when experiencing an acute discrete threat from within or without, and corruption over violence when experiencing a "business-as-usual" atmosphere; (3) violence over corruption when feeling extreme emotions about their own power—either desperate for their very survival or cocky about their superiority—and corruption over violence when calmly and dispassionately assessing opportunities and limitations based on their capabilities; (4) violence over corruption when dealing with a stronger state government capable of interfering regulation (keeping in mind that "high levels of organized crime rarely go together with strong policing and effective maintenance of the rule of law"[3]), and corruption over violence when dealing with a weaker or failing state government; (5) violence over corruption when viewing the national state government as a key adversary, and corruption over violence when viewing the national state government as a potential ally; and (6) violence over corruption when dealing with high-profile targets, and corruption over violence when dealing with low-ranking officials. Within today's global

Table 6.1. Corruption versus violence syndromes exhibited by transnational criminal organizations

Element	Corruption syndrome	Violence syndrome
Bargaining situation	Non-zero-sum cooperative	Zero-sum competitive
Decision setting	Routine—"business as usual"	Crisis—acute internal or external threat
Emotional attitude	Calm and detached—systematic	Extremely on edge—desperate or cocky
Regime power	Weaker or failing government	Stronger regulation-capable government
State relationship	Government seen as a potential ally	Government seen as a key adversary
Primary target	Low-ranking officials	High-profile leaders
Underlying triggers	If status quo persists	If non–status quo change is imminent
	If no intrusion of rival groups	If entrance of rival criminal groups
	If no disobedient group members	If blatantly disobedient group members
	If no new state anticrime measures	If new major state anticrime measures

security setting, these two contrasting tactical syndromes suggest that transnational criminal organizations rely on corruption more when they perceive predicaments as routine, and these groups rely on violence more when they perceive predicaments as involving an impending or ongoing crisis.

Given these two syndromes, one might ask, What might trigger a transnational criminal organization's perceiving the kind of threat associated with the kind of crisis mentality that leads to a preference for the use of violence over corruption? The typical triggers for a transnational criminal organization's developing a crisis mentality associated with violence include the entrance of rival criminal groups into the particular geographical area, preferred market, or commodity transactions it currently dominates; blatant disobedience or violation of internal rules by one or more of its members; or the emergence of a new sweeping anticrime detection and prosecution initiative by an affected national government. In contrast, the typical triggers for a transnational criminal organization's remaining in a routine mind-set leading to a preference for corruption over violence include persistence of the status quo, no intrusion of rival criminal gangs, no blatantly disobedient members of one's own group, and no new significant government anticrime measures. Given the increasing global proliferation of transnational criminal organizations, competition seems likely to increase among them, and thus without adaptation to this development the perception of crisis could escalate in the future.

In light of this analysis, there appears to be no built-in preference from a law enforcement or defense standpoint about transnational organized crime's reliance on corruption tactics versus violence tactics. In other words, unless particular societal values point in one direction or the other, normatively there seems to be no reason to attempt to push criminals away from corruption toward violence or, alternatively, to push criminals away from violence toward corruption. Both tactics threaten security in different ways, and neither is inherently more susceptible to successful countermeasures. The value in this conditional analysis thus lies more in differentiating among effective policy responses than in judging the overall acceptability of criminal behavior.

CONDITIONS PROMOTING INDIVIDUAL INSECURITY VERSUS STATE INSECURITY

In a parallel manner, this study's case findings reveal patterns, summarized in figure 6.4, about the conditions surrounding transnational criminal activities having a primary negative impact on individual/human security versus national/state security. Background influences affecting whether the security impact of criminal activities focuses on the individual or the state can include the scope of operations and goals of transnational criminal activities, the historical experience of a target state with transnational organized crime, the relative preparedness and vulnerability of the government regime vis-à-vis the society at large, and the manner in which the dominant cultural values relate to prevalent transnational criminal activities. Thus relevant here are both the characteristics of the criminal activity and the nature of the setting in which the activity occurs.

Four clusters of conditions help to explain when transnational criminal activities are likely to have their primary impact on individual/human security. First, individual security is likely to be the focus of disruption when within target societies unhealthy lifestyles are already prevalent, involving widespread addiction to dangerous substances or habits (associated with vice); high susceptibility to contagion of debilitating infectious diseases (as a result of unsanitary living conditions and/or poor health care); and a pervasive sense of terror and lack of safety, promoting psychological trauma about an unsettling domestic atmosphere. Second, a primary individual security

Figure 6.4. Conditions promoting transnational criminal activities' impact on individual security versus state security

---

CONDITIONS WHEN CRIMINAL ACTIVITIES ARE MOST LIKELY TO IMPACT INDIVIDUAL SECURITY

When a society has rifts and internal friction, but a national government is popular, well entrenched, and difficult to undermine

High Personal Exposure to Danger

Pre-existing prevalence of unhealthy lifestyles
Widespread addiction to dangerous substances or habits
High susceptibility to contagion of debilitating infectious diseases
Pervasive sense of terror and lack of safety promoting psychological trauma

Vulnerability to personal damage
Frequent death threats aimed at innocent citizens and gang members
Ongoing abuse of persons or property
Commonplace extortion

Low Protective Societal Norms and Institutions

Nonexistent or eroded civil society norms
Weakened functioning of financial institutions, stymied economic development, and economic havoc
Vocal domestic cultural intolerance, avoidance, and bigotry among different societal groups
Declining human dignity, human rights and freedoms, and sense of protection

Setting dominated by lawlessness
Attraction of numerous criminal groups into area and burgeoning prisoner population
Regularity of street crime and common nonreporting of crime
Inflamed ongoing societal tensions and conflicts

CONDITIONS WHEN CRIMINAL ACTIVITIES ARE MOST LIKELY TO IMPACT STATE SECURITY

When a national government is in transition, divided, or failing, but a society is unified and resilient

Eroded National Political Authority

Pre-existing challenges to state sovereignty
Funding of antigovernment insurgents and terrorists
Frequent violation of border control
Usurpation of government authority to rule

Tarnished external state image
Diminished attractiveness of country for tourism
Undermined perceived government legitimacy and reputation
Vulnerability signaled and instability spread to neighbors due to state not reining in undesired activities

Decreased State Capacity to Respond Effectively to Threats

Deteriorated state government apparatus
Weakened democratic institutions, transparency, and the rule of law
Coercive elimination or marginalization of political groups opposing organized crime
Government officials lacking integrity in law enforcement agencies, police forces, and courts of justice

Diminished state ability to resolve disputes effectively
Low public support for state interdiction of sources of undesired unruly activities
Difficulties in reaching or enforcing postwar peace accords if profitable commodities are at stake
Continued unrestrained disruptive behavior thwarting agreements

impact seems likely when vulnerability to personal damage exists, including frequent death threats against innocent citizens and gang members; ongoing abuse to persons or property; and commonplace extortion. Third, this primary disruption of individual security is associated with the presence of eroded or nonexistent civil society norms, including weakened functioning of financial institutions, stymied economic development, and economic havoc; vocal domestic cultural intolerance, avoidance, and bigotry among different societal groups; and declining human dignity, human rights and freedoms, and sense of protection. Finally, individual security diminishes most within a setting dominated by lawlessness, one that attracts numerous criminal groups into the area and has a burgeoning prison population; regularity of street crime and common nonreporting of crime; and inflamed ongoing social tensions and conflicts. Thus the combination of high personal exposure to danger and low protective societal norms and institutions seems most conducive to transnational criminal activities degrading individual/human security.

On the other hand, four different clusters of conditions explain when transnational criminal activities are likely to have their primary impact on state/national security. First, this primary state disruption is likely if pre-existing challenges to state sovereignty exist, including funding of anti-government insurgents and terrorists; violation of border control; and usurpation of government authority to rule. Second, primary interference with state authority is likely if a tarnished external state image exists, including diminished attractiveness of a country for tourism; undermined perceived government legitimacy and reputation; and vulnerability signaled and instability spread to neighbors due to states not reining in undesired activities. Third, state security is most lessened if the state government apparatus has deteriorated, including weakened functioning of democratic institutions, transparency, and the rule of law; coercive elimination or marginalization of political groups opposing organized crime; and government officials lacking integrity in law enforcement agencies, police forces, and courts of justice. Finally, state security is degraded most when there exists a diminished state ability to resolve disputes effectively, including low public support for state interdiction of sources of undesired unruly activity; difficulties reaching or enforcing postwar peace accords if a profitable commodity is at stake; and continued disruptive behavior thwarting constraining agreements. So the combination of eroded national political authority and decreased state capacity to respond effectively to threats appears to maximize the potential for transnational criminal activities to interfere with national/state security.

Table 6.2. Individual security versus state security syndromes generated by transnational criminal activities

Element	Individual security syndrome	State security syndrome
Promotion of distrust	Rifts promoted among societal groups	Lowered confidence in government
Fostering of disruptive links	Collaboration with local warlords	Collaboration with terrorists and insurgents
Undermining of stability	Social groups disbanded or disintegrated	Political parties/officials bought/eliminated
Erosion of institutions	Weakened financial and social institutions	Weakened political institutions/legitimacy
Heightening of intimidation	Pervasive fear among citizenry	Pervasive fear among government officials
Intensification of anarchy	Loss of dignity, health, or life	Eradication of border control
Underlying triggers	Can enter authority vacuum as savior	Can make political system unworkable
	Can cloud legitimate/ illegitimate divide	Can empower opponents of regime
	Can mask vice as consumption freedom	Can function as shadow government
	If government is popular and entrenched	If society is unified and resilient

In pondering these conditions, two alternative syndromes—summarized in table 6.2—characterize individual security versus state security impacts. Looking first at the promotion of distrust, transnational criminal activities primarily disrupt individual security when causing social distrust, rifts, and friction among societal groups, often with some groups serving as scapegoats for the most severe societal problems and with a "might-makes-right" mentality for resolving disputes present among them; and they primarily disrupt state security when causing a loss of internal and external trust and confidence in government. Turning to links with disruptive elements, transnational criminal activities primarily disrupt individual security when working closely with local warlords and attracting into an area other unruly societal groups whose goals allow coexistence with the existing state government; and they primarily disrupt state security when working closely with or fueling terrorists or insurgents/rebels and attracting into an area other unruly political groups whose goals require overthrow of the national government. Moving to the elimination of stabilizing influences, transnational criminal activities primarily disrupt individual security when causing existing functional and integrity-promoting social groups to disband or disintegrate and promoting widespread poverty; and they primarily disrupt state security when eliminating political groups, rendering law enforcement ineffective, or buying elections, candidates, and parties. Examining the weakening of institutions, transnational criminal activities primarily disrupt individual security when weakening financial or social institutions; and they primarily disrupt state security when weakening political institutions and tarnishing the reputation and legitimacy of the government. Considering intimidation, transnational criminal activities primarily disrupt individual security when instilling fear in the citizenry, and they primarily disrupt state security when instilling fear among government officials. Finally, looking at anarchy intensification, transnational criminal activities primarily disrupt individual security when spreading rampant disease, lawlessness, loss of dignity, and death within a country; and they primarily disrupt state security when functionally eradicating border control over who or what can enter and leave a country.

In some ways, however, these two alternative syndromes leave open the basic question of exactly when transnational organized crime might choose to focus on societal or governmental disruption. Typically, transnational organized crime appears to concentrate on societal impacts when it feels it can maximize benefits and minimize costs most from societal discord—by entering a vacuum of authority full of friction and hostility as a potential savior to those fearful and disaffected; by obfuscating the capacity to differentiate between legitimate and illegitimate activity; and by promoting a kind of vice-oriented social order that appears, on the surface, to allow for complete freedom of choice about consumption of illicit commodities. In similar fashion, transnational organized crime seems to concentrate on state impacts when it feels it can maximize benefits and minimize costs most from national government dysfunction—by making the existing political system unworkable; by empowering those who oppose it; and by in reality serving as a shadow government. The cost-benefit ratio may tilt toward society security disruption when a society already has lots of rifts and internal friction, but the national government is popular, well entrenched, and difficult to undermine; it may tilt toward state security disruption when a national government is in transition, divided, weak, or failing, but a society is unified and resilient. Considering the ongoing direction of transnational criminal activities, it appears that developing countries may be more susceptible to state security disruption, and advanced industrial societies—despite the pervasiveness of civil discourse—may contain the greater potential for individual security disruption.

Regardless of whether transnational criminal activities have their primary impact on individual/human security or on national/state security, the future implications appear dire. The bottom-up individual impact may remove any sense of order within a country in such a way that individual citizens and the society as a whole could find themselves completely unable to function, and the top-down state impact may eliminate the possibility of guidance from a central political authority in such a way that no regime could operate effectively, resulting in a failed state (Colombia in many ways exemplifies both patterns). The ensuing chaos would suit perfectly the interests of transnational organized crime, as through their activities they could take advantage of and amplify any existing societal vulnerabilities and state political frailties. Regardless of transnational criminals' awareness about how their cross-border activities disrupt individual and state security, however, as mentioned earlier, they cannot push this disruptive impact too far, for they need a certain minimum threshold of stability and predictability within operating areas to carry out their highly profitable illicit global transactions.

CONCLUDING THOUGHTS

This chapter's analysis sets the stage for application of unconventional tools to counter the ravages of the modern growth and spread of transnational organized crime. The first part of the chapter demonstrates that it is possible to evaluate systematically the relative predominant tactical preferences associated with the major transnational criminal organizations and the relative primary security impacts associated with the major transnational criminal activities, allowing those wishing to constrain these dangers to have a better idea about where to start in their efforts. The second part of the chapter presents a conditional analysis that makes it evident that one could develop for policy purposes far deeper situational insight about when transnational criminal organizations select certain tactics and when transnational criminal activities generate security impacts.

These new understandings open up some different avenues to cope with the challenge of managing transnational organized crime within today's complex global security environment. They provide not a new definitive set of solutions to the problem but rather a richer interpretive context in which a much wider range of responses can be evaluated, developed, and implemented. Once the veil is lifted on the underlying dark logic associated with illicit cross-border crime, then a dramatically more realistic potential emerges to undertake effective countermeasures.

Nonetheless, stubborn resistance to this kind of highly differentiated conditional analysis of transnational organized crime should not be underestimated. As long as many concerned government and private-sector authorities continue to depict the participants in transnational criminal organizations as an impenetrable or irrational set of thugs, no progress can be made in the direction of fine-tuning ways of restraining and thwarting them. As long as many of those responsible characterize the mode of operation of transnational organized crime—and the essential nature of transnational criminal activities—either as rigid, fixed, and monolithic or, alternatively, as random, chaotic, and unpredictable, no meaningful policy responses different from the largely unsuccessful ones ongoing today seem likely to emerge. As long as many of these officials view the targets of transnational organized crime as inherently impossible to protect—or completely responsible for their own protection—from the transnational criminal threat, vulnerability to the worst kinds of security consequences will continue and escalate.

7 LINKS BETWEEN TRANSNATIONAL CRIMINALS AND TERRORISTS

HAVING IDENTIFIED THE CONDITIONS under which transnational criminal organizations use corruption versus violence and under which transnational criminal activities influence individual and state security, these insights need to be situated in the context of major nonstate forces with which criminals conspire and collude, with special attention to transnational terrorism. After presenting the general context of these other disruptive elements, this chapter uncovers similarities and differences and mutual connections between transnational crime and transnational terrorism, as well as modes of criminal facilitation of terrorism. The resulting security challenges merit special attention, for contrasting interpretations of them have led to quite different—and sometimes mutually undercutting—defensive orientations by restraining authorities toward transnational criminals and transnational terrorists.

CRIMINALS IN THE CONTEXT OF OTHER DISRUPTIVE NONSTATE FORCES

Understanding fully the important interaction between transnational criminals and transnational terrorists requires explicit consideration of the broader security-threatening context within which criminals and terrorists operate. Today's anarchic international system encompasses a multiplicity of globally disruptive nonstate parties such as militant religious movements, unruly ethnopolitical groups, ecoterrorists and anti-globalizationists, warlords, and insurgents/rebels.[1] These groups have re-emerged in the twenty-first century to fill the voids where effective governance is missing, yet they do not possess the traditional characteristics of strong stable states—"high levels of legitimacy and authority, adequate levels of provision of collective goods, sound economic management, the primacy of the collective, and a high degree of inclusiveness."[2] Members of these groups all seek directly or indirectly to undermine or circumvent state authority, and they often have ties with members of the other groups, yet particular patterns can vary markedly:

> In many cases these groups are challenging the state; in others they are cooperating and colluding with state structures; in some, the state is a passive by-stander while they fight one another. In several instances they are both fighting one another and confronting state structures that seek either to destroy them or to bring them under control.[3]

Indeed, "conflicts fought without the involvement of governments—among militias, rival guerrilla groups, clans, warlords, or communal groups—are now more numerous than state-based conflicts"; contributing to the emergence and perpetuation of such conflicts are transnational organized crime's huge revenues, which simultaneously make resorting to violence less expensive and make alternatives to violent resolution of disputes less appealing.[4]

Enhancing the confusion surrounding the relationship between transnational organized crime and these other globally disruptive groups is the tendency of some policy makers to classify inappropriately any form of private violence as terrorism because of (1) the difficulties in distinguishing among various types of unruly parties—at least in part reflecting the many interconnections among them—or (2) the desire to attract more resources and justify strong retaliation.[5] Although these groups' relationships and strategies continue to evolve in response to changing vulnerabilities and counterpressures, stable distinctive patterns do persist. Because of these differences in orientation and the distinctive challenges posed, conceptually lumping all of these nonstate forces together can undermine the effectiveness of countermeasures in confronting these disruptive elements. Thus a pressing need exists to differentiate carefully at least among the four principal "ideal types" of global privatized violence—criminals, warlords, insurgents/rebels, and terrorists.[6]

Table 7.1 displays an overarching comparison among these four unruly forces in today's world. Each disruptive subnational or transnational group has a distinctive basic orientation, primary motivation, organizational style, relationship with the state, primary set of targets, typical choice of tactics, geographical scope, and desire for visibility. In terms of their basic orientation, criminals are more economically oriented, terrorists and insurgents/rebels are more politically oriented, and warlords are a mix of the two ori-

Table 7.1. Distinctions between transnational organized crime and other internationally disruptive nonstate forces

	Criminals	Warlords	Insurgents/rebels	Terrorists
Basic orientation	Economic	Economic/Political	Political	Political
Primary motivation	Global networking of trading or smuggling so as to dominate illicit flows to maximize profit	Defense or liberation of population and territory from external control so as to acquire power and resources	Defense or liberation of population and territory from external control so as to take over or replace the state	Global networking to discredit the state by provoking state repression in response to violence
Organizational style	Mixture of hierarchy and network, with movement toward network	Charismatic leadership, hierarchical control, and patronage systems	Operational decentralization in revolutionary activities	Horizontal networks of loosely connected subversive cells
Relationship with the state	Undermining state political and judicial process, with no interest in state collapse	Pragmatic maintenance or acquisition of autonomy and monopoly on force	Hostility toward the state and attempted acquisition of predominance of force	Hostility toward the state and push for fundamental change in ideology or political system
Primary targets	Unnamed civilians	Government security forces and competing disruptive groups	Government security forces and competing disruptive groups	Unnamed civilians
Typical tactics	Corruption and violence	Corruption and violence	Violence	Violence
Geographical scope	Global influence	Local population and territory control	Local population and territory control	Global influence
Desire for visibility	Low	High	High	High

entations. In terms of their primary motivation, criminals want to establish global networks of trading and smuggling and dominate illicit cross-national flows so as to maximize profit; warlords want to defend or liberate the population and territory from external control so as to acquire power and resources; insurgents/rebels want to defend or liberate the population and territory from external control so as to take over or replace the state; and terrorists want to discredit the state by provoking repression in response to violence.[7] In terms of their organizational style, criminals display a mixture of hierarchy and network, with noticeable movement in the direction of network structures; warlords display charismatic leadership, hierarchical control, and patronage systems; insurgents/rebels display operational decentralization in revolutionary activities; and terrorists display horizontal networks of loosely connected subversive cells.[8] In terms of their relationship with the state, criminals reflect a mode of undermining the state's political and judicial processes but without any interest in the collapse of the state; warlords reflect a mode of pragmatic maintenance or acquisition of autonomy and of monopoly on the use of force; insurgents/rebels reflect a mode of coercive hostility toward the state and acquisition of a monopoly on the use of force; and terrorists reflect a mode of coercive hostility toward the state and pushing for change in state political ideology and political system.[9] In terms of primary targets, criminals and insurgents/rebels mainly focus on official security forces and competing groups, whereas warlords and terrorists principally concentrate on unarmed civilians.[10] In terms of the typical tactics chosen, criminals and warlords rely on a mix of corruption and violence, whereas insurgents/rebels and terrorists rely more exclusively on violence and the threat of violence. In terms of the geographical scope of activity, criminals and terrorists seek global influence, whereas warlords and insurgents/rebels seek local control of the population and territory.[11] Finally, in terms of the desire for visibility, criminals usually prefer to operate under the radar, whereas warlords, insurgents/rebels, and terrorists prefer high visibility to attract new members, convey an image of strength, and/or exact concessions.

Transnational criminal organizations are thus distinctive when placed in this broader context of unruly global nonstate forces. Criminals are alone in wishing to avoid both the collapse of the state government and the glare of the media spotlight. Unlike terrorist groups, trafficking enterprises generally do not seek "to instill fear and dread in civilian populations"; unlike warlords and insurgents/rebels, criminal enterprises do not seek "to implement political change."[12] Given that the security challenges of these disruptive nonstate forces are likely to grow in the future,[13] management efforts should take into account the differences among their motives, tactics, power levels, and security impacts.[14]

Despite these distinctions, one kind of violent global nonstate group can easily morph into another kind of group, and the boundaries among them are blurring, with transnational organized crime is at the center of this process:

> Part of the reason for this blurring is that criminal activities have become the common denominator. To put it simply criminal activities are no longer the excusive prerogative of criminal organizations. Terrorists, insurgents, warlords, militias and paramilitary forces all engage to one degree or another in criminal activities. Indeed, these activities, their involvement in the illegal global economy, and the connections that they make have made them much more formidable challengers to the state.[15]

For example, the 2004 Madrid bombers had morphed from transnational criminals into transnational terrorists. This blurring also applies increasingly to the organizational structure of the different unruly groups, as they now appear "in a variety of shapes, sizes, and shades of organizational sophistication, from transnational wheel networks that use core groups to steer their far-flung operations, to decentralized chain networks that rely on ad hoc coordination among largely independent nodes, to numerous cross-mutations that mix and match features of these 'ideal types.'"[16]

Just as transnational criminal organizations maintain some ties and undertake some joint activities with each other (and with governments and multinational corporations), so these criminal groups occasionally have ties and joint activities with warlords, insurgents/rebels, and terrorists. Recently, such groups have responded to international police pressure by extending their cooperation with one another and engaging in "marriages of convenience," recognizing, in the process, common underground tactics; reliance on similar weaponry; and use of the same international financial, commercial, transportation, and communication infrastructure systems that provide both anonymity and multiple access points.[17] For example, illicit arms smuggling often involves institutions and individuals not part of criminal organizations, including a wide variety of unruly groups involved in the internal power struggles within states.[18] The guiding principle behind such collusion among disruptive nonstate forces, presenting for security policy makers "a cauldron of traditional and emerging threats that interact with each other and at times converge,"[19] appears to be not ideological affinity but rather pragmatic operational opportunism. With their complex web of external ties, transnational criminals seem willing to work with anyone else—legitimate or illegitimate—who can help them turn a profit; in that way, these groups seem open to and accepting of a much wider array of temporary allies in dealing with global challenges than are national state governments.

SIMILARITIES AND DIFFERENCES BETWEEN CRIMINALS AND TERRORISTS

Disagreements and misconceptions exist among both analysts and policy makers about the level of commonality between transnational criminals and transnational terrorists. Some observers lump transnational criminals and terrorists into the same category—disruptive thugs who undermine global stability—seeing terrorism as simply a form of transnational organized crime[20] or seeing any distinctions between the two as "fading fast."[21] Other onlookers conversely claim that the logic behind criminal and terrorist behavior is quite different, sometimes to the point of being mutually exclusive, and that the two types of groups diverge sharply in their motives, methods, and impacts.[22] As with many debates, the truth appears to lie somewhere in between the two common extremes, for, in reality, both similarities and differences characterize transnational criminal organizations and transnational terrorist groups.

Similarities between transnational criminals and terrorists include that both are rational, threaten and use extreme violence, operate secretly, defy the rule of law, and are highly adaptable and resilient.[23] On that last point, law enforcement officials have recently been frustrated by the reality that al-Qaeda shares numerous qualities with transnational criminal enterprises, including "flat decision-making hierarchies, compartmented networks, and the ability to gather information and change practices in response to experience."[24] Similar personalities seem to be attracted to the two sordid professions (although transnational criminals tend to come from lower socioeconomic classes and transnational terrorists tend to be from the middle classes): both types of groups usually recruit new members from the same pool of frustrated marginal segments of the population, involving "people who are prepared to take risks, enjoy excitement and thrills, and scorn the norms of regular society."[25] Transnational criminal organizations and terrorist groups both are "violent non-state actors" that "are inherently illegitimate vis-à-vis the classical state system in part because the essence of being a state is having a monopoly on the legitimate use of violence"; both of these nonstate groups, however, "often provide alternative governance, offering services and supplying collective goods that the state is unable or unwilling to offer and provide."[26] Indeed, the two groups "emerge in response to inadequacies, deficiencies or shortcomings in many states and to one degree or another seek to compensate for those shortcomings."[27]

These two types of organizations both seek to undermine public confidence in national governments, albeit in differing ways. Both "people who commit crimes and people who throw bombs" usually have a common enemy in the state and its law enforcement agencies.[28] So terrorists through violent acts cause the mass public to doubt their state government's ability to provide protection, and criminals (despite occasionally colluding with governments) through breaking accepted rules and creating a vacuum of law and order cause citizens to lose confidence in the integrity of governing institutions.[29] With both terrorists and criminals targeting innocent members of the mass public, "substantial numbers of citizens have lost faith in the integrity and capacity of the legal process,"[30] and, as a result, "citizens alternate between indifference and skepticism that anything will change to outrage that the government is incapable of maintaining even the most basic order in the country."[31]

On the other hand, transnational criminals differ from transnational terrorists in crucial ways. No organized crime outfit operates exclusively according to the tenets of religion or political ideology,[32] and, correspondingly, no terrorist group is built around pure profit motivations. Although trivialized by some skeptical analysts, who emphasize, for example, the existence of narco-terrorists, this distinction between political and economic motivations appears to be quite significant from a security perspective, as transnational terrorists seek to overthrow the state regime, whereas transnational criminals seek simply to circumvent its rules and practices.

A closely related critical distinction between criminals and terrorists revolves around the relationship between these groups' goals and the status quo: transnational terrorists seem much more overt about wanting to disrupt the status quo, whereas transnational criminals tend to favor the status quo and to want to keep a lower profile and blend in more with legitimate activities,[33] even though they occasionally engage in the high-risk strategy of "daring authorities to crack down on them."[34] Indeed, with some exceptions, most transnational criminals do everything in their power to avoid being perceived as political terrorists, for that could impede their business success:

> For real career criminals, the conduct of politically motivated terrorists is incomprehensible and even weird. Why would anyone take such extreme risks

without any prospect of eventually enriching themselves? Who would want to openly confront the authorities, instead of evading or corrupting them? Is it not more sensible to keep illegal activities as concealed as possible? It is foolish to draw attention to oneself by using disproportionate violence. The opportunities for organized crime are largely based on the idea of exploiting the existing imperfections in the economic and moral system of the state. . . . Viewed from this perspective, organised crime is conservative.[35]

Newer transnational criminal organizations may not depend on the state and the established global economy as much as in the past,[36] and these organizations—in stark contrast to terrorist groups—usually persist in not wanting media, public, or government attention.[37] Overall, whereas some distinctions between these two types of groups have blurred in recent years, crucial conceptual differences remain.

CRIMINAL-TERRORIST CONNECTIONS

Considerable controversy also exists over whether "a deadly nexus" exists between organized crime and terrorism in multiple regions of the world, with widespread and dangerous links between them,[38] or, alternatively, little meaningful cooperation exists between the two groups.[39] Once again, these two common opposing views may be too extreme: what links do exist between the two groups seem opportunistic and sporadic,[40] functioning only as long as they benefit both parties. For example, the interest in illicit arms transfers, illicit drug transfers, and illicit human transfers is often mutual, as is that in clandestine means of transportation and finance, but cooperative arrangements rarely convey a flavor of permanence. Because both criminals and terrorists thrive under a certain degree of political instability, ties between the two appear most commonly in developing countries rather than in the advanced industrial societies of Western Europe and North America.[41]

In particular, supplier linkages between criminals and terrorists are common when dealing with drugs and weapons. After the Cold War, small and light arms became widely available for illicit trafficking by criminals to terrorists for operational use, and many transnational terrorist groups rely heavily for funding on illegal narcotics revenues.[42] In 2004, of the thirty-six groups on the U.S. State Department's terror watch list, fourteen were linked to narcotrafficking.[43] In the Madrid terrorist bombings of March 11, 2004, Moroccan drug traffickers, who had become radicalized and had merged into a local terrorist group,[44] provided the money for the preparation and implementation of the attacks, implemented by bombers who themselves were involved in mobile phone fraud, and it was these criminal drug smugglers who provided all the money and the know-how for the attack: indeed, a perfect illustration of how "terrorists often are supporting themselves through a range of seemingly petty yet organized crime activity" is that "one of the central members of the Madrid terror cell, Jamal Ahmidan, was a former international drug dealer who converted to Islam while in prison and tapped his criminal past after his release to supply the cell's logistical needs—including the exchange of drugs for the explosives used in the attacks."[45] Terrorists often find low-level crime to be useful to pursue their politically disruptive goals and sometimes use counterfeiting or protection rackets to finance their activities. In recent years, terrorists have become much more involved in the traditional criminal domains of illicit arms transfers, illicit drug transfers, and illicit human transfers.

The connection between transnational criminals and terrorists can certainly go the other way, where transnational criminals engage in terrorist activities. One example of crime bosses dabbling in terror is the Dubai-based Indian mobster Aftab Ansari, who "is believed to have helped fund the September 11 attacks with ransom money earned from kidnapping."[46] Another illustration occurred when a member of the Japanese Yakuza joined Aum Shinrikyo, the Japanese terrorist group that released nerve gas in a Tokyo subway station in March 1995, leading to both high status within Aum Shinrikyo as a rare convert and rising stature in the Yakuza due to new business generated.[47] Once again, this collaboration appears to be most likely when there is a convergence between the economic interests of criminals and the political interests of terrorists.

The linkages between transnational organized crime and transnational terrorism are not universal but rather appear to be a function of the type of group, activity, and objective involved. In particular, "it is more profitable for terrorists to collaborate with production, smuggling and sales organisations than with organised crime of the type that organises the underworld as a whole; and conversely, it is more advantageous for organised crime to collaborate with substantial organisations that really exert political influence than the lone fanatic who attacks unexpectedly and only generates temporary panic."[48] Because groups, activities, and objectives change over time, collaborative preferences usually are temporary rather than permanent. It is interesting to note that the global distribution of terrorist attacks and the global distribution of organized crime activity differ markedly: terrorist incidents are most prevalent in the Middle East, where rates of organized crime are relatively low; terrorist incidents are infrequent in Eastern Europe and sub-Saharan Africa, where rates of organized crime are relatively high.[49]

Regardless of the tightness and enduring quality of criminal-terrorist ties, the collusion between transnational criminal organizations and transnational terrorist groups poses a major threat to democratic institutions.[50] This danger is compounded when transnational criminal organizations provide logistical support not only to transnational terrorists but also to unfriendly foreign intelligence services and governments.[51] For example, in 2006 an Indonesian smuggling ring conspired to export a variety of state-of-the-art military weapons systems from the United States to the Tamil Tigers to be used to fight against Sri Lankan government forces, and in March 2008, global arms trafficker Viktor Bout was charged with conspiring to sell millions of dollars of weapons to the Revolutionary Armed Forces of Colombia (FARC).[52] Ironically, the global war on terror—involving considerable American pressure on governments aiding terrorists to cease this assistance—has indeed led to reduced state sponsorship and financial support for terrorists, but, in the process, may counterproductively have pushed terrorist groups to become more reliant on transnational criminals.[53]

CRIMINAL FACILITATION OF TERRORISM

In light of these criminal-terrorist connections, perhaps the most dire security threat occurs when transnational criminals facilitate the disruptive activities of transnational terrorists. Figure 7.1 displays the five facilitation modes affecting terrorist success in achieving political objectives and in evading law enforcement surveillance and interdiction. The first mode highlights a coordination threat, involving functional networking linked to the adaptive and decentralized nature of transnational activities, as transnational criminals provide robust cross-border transportation, communication, and logistics for transnational terrorists. This multifaceted networking can make both apprehension of perpetrators and interruption of illicit activities much more difficult. The second mode highlights an invisibility threat, involving operational secrecy linked to the ability of transnational activities to remain shielded from scrutiny, as transnational criminals provide transnational terrorists cover, clandestine movement of people and goods, and concealment of fixed assets. This invisibility can make detection of both transnational criminals and transnational terrorists much more difficult, and seems particularly problematic with respect to terrorism because terrorist actions would otherwise normally be more overt. The third mode highlights a social threat, involving thug im-

Figure 7.1. Transnational criminal modes of facilitating transnational terrorism

---

COORDINATION THREAT

Functional Networking
Linked to the adaptive and decentralized nature of transnational activities.
Transnational criminals provide robust cross-boundary transportation, communication,
and logistics for transnational terrorists.

INVISIBILITY THREAT

Operational Secrecy
Linked to the ability of transnational activities to remain shielded from scrutiny.
Transnational criminals provide transnational terrorists cover, clandestine movement
of people and goods, and concealment of fixed assets.

SOCIAL THREAT

Thug Importation
Linked primarily to illicit human transfers.
Transnational criminals facilitate the illegal entrance into Western states of disruptive
unruly elements, including transnational terrorists.

ECONOMIC THREAT

Financial Support
Linked primarily to illicit drug transfers.
Transnational criminals engage in activities that generate profits that end up funding
subnational insurgents and transnational terrorists.

POLITICAL-MILITARY THREAT

Coercive Power
Linked primarily to illicit arms transfers.
Transnational criminals directly supply and sell weapons and weapons components
to subnational insurgents and transnational terrorists.

---

portation linked primarily to illicit human transfers, as transnational criminals facilitate the illegal entrance into Western states of unruly elements, including transnational terrorists. When transnational terrorist activities end
up having strong ties to internal groups—as can be the result of criminally-
induced illegal migration—these activities become much more difficult to root
out and control. The fourth mode highlights an economic threat, involving
financial support linked primarily to illicit drug transfers, as transnational
criminals engage in profitable activities that end up expanding the scope of
disruptive behavior by both subnational insurgents and transnational terrorists. This economic threat can readily undermine any success states have
in bottlenecking the funding of these unruly groups by freezing suspected

terrorist bank accounts and sanctioning state patrons of terrorism. Finally, the fifth mode highlights a political-military threat, involving coercive power linked primarily to illicit arms transfers, as transnational criminals directly supply and sell weapons and weapons components to subnational insurgents and transnational terrorists. As with the economic threat, this political-military threat can negate any gains in restricting terrorist arms access from the enactment of domestic gun control and international arms control legislation. Illegitimate criminal weapons sources can be just as predictable and yield just as high quality arms as legitimate sources.

Of these five modes of criminal facilitation of terrorists, state security policy makers appear to be most concerned about the last two, involving criminal generation of profits that help to fund terrorists and criminal supply of weapons systems to terrorists. One of the most notorious examples of this kind of criminal facilitation of terrorism is al-Qaeda's well-developed connections with criminal syndicates in Central Asia, including Pakistani and Afghani opium traffickers.[54] Indeed, from the vantage point of the American war on terror, the most debilitating case has to be the persistent links between criminal and terrorist networks in Afghanistan. Special concern about these last two types of criminal facilitation of terrorism seems warranted because they undermine oft-pursued state-to-state multilateral agreements to freeze terrorist funding, to deny terrorists safe havens, and to place an embargo on the flow of arms to terrorists and their state supporters. In effect, transnational organized crime, which is willing to engage in business if profits can be made with any group regardless of its implicit or explicit political agenda, can in these ways render irrelevant and ineffective the most common countermeasures state governments and international organizations traditionally launch against transnational terrorist groups.

SECURITY LESSONS

Some key security lessons, summarized in figure 7.2, emerge from studying transnational criminal facilitation of transnational terrorism. These lessons surrounding criminal-terrorist collusion pertain to (1) improving relations between state and society, (2) promoting cooperation among responsible parties, and (3) expanding the scope of policy responses. Each area where criminals facilitate terrorists deserves not just more attention but also a somewhat different kind of attention than it has so far received, and this change in focus necessitates a much greater understanding of the strategic calculus of those who supply terrorists with their needs than we have today.

Figure 7.2. Key lessons from collusion between transnational criminals and transnational terrorists

---

Improving Relations between State and Society

National governments may need to keep lines of communication open within democracies to their citizenry so as to maintain trust and confidence.

Mass publics may need to remain informed and attentive so as to discriminate between security threats caused by incompetent government and those caused by nonstate disruptive forces.

Promoting Cooperation among Responsible Parties

More coordination may be needed both across agencies within a government and across governments of the world's countries in managing the criminal and terrorist threats.

Reduced compartmentalization may be needed to avoid mutually undercutting policies among those fighting criminals and terrorists.

Expanding the Scope of Policy Responses

Interdiction may be needed of the supply of weapons provided by criminals to terrorists and the demand for goods and services provided by terrorists for criminals.

Broader longer-term planning may be needed for both intelligence gathering and policy actions due to the greater money, personnel, and logistical support available to criminals working with terrorists.

Improving Relations between State and Society

In terms of improving relations between state and society, because both transnational criminals and transnational terrorists directly or indirectly attempt to undermine state authority, it appears that governments have an especially great need within democratic societies to keep the lines of communication open to their citizenry so as to be able to restore trust and confidence when necessary. Nontransparency or deception in national security affairs—when done specifically in the context of government policies toward these violent nonstate groups—could easily backfire and leave a state with little credibility in the eyes of its citizenry. Similarly, well-publicized apprehension and prosecution of suspected transnational criminals or terrorists can create massive embarrassment for national governments in cases where those arrested turn out to be innocent. Although fear of transnational organized crime and transnational terrorism may induce a public willingness to make sacrifices[55] in finances and freedoms, such willingness may decline over time as terrorist and criminal successes—often due to the interconnections between the two groups—undermine public confidence in national governments' integrity and protection capabilities.

Given the criminal and terrorist desire to undermine state authority, the mass public at the same time bears some responsibility to stay informed and to avoid focusing just on dramatic disruptions. Private citizens need especially to remain attentive to what kinds of security problems associated with transnational criminals or terrorists are directly a result of government ineptitude and what kinds of these problems are immune to effective management, even with the most adept regime in place. Having the mass public stay attuned to nonstate group threats and government policies to address these threats is indeed a tall order, for the threats are constantly changing and the problems, policies, and perpetrators may not always be easy to discern.

Promoting Cooperation among Responsible Parties

In terms of promoting cooperation among responsible parties, it appears that, even though transnational criminals and transnational terrorists are not in permanent formal conspiratorial arrangements, there should be more coordination than there is today both across government agencies and across national governments in managing these two threats. Because within most national governments the institutional mechanisms focusing on restraining transnational organized crime are quite separate from those focusing on restraining transnational terrorism, with the former largely housed within domestic law enforcement agencies and the latter mostly situated within international defense ministries, new ways are needed to overcome these bureaucratic barriers and develop new institutional arrangements that foster more cross-agency cooperation in intelligence and action efforts. Similarly, across national governments, the usual "need-to-know" compartmentalization barriers interfering with intelligence sharing and joint-action planning about criminals and terrorists need to be overcome.

Having anticrime and counterterrorist policies formulated and implemented separately and independently by each country or government agency seems highly counterproductive. Compartmentalization can easily lead to mutually undercutting policies or to those waging the battle against either criminals or terrorists unintentionally making matters worse for those waging the other battle. The complexity of the challenge posed by the criminal-terrorist threat requires the combined best efforts by the best minds available.

Expanding the Scope of Policy Responses

In terms of expanding the scope of policy responses, there needs to be greater realization that eradicating terrorism cannot be done in "splendid isolation" from other threats. Sometimes the best way to curtail transnational terrorist activity may be to cut off the supply of weapons provided by transnational criminal organizations for terrorists to undertake global violent acts, and sometimes the best way to curtail transnational criminal activity may be to cut off the demand for criminal goods and services provided by the sustaining market of transnational terrorist customers. Current counterterrorist policy focuses more on making sure that state suppliers of terrorist funding are cut off than on making sure that terrorist reliance on transnational organized crime is diminished. Despite the reality that these battles are decidedly a two-pronged effort—with the most effective countermeasures against transnational organized crime significantly different from the most effective countermeasures against transnational terrorism—policies fighting against transnational organized crime and those fighting against terrorism need broader integration.

Although joint disruptive behavior from transnational criminals and transnational terrorists could involve both double-crossing each other, security officials need to prepare for a challenge that might be much more difficult to manage because of the involvement of the greater planning capacity, logistical support, money, technology, and personnel from two different types of dispersed groups. To counter this more formidable threat, security policy makers seeking to constrain the joint threat need to engage in wider and more long-term planning themselves. As a part of this effort, some of the global war on terror should have resources expended not just directly against the terrorists themselves, and not just on states providing them with safe havens, but rather also on those unruly nonstate groups that collude with terrorists and supply the terrorists with their needs. As a first step, intelligence monitoring systems for both groups should be broadened, intertwined, and follow more parallel modes, with a key focal point for intelligence collection being tracking the fluid links between transnational criminals and transnational terrorists. As a second step, because of similarities in organizational structure involving fluid decentralized autonomous cells, action responses to one type of group should take into account those toward the other.

CONCLUDING THOUGHTS

It is readily evident from this analysis that to confront successfully transnational criminal facilitation of transnational terrorism, there is a need for considerable creativity and "outside-the-box" thinking, entailing "pressing all the buttons at once" in such a way as to place maximum possible pressure on all five modes of criminal facilitation of terrorism at the same time. The type and amount of pressure that optimizes this effort should be driven by available defense resources: for example, if a solid intelligence source is available somewhere, it should be immediately exploited, and if new ways are found to interdict illicit movement, they should be readily undertaken. Government responses to the criminal-terrorist link need to be dynamic, devoid of a predetermined type and level of activity, in order to promote flexibility in reallocating personnel and resources as opportunities or constraints present themselves. The primary means of bottlenecking needed resources facilitating transnational terrorism appears to be to shut down the criminally induced supply of disaffected people, laundered cash, and lethal arms they regularly receive. Because transnational criminal organizations have few, if any, political ideology ties, are relatively indiscriminate about whom their customers are, and are used to rapidly changing markets for their illicit goods and services, they would likely quickly find substitutes if terrorist markets were to disappear or dramatically diminish; however, from a security standpoint, this resource bottlenecking seems likely to foster the emergence of substitute criminal markets that are likely to be more socially acceptable and less dangerous than those markets that would be lost.

If the primary security concern is combating terrorism, and transnational organized crime is not seen as much of a direct security threat, there would still be a need to devote considerable intelligence and defense resources to increase understanding, monitoring, and manipulation of transnational criminal organizations so as to help make counterterrorist strategies successful. In this regard, many counterterrorist strategies downplay the role of transnational organized crime in facilitating terrorism and instead focus on freezing terrorist bank assets as a means of bottlenecking terrorist groups' capacity to undertake their activities; yet from a conceptual vantage point, there is no reason to assume that preventing terrorists from accessing funds (through freezing bank assets) would be any more effective than preventing terrorists from accessing weapons (through constraining transnational criminal organizations involved in arms smuggling).

Similarly, if the primary security concern is combating transnational organized crime, and not on containing transnational terrorism, there would still be a need to gather intelligence and maximize defense against terrorists because they constitute one of the primary markets for the goods and services criminals have to offer. For certain types of transnational criminal activity, especially but not exclusively arms, a key segment of target purchasers may be not law-abiding citizens but rather people just as unscrupulous and unruly as the criminals themselves. No matter how many transnational criminal organizations government authorities are able to shut down, revenues from terrorist (and insurgent) customers can keep revitalizing otherwise depleted criminal coffers. The links between transnational criminal and transnational terrorists seem sufficiently tight to elicit concerted simultaneous action against both.

So if security policy makers desire to contain and constrain both transnational terrorist and transnational criminal activities, where should one begin and which group should one choose as one's initial primary focus? Because transnational criminals and transnational terrorists mutually benefit from their relationship, on the surface this would appear to be an unanswerable "chicken-and-egg" inquiry. Nonetheless, there are certain strategic ingredients to making sound decisions concerning such dual countermeasures in dealing with a particular predicament at a particular point in time. First, one could look at which of the two groups—criminals or terrorists—is more immediately vulnerable to outside interference; this vulnerability could be a function of the current intelligence one has on the two groups, the array of constraining options one has at one's disposal for addressing each group, and the vigilance of each group has with regard to external intervention in its activities. Second, one could look at which of the two groups poses a more immediate threat to target populations, involving both the level of preparedness of the group initiating unruly behavior for undertaking offensive actions against desired targets and the level of preparedness of these targets to resist or respond to such actions. Finally, one could look at the relationship between the particular transnational criminal organization and transnational terrorist group in question to see who is more dependent on whom and who is calling the shots, with the underlying assumption that one would want to undertake countermeasures first against the group in the driver's seat.

Managing transnational organized crime turns out to be the crux of addressing a host of other national and international security disruptions. Because the conditions conducive to transnational criminal activity tend to spawn disruptive behavior by other unruly nonstate forces as well, it is crucial to approach this management of transnational organized crime in an integrated way within a much broader security framework. Through this method, there is a much lower chance that attempts to contain or reduce criminal activities would unwittingly amplify other important security threats.

8 CONCLUSION
Policy Implications

GIVEN THE DEBILITATING LINK between transnational organized crime and transnational terrorism, the differentiated use by transnational criminal organizations of corruption tactics versus violence tactics, and the distinctive impact of transnational criminal activities on individual security versus state security, determining appropriate responses to this threat is not an easy task. Indeed, in the fight against illicit global cross-border transactions, observers generally agree that "governments are failing,"[1] "traditional diplomacy has little or no prospect of being effective,"[2] and few successful international controls exist.[3] This pessimistic outlook is not due to regulators' being uninformed or uncaring, and it cannot be remedied simply by enhancing their authority or by throwing more money at the problem. This chapter presents the security paradoxes surrounding effective management, the changes in orientation needed to overcome these challenges, and the concrete policy recommendations with a potential for effective management of transnational criminal threat.

SECURITY PARADOXES IN ADDRESSING THE PROBLEM

Attempting to constrain effectively transboundary "transsovereign" problems faces difficult challenges. The reasons behind this predicament include the need for (1) state governments and the private sector to control or contain these problems without closing off economies, societies, or technologies; (2) cooperation and commitment among a great number of sometimes reluctant parties; (3) involvement of nonstate as well as state parties in any solution; (4) action taken by state governments to affect economic and social spheres "where the arm of liberal capitalist states has the shortest reach";

and (5) bypassing state sovereignty to manage these problems.[4] As a special transboundary problem, transnational organized crime poses particular difficulties because it is covert, subtle, and deeply embedded not only in the web of corruption and violence within states but also in the conflicting impulses between private citizens and government officials.

One basic deficiency in the ongoing efforts to manage transnational organized crime has been the reluctance among those responsible to recognize how profoundly this threat is facilitated by a highly conducive global setting. The intensification of globalization, the proliferation of weak failing or failed states, and the accelerating development of technologies that facilitate illicit transfers all appear to be deep-rooted, pervasive, and persistent patterns for the foreseeable future. Furthermore, despite the homogenizing of certain beliefs, the current international system is characterized by a multiplicity of conflicting values when it comes to illicit cross-border transactions. Undertaking in a vacuum policy initiatives against this activity that fly in the face of and are directly undermined by the current international relations system and rules of the game seems to be naive.

A second basic deficiency in attempts to manage transnational organized crime has been an inability among responsible authorities to keep pace with the rapid transformation of this threat. Transnational organized crime is dynamic, fluid, and adaptive, often employing asymmetric means[5] and the most advanced technology to achieve its ends. In contrast, the flexibility and speed of adjustment of most inertia-laden government bureaucracies opposing transnational organized crime appears to be consistently a lot lower. An "information asymmetry" occurs in this regard: transnational criminal networks "contain relatively flat authority structures that facilitate rapid decision cycles and quick information flows," whereas, in contrast, government law enforcement bureaucracies have "tall management hierarchies, cumbersome decision procedures, and interagency coordination challenges" that are associated with "significantly higher information costs than their illicit adversaries."[6] Because illicit criminal networks are notorious for adapting quickly and being highly resilient in the face of new government regulatory controls,[7] and because many responsible officials seem to be resigned fatalistically to tacit acceptance of their own sluggish pace, it is a struggle to develop coherent effective countermeasures. Undertaking responses to transnational organized crime that are consistently one step behind adept changes by targeted criminals appears to be a recipe for disaster.

In light of these challenges and deficiencies, four key security paradoxes—highlighted in figure 8.1—emerge in addressing transnational organized crime: failures associated with ineffective international legislation, overzealous coercive responses, halfhearted national sanctions, and conflicted mass public outcry. These paradoxes reveal significant underlying tensions reflect-

Figure 8.1. Debilitating security paradoxes in addressing transnational organized crime

---

Failure Associated with Ineffective International Legislation

Implementing international laws to ban undesired transfers across boundaries may help in the short run, but such action may increase crime in the long run by pushing such transactions underground and by making criminal recruitment easier in response to blunt constraining action.

Effective international initiatives to thwart international smuggling operations may require the ability by law enforcement authorities to cross borders expeditiously, but most states are not willing to give up sovereignty to facilitate the seamless transfer of prosecutorial ability.

Failure Associated with Overzealous Coercion

Using the military and the police to interdict transnational criminals can deter their activities, but strengthening coercive elements within fragile states can backfire and end up short-circuiting democratic governance processes and civil discourse societal norms.

Increasing the size and strength of forces opposing cross-border illicit activity can lessen criminal intrusion, but such a move will also make these forces more likely to be targeted by transnational criminals for corruption and violence and stimulate a dysfunctional action-reaction cycle.

Failure Associated with Halfhearted National Sanctions

Vulnerable states may be devastated by transnational organized crime, but desperate governments may find such illicit activity to be one of the only sources for economic resuscitation or foreign currency and thus may turn a blind eye to the questionable origins of revenues received.

An effective state countermeasure to deal with transnational organized crime may require all-pervasive intrusive surveillance combined with all-pervasive ruthless security forces, but such a firm response is usually off the table because of the civilized values of self-restraint within victim societies.

Failure Associated with Conflicted Mass Public Outcry

Members of the mass public may complain loudly about transnational organized crime because they bear many of the costs—suffering great personal misery and loss—but they also may reap many of the benefits because illicit trade can provide jobs and buoy sagging economies.

The covert low-profile nature of transnational criminal activities may decrease the potential for overt harm to be done to individuals, but it also may decrease the visibility of illicit activities to the mass public and thus its willingness to take steps to stop them.

ing unintended and unanticipated backfire effects and limited flexibility on the part of private citizens and national governments. When placed in the context of an international system that facilitates cross-border illicit activity and of regulatory institutions unable to keep pace with criminal adaptability, these tensions are amplified. Ultimately, these paradoxes call into question several widely advocated approaches for containing the global criminal threat.

The Failure Associated with Ineffective International Legislation

Coordinated international legislation restraining transnational organized crime can frequently fail. The two causes of this failure are (1) implementing international laws to ban the transfer of undesired goods across boundaries may help in the short run, but such action may actually increase transnational criminal activity in the long run by pushing such transactions into a seamy underground black market; and (2) effective international initiatives to disrupt cross-border illicit transfers may require a level of coordination that does not yet exist. The underlying security paradox here is that national governments may push ahead blindly in formulating and signing international agreements that, despite their signaling of symbolic commitment, embody little realistic hope of accomplishing anything other than stimulating more criminal activity. Overall, there appears to have been far too much effort expended exclusively on trying to find the right set of laws, agreements, prohibition regimes, or enforcement mechanisms to prosecute international criminals and to deter future transnational criminal activity.

A strong counterargument certainly merits discussion in this regard. Regardless of their direct effectiveness in eradicating transnational organized crime, international policing initiatives and global prohibition regimes against illicit cross-border activities have "evidenced progress toward an ever more powerful capacity to immobilize transnational criminals" and can generate "politically useful perceptual effects and symbolic uses that are often taken for granted or overlooked," expressing a state's moral resolve in a way that "can have substantial payoffs for both political leaders and law enforcement practitioners by impressing and appeasing various domestic and international audiences."[8] However, the perceptual and symbolic victories, the expression of moral resolve, and the appeasement of various audiences do not appear to make a significant dent in actually reining in the behavior of transnational organized crime. Thus, although global and regional cooperation is important to successful responses, the prospects for effective containment of transnational organized crime through coordinated legislation appear decidedly dim.

Looking at the first problem of negative long-term effects of international legislation against transnational organized crime, even with sufficient cross-national will to formulate or harmonize international regulations, backfire effects and undesired consequences can emerge:

> There is certainly an enormous gap between stated policing goals and actual outcomes. More law enforcement can also simply prompt more sophisticated and geographically dispersed law evasion techniques; this, in turn, can make law enforcement more difficult and complicated, providing a rationale to further empower, fund, and expand the international reach of crime control efforts. Law enforcement pressure can perversely turn disorganized crime into more organized crime, as is evident in the transformation of professional migrant smuggling in recent years. It can also exacerbate problems of corruption by creating incentives for criminals to spend more on bribes and payoffs.[9]

In this manner, "the existence of organised crime so often depends on the way in which the criminal law is enforced and administered,"[10] with, for example, blunt coercive governmental responses to the threat having the potential to contribute positively to the ability of these violent nonstate parties to recruit new members.[11] Evidence suggests that usually "the more states seek to raise barriers against the flow of illicit goods, services, and labor, the more the traffickers stand to profit from their trade,"[12] and the burgeoning of black markets in response to expanding international laws against transnational criminal activity provides a telling lesson about how unintended backfire effects can result when states undertake certain knee-jerk responses to illicit cross-state transfers without forethought about undesired long-term ramifications.

Although some of these international agreements do not backfire, they can still fail to achieve their ends when states functionally ignore their provisions or these provisions do not cover crucial dimensions of the threat. A general example of ignoring provisions is the United Nations Convention against Transnational Organized Crime (UNTOC), signed by 147 member states in 2000, entered into force in September 2003, and designed to establish the legislative framework for addressing transnational organized crime and for building the mechanisms for international cooperation. Even from the perspective of the United Nations itself, "there are large gaps in its ratification and in the implementation of its provisions," there is "ineptitude in promoting implementation of the UNTOC," and "the international community does not seem to be taking its own instrument seriously."[13] A specific example of omitting crucial threat dimensions occurs in illicit arms smuggling, where the dominant set of policy recommendations are attempts to strengthen market regulation possessing limited potential to be effective against covert collusive networked processes that evade such legal action.[14] International regulation of illicit trade has been markedly slow to deal with the activities of nonstate groups and to enforce accountability regarding state sponsorship of such groups, opening up significant strategic options to transnational criminals.[15]

Turning to the second problem of inadequate existing coordination in international legislation against transnational organized crime, the tensions among anarchy, sovereignty, and interdependence discussed in chapter 2 specifically work against states' willingness to subordinate their own interests to agree to abide by such international agreements. Most states today are still reluctant to facilitate the seamless transfer of prosecutorial powers: "The nature of international smuggling means that any effective international effort to thwart smuggling operations would necessarily include the ability by law enforcement authorities to cross borders expeditiously," yet "with only minor exceptions, the nations of the world have not found themselves willing to give up sovereignty to permit officials from either another nation or from an intergovernmental organization to cross their borders without explicit permission."[16] The motivation behind this steadfast state resistance and maintenance of "sovereign walls" is a justifiable concern about preserving cultural autonomy in a globalizing world, one in which the prospect of multilateral responses to transnational security challenges may elicit different reactions depending on how these responses relate to national interests.[17] Because criminal activities emerge from distinctive cultural contexts, "behavior that is acceptable in one country may be illegal in another."[18]

The Failure Associated with Overzealous Coercion
In a parallel manner, failure can surround overzealous use of coercion by states or intergovernmental organizations to respond to transnational organized crime. The two dimensions of this problem are (1) using the military and the police to interdict transnational criminals can deter their activities, but strengthening coercive elements within fragile states can backfire and end up short-circuiting democratic governance processes and civil discourse societal norms; and (2) increasing the size and strength of forces opposing

cross-border illicit activity can lessen criminal intrusion, but such a move can also make these forces more likely to be targeted by transnational criminals for corruption and violence and could stimulate a dysfunctional action-reaction cycle.[19] Illustrating both elements are the problems ensuing from the recent crackdown by the Mexican government to curtail illicit drug smuggling into the United States. The security paradox embedded in this failure is that the stern sanctions needed to interdict transnational criminal activities frequently can change the complexion of a country's political landscape, empowering those elements used to resolving differences through the use of force instead of through civil discourse.

Examining the first problem of coercion against criminals short-circuiting democratic governance, one advantage is that, even though transnational criminals have an information advantage over law enforcers, "law enforcers enjoy a force advantage over traffickers."[20] Because transnational organized crime so deeply embeds itself within countries where it operates, however, it would be extremely difficult to apply such coercion without it being highly visible and disruptive within the normal day-to-day activities of ordinary citizens. The militarization of anticrime initiatives can alienate citizens against their government, reduce support for anticrime and law-and-order initiatives, and ultimately increase political and social turmoil. Moreover, the implementation of large border patrols has in many societies appeared to escalate criminal-induced bribery and bloodshed more than dramatically lessening the movement of illicit goods, services, and people across national boundaries. When democratic countries find themselves having to rely on the threat of force rather than on public consensus to maintain law and order, the result usually makes domestic political stability highly fragile. Even if a national government's coercive measures effectively reduce transnational criminal activities, unless such policies are globally harmonized—and international agreements on coercive responses appear even less likely than agreements on passing legislation—the net effect could be simply to push these illicit activities into another more vulnerable part of the world.

Turning to the second problem of coercion against criminals triggering an unending action-reaction cycle, because transnational organized crime has secure nonstate sources for money and arms, it would be extremely difficult for governments or intergovernmental organizations to get into coercive tit-for-tat exchanges with criminals without incurring huge costs. Because law enforcement/defense agencies and transnational criminal organizations are both involved in organizational learning and competitive adaptation in response to each other's strategies,[21] an unending "cat-and-mouse" chase can develop in which there may be no long-term winners. Although the first problem would mainly be of concern to developing countries, the second applies at least as much—and perhaps more because of massive state firepower—to advanced industrial societies.

The Failure Associated with Halfhearted National Sanctions

Failure can also result from undercommitted national government sanctions directed against transnational organized crime. The two dimensions of this problem are that (1) vulnerable states may be devastated by transnational organized crime, but desperate governments may find such illicit activity to be one of the only sources for economic resuscitation or foreign currency and thus may turn a blind eye to the questionable origins of revenues received; and (2) an effective state countermeasure to deal with transnational organized crime may require all-pervasive intrusive surveillance combined with utterly ruthless security forces, but such a firm response is off the table because of the civilized values of self-restraint within victim societies. The underlying security paradox is that governments often seem to operate under a delusion that both unified opposition to transnational organized crime and complete societal acceptance of effective countermeasures exist.

Regarding the first problem of desperate states ignoring the origins of illicit revenues, the three major transnational criminal activities shed light on this conflicted behavior common especially among developing states. With respect to illicit arms transfers, government tolerance may result from a pragmatic emphasis on "economic advantage and political expediency."[22] With respect to illicit drug transfers, in practice foreign defense agencies have been reluctant to participate in the war on drugs,[23] and consuming states often functionally tolerate or underpunish the use of illegal drugs because of either the widespread social demand for them or the economic profits deriving from their sale. Finally, with respect to illicit human transfers, government tolerance may be a function of its awareness that its own companies have privately arranged to import cheap illegal aliens for economic profit.[24]

Regarding the second problem of draconian responses being off the table, because attempts by advanced industrial society governments to interfere with personal freedoms (particularly the right to privacy) have encountered substantial domestic resistance even when responding to transnational terrorism's highly visible threat (such as with the Patriot Act), such difficulties would appear to be even worse when addressing transnational organized crime's covert dangers. Although similar limitations characterize national government sanctions on virtually all nonstate transnational groups, special complexities emerge with respect to transnational organized crime.

Furthermore, the emphasis of many national governments on supply-side sanctions—reducing the influx of foreign illicit goods and services rather than reducing consumer demand within their own societies for these illicit goods and services—represents a dodging of the tough choices and tradeoffs involved. In particular, "supply-side law enforcement initiatives abroad often endlessly chase the international symptoms rather than the source of the problem at home," and such initiatives are in some sense cowardly because "blaming and targeting international drug traffickers and migrant smugglers is politically easier than dealing honestly with the enormous consumer demand for psychoactive substances and cheap migrant labor."[25] Instead of realizing that without addressing demand illicit trafficking will continue uninterrupted, this rather fatalistic orientation assumes that directly addressing undesired domestic demand for illicit goods and services within societies emphasizing freedom of choice would turn into an exercise in futility.

The Failure Associated with Conflicted Mass Public Outcry

From a bottom-up perspective, failure can be associated with subdued mass public outcry against transnational organized crime. In many cases, citizens do not seem to be very concerned about this illicit activity because they are either unaware of it or benefit from it; alternatively, the mass public reaction "is polluted by a moral panic" that can lead to countermeasures not working properly because they are not well thought out.[26] More specifically, (1) although members of the mass public may bear many of the costs and suffer great personal misery and loss from transnational organized crime, they also may reap many of the benefits because illicit trade can provide jobs and buoy sagging economies; and (2) the covert low-profile nature of many transnational criminal organizations may not reduce the potential for overt harm to be done to individuals, but instead decrease the visibility of illicit activities to the mass public—and of the links between disruptive occurrences and transnational organized crime—and thus lower public willingness to take steps to stop these activities. The security paradox behind the mass public lack of concern and vigilance within societies affected by transnational organized crime is that under some circumstances people assume that responsible authorities will effectively interdict criminal dangers when their lives are unpleasantly disrupted, but at other times these same private citizens may be tolerant of or even complicit with transnational criminal activities.

With respect to the first problem of high criminal enticement of the public, "citizens are lured into these illicit trades, either by the vast amounts of money involved or through extortion by the criminal bosses who run them"; although many illicit cross-border activities cause human misery, at the same time these activities may provide employment and boost depressed economies.[27] A slippery slope emerges for members of the public, when engaging in seemingly minor offenses such as buying a bootleg watch overseas or illegally downloading movies, music, or games can readily escalate into complicity in far more serious transnational criminal operations. The persistent demand for illicit weapons for offensive and defensive purposes, illicit drugs for personal escape, and illicit migrants for personal sexual pleasure or for cheap labor prevents bottom-up pressure on legislators within responsive democratic societies to rein in transnational criminal activities.

With respect to the second problem of low criminal visibility to the public, many people are simply not in a position—because of their ignorance of criminal operations or the skewed roots of their passionate outrage—to evaluate properly what illicit cross-border transactions need most urgently to be stopped. Moreover, many private citizens are so fearful of criminal reprisals that they would prefer not to know if some purchased good or service or some paycheck-issuing employer is embedded in the web of transnational organized crime. Even those being exploited are sometimes reluctant to learn the complete picture about criminal perpetrators, playing right into the hands of the exploiters. Moreover, public norms reflect ambivalence: for example, if anticorruption voters face a democratic election race between "a candidate who is seen to be corrupt but effective" and "another with a cleaner but less dynamic and effective reputation," citizens often pick the first over the second.[28] If Western publics were as unified and vocal in opposing transnational organized crime as they are in opposing terrorism, more progress would be possible.

Despite the severe concrete security dangers and the rhetorical condemnation of illicit cross-national transfers, neither states nor mass publics seem eager to act quickly and effectively to restrain transnational organized crime. With "so many segments of the society having a vested interest in the perpetuation of crime," the ability to respond decisively is blunted:[29] the proceeds from illegal contraband can extend, even within countries like the United States and the United Kingdom, "from consumers who prefer the better/ lower priced goods, to smugglers who make a large profit, to middlemen and authorities with their propensity for bribery and corruption."[30] Indeed, "as consumers, we are all involved—often unwittingly—in the shadowy world of transnational organized crime"; for example, migrant labor smuggling has driven down costs in the agricultural industry and kept food prices relatively low for the last fifteen years.[31] If abolished, illicit business "would be sorely missed" because it performs such high-demand services.[32]

NEEDED CHANGES IN ORIENTATION

To overcome these obstacles, those seriously interested in constraining transnational organized crime cannot continue to operate on past premises. Openness to change is essential to address a highly adaptive threat. As a key part of this transformation, to make the tough decisions necessary, responsible authorities need to move from conventional thinking to counterintuitive thinking, integrate treatment of interrelated security challenges, and differentiate responses to distinct threats. Figure 8.2 summarizes the basic changes in orientation conducive to effective management.

Move from Conventional Thinking to Counterintuitive Thinking

First, there is a need to abandon some elements of conventional security thinking and embrace key counterintuitive assumptions. These assumptions include the following: (1) the dangers that are most visible are not necessarily those that deserve the highest policy priority; (2) well-intentioned efforts vis-à-vis transnational organized crime—such as passing more national and international laws to ban illicit activities—can often backfire; and (3) the spread of global values emphasizing material success and moral relativism means that virtually anyone can be seduced through the lure of quick large profits[33] into participating, knowingly or unknowingly, in transnational criminal activity. All three imply that relying on standard practices is exactly what transnational criminals would anticipate and thus is likely to fail miserably.

A crucial starting point is to recognize that relying on existing national and global authority structures using standard operating procedures is not sufficient to stop transnational organized crime. Because criminals "are con-

Figure 8.2. Changes in orientation needed to deal with transnational organized crime

---

Need to Move from Conventional Thinking to Counterintuitive Thinking

Dangers that are most visible are not necessarily those that deserve the highest policy priority.

Well-intentioned efforts vis-à-vis transnational organized crime can often backfire.

Anyone can be seduced through the lure of profits into participating in transnational criminal activity.

Existing national and global authority structures using standard operating procedures are not sufficient to manage the demise of transnational criminal transactions.

Need to Integrate Treatment of Interrelated Security Challenges

Transnational organized crime's complication of the identification and prosecution of disruptive nonstate forces, interference with civil society practices, and facilitation of transnational terrorism merit more integrated treatment.

The five major transnational criminal organizations and the three major transnational criminal activities should receive unified treatment because of the extensive cross-linkages among them.

Concerted efforts need to build multiagency and international partnerships to fight transnational organized crime, involving, where possible, public-private cooperation and coordination.

Barriers impeding mutual protection efforts both within countries and across countries need to be lowered because of transnational criminals' capacities to evade narrow interdiction efforts.

Need to Differentiate Responses to Distinct Threats

There is a need to address separately the demand end as well as the supply end of illegally transferred people, goods, and services.

The criminal tactics of corruption and violence need to be addressed in different ways.

The criminal impacts on individual/human security and national/state security need to be addressed in different ways.

The strategic response to transnational organized crime needs to be a multipronged effort targeting both (1) domestic changes to lower demand, prevent bribery, and alert citizens to dangers; and (2) foreign changes to cordon off supply sources, dampen the tendencies toward violence, and forestall regime destabilization.

Need to Re-evaluate Metrics for Gauging Anticrime Success

There is a need to move away from reliance simply on reduction in the aggregate level of violence and corruption, capture or killing of criminal leaders, reduction in the size of a transnational criminal organization, or reduction in the scope of criminal activities.

There needs to be an emphasis on long-range strategies rather than on short-term solutions to transnational criminal threat.

States should undertake policy options designed to shape and manage rather than eradicate transnational organized crime in such a way that these states and their citizenry deem remaining illicit activities undertaken to be more acceptable and less dangerous.

In the end, criminal activities could then complement rather than undermine state control.

stantly challenging sluggish state-centric responses to their asymmetrical, adaptable organizations and methods,"[34] to cope with this threat, security policy makers need to go well outside of their law enforcement and defense institutions and their standard operating procedures. For example, a need exists to move away from reliance on largely unilateral, reactive, and retributive policies and practices as the primary means to combat transnational organized crime.[35] To rest confidently with the thought that everything will work out if one persists in pursuing ongoing strategies (comforted by the underlying delusion that existing policies simply need to continue longer to be successful), without reconsideration of alternative options, would enhance dramatically vulnerability to these criminally induced ominous flows in the future.

Integrate Treatment of Interrelated Security Challenges

Second, a need exists to integrate treatment of interrelated security issues regarding transnational organized crime. The main issues are (1) three highly interconnected dangers triggered by transnational organized crime—its complicating the identification and prosecution of disruptive forces, its interference with civil society practices, and its potential facilitation of transnational terrorism—merit more integrated management; (2) the growing links among the five major transnational criminal organizations and the three major transnational criminal activities, as well as among newly emerging criminal groups and illicit behaviors, are sufficiently tight to justify joint consideration of policies addressing them; (3) within countries, multiagency cooperation and coordination (including public-private partnerships) should be pursued wherever feasible;[36] (4) across countries, concerted efforts should occur (though difficult to attain) to build international partnerships to fight transnational organized crime;[37] and (5) cross-national barriers impeding mutual protection efforts should be lowered.[38] The potential risks associated with these proposals are sufficiently multifaceted, and their scope is sufficiently wide, that some might find this challenge more than a bit daunting, but this integration seems crucial because of the ability of transnational criminals to alter their focus continually and to evade the thrust of narrower interdiction efforts.

A key first step in this integrated approach is to avoid the reductionist tendency to break down transnational organized crime into its component parts, each to be addressed separately and sequentially. Many of those wanting stricter anticrime policies advocate doing so in a piecemeal manner, exemplified by frequent calls for a special exclusive focus on global illicit arms transfers, illicit drug transfers, or illicit human transfers, but such action seems futile because of the tight linkages among the various criminal activities. Government agencies tasked with only small discrete chunks of the emerging criminal security challenges need to coordinate with other relevant agencies and broaden their mandates. Countries attempting to fight transnational organized crime on their own using methods that differ markedly from those of everyone else need to participate in more harmonized responses.

Differentiate Responses to Distinct Threats

There is a need to differentiate responses to distinct threats posed by transnational organized crime. This differentiation involves the following: (1) any effective solution to transnational organized crime should address separately the demand end as well as the supply end of illegal global transactions, because of the high frequency of private individuals and groups eagerly taking advantage of these illicit people, goods, and services;[39] (2) because the criminal tactics of corruption and violence operate very differently from each other, they need to be addressed in very different ways; and (3) equal but differentiated attention should be paid to transnational organized crime's individual/human security impacts and national/state security impacts. This increased differentiation may produce greater wariness about whom one associates with, whose goods and services one buys, and whom one views as a legitimate business.

A key impetus to this orientation would be to ensure that the strategic response to transnational organized crime is a multipronged effort, hitting demand and supply, corruption and violence, and individual security and state security simultaneously but in very different ways. This multifaceted approach involves targeting both domestic changes to lower demand, prevent bribery, and alert citizens to dangers as well as foreign changes to cordon off supply sources, dampen the tendencies toward violence, and forestall regime destabilization. In this effort, democratic societies championing freedom of choice, individual self-gratification, and the unrestricted functioning of the free market may find themselves facing even greater obstacles (1) when attempting to reduce demand for illicit goods and services from their citizens than when attempting to keep these goods and services from crossing their borders, (2) when attempting to alter societal norms concerning corruption and violence than when attempting to alter government policies regarding corruption and violence, and (3) when attempting to protect individuals from criminal harm than when attempting to protect state regimes from criminal harm. Such a diversified strategy should incorporate multiple targets, including various illicit commodities and services, criminal gangs, geographic regions, and vulnerable economic sectors,[40] for no linear sequential monolithic orientation seems likely to succeed.

Re-evaluate Metrics for Gauging Anticrime Success

Finally, in the battle against transnational organized crime, there is a need to reconsider the metrics used to measure success. Conventionally, anticrime policy makers have looked at (1) the decrease in the aggregate levels of violence and corruption, (2) the capture or killing of criminal leaders, (3) the drop in the size of a transnational criminal organization, and/or (4) the reduction in the scope of criminal activities. However, these can easily turn out to be false measures of anticrime effectiveness: violence may decrease while debilitating corruption increases or simply becomes more covert and harder to detect; captured or killed criminal leaders may turn into martyrs and are easily replaced; a particular criminal syndicate may shrink specifically because new ones are forming; and success in narrowing the geographical scope of criminal activity in one part of the world may simply increase such illicit activity elsewhere. Moreover, the time frame for judging anticrime efforts is frequently too limited, for apparent short-term success in achieving anticrime objectives frequently can create long-range security problems, including severe unintended side effects. Going for easy-to-measure benchmarks to determine the success of one's anticrime efforts can be misleading and, as history demonstrates, can lead to a false sense of victory in the war on transnational organized crime.

In contrast, it seems preferable to evaluate anticrime success in terms of managing rather than eliminating the transnational criminal threat. More specifically, states should undertake a long-range strategy to shape rather than eradicate criminal disruption in such a way that what remains is more acceptable. It is crucial to prioritize anticrime measures, carefully selecting and targeting those organizations and activities that pose the greatest disruptive threat,[41] with the determination of which are most and least tolerable based on the severity (discussed in chapter 3) of corruption and violence tactics and of individual and state security impacts. Rather than a broad scattershot approach attempting to address all undesired criminal behavior simultaneously, this more selective approach would allow more coherent concentration of effort with limited resources. For example, in Russia (with Putin continuing to have a major policy influence today), "as long as the balance between organized crime and the state favors the state, Putin will be content to live with a manageable level of crime (by Russian standards) that can be controlled and monitored by the police so that the executive branch can focus its energy on strengthening the state instead of wrestling over control of it";[42] in Myanmar, the government considers drug trafficking to be acceptable but does not approve of violence, so the state can focus mainly on an antiviolence crackdown. If formulated and implemented properly, such anticrime policies could result in criminal activities complementing rather than undermining state control.

POLICY RECOMMENDATIONS

Any specific recommendation dealing with transnational organized crime needs to be considered within the broader framework: (1) placing every kind of pressure possible on the criminal system—financial interdiction, negative public relations campaigns, direct attack, and deception; (2) keeping the pressure on for a sustained period; (3) working to establish or restore the integrity and legitimacy of political, economic, and social institutions tainted by criminal ties; (4) changing countermeasures continually to keep criminals off balance and to keep pace with their own changes in behavior; (5) fostering international cooperation to dismantle criminal networks[43] through concerted multilateral rather than unilateral action; and (6) enlisting the aid of third parties, such as host governments and international law enforcement organizations. One example here of the latter two thrusts is the Merida Initiative, a cooperative effort, initiated by the U.S. State Department in June 2008, between the United States and the governments in Mexico, Central America, Haiti, and the Dominican Republic to confront transnational organized crime in the region. A flexible and versatile toolbox of approaches needs to be available for simultaneous use, employing both positive and negative incentives to confront transnational organized crime on all fronts: seek to deny it financial support and safe havens; attempt to interfere with and jam its use of advanced technologies; make unavailable or interfere with its modes of transportation; pressure third parties not to support it; create a generally inhospitable environment for it; conduct aggressive intelligence operations against it; take action to disrupt its operations as much as possible, especially apprehending leaders and key operatives; visibly harden security to deny its objectives by making it physically much more difficult to achieve its goals; showcase one's victories against it; and mount one's own strategic communication campaigns.

Although transnational criminals are extremely clever and resilient and adjust quickly to changing circumstances and countermeasures, taking advantage of the combined resources of defense and law enforcement institutions—using both police and military forces—provides the best chance for containing unruly corrupt or violent transnational activity. Using these combined resources should result in at least a delay and possibly a long-term reduction in criminal disruption. This combination should not be difficult to achieve because of the recent fusion of criminal justice and national security concerns within advanced industrial societies.[44]

This study's specific policy recommendations differ markedly from those most commonly used today by the world's governments. These policy recommendations are (1) redirecting intelligence collection, (2) substituting preventative for reactive responses, (3) implementing distinctive means to contain corruption and violence, (4) implementing distinctive means to protect individual and state security, and (5) undertaking target-centered threat management. These somewhat unorthodox prescriptions explicitly take into account both feasibility and desirability and short-term and long-term concerns. Figure 8.3 highlights this wide-ranging policy advice for managing transnational organized crime.

Redirecting Intelligence Collection

Once policy makers move away from standard operating procedures, a cornerstone supporting new policy approaches involves recognizing that traditional forms of intelligence have not been and will not be sufficient to track transnational organized crime. Widespread agreement exists about the inadequacy of current intelligence in this area: according to a 2008 report from the U.S. Department of Justice, "there are large gaps" in intelligence on transnational organized crime, which place in jeopardy the ability to track emerging threats emanating from illicit cross-border transactions.[45] Indeed, it wasn't until September 1995 that the Central Intelligence Agency, under pressure from Congress, "agreed to include the investigation and infiltration of global criminal gangs as part of its mission."[46] With domestic intelligence agencies such as the Federal Bureau of Investigation far more used to covering these disruptive groups than foreign intelligence agencies such as the Central Intelligence Agency, a long tradition exists in the United States and elsewhere of poor information sharing between local law enforcement operations and international intelligence operations.[47]

The expanding global scope of criminal activities requires an explicitly transnational intelligence thrust. Aside from having a more systematic picture of the scope and nature of transnational criminal activity, states need to have

Figure 8.3. Policy recommendations for managing transnational organized crime

General Framework

Place every kind of pressure possible on the criminal system—financial, public relations, direct attack, and deception—for a more sustained period in order to convince criminal targets of one's determination and credible commitment.

Change countermeasures continually to keep criminals off balance, incorporating a flexible and versatile toolbox of approaches using both positive and negative incentives to confront them on all fronts simultaneously.

Redirect intelligence about the tactics and security impacts of transnational organized crime, undertaking more long term and aggressive intelligence operations against it.

Enlist the aid of third parties, such as host governments and international law enforcement organizations, while simultaneously encouraging third parties to harmonize policies against transnational organized crime.

Seek to deny transnational organized crime financial support and safe havens, taking action to disrupt its operations as much as possible, including interfering with its use of advanced technologies and apprehending its leaders and key operatives.

Visibly harden security targets to deny transnational criminal objectives by making it physically more difficult to succeed while simultaneously showcasing one's own victories against criminal organizations.

Work to establish or restore the integrity and legitimacy of political, economic, and social institutions tainted by criminal ties, particularly addressing positive reforms within the justice system.

Create a generally inhospitable environment for the operations of transnational organized crime, prioritizing when nonstate governance from below is most disruptive to the civil functioning of both state and society.

Specific Strategies

Acquire better knowledge about the strengths, goals, plans, and intentions of criminal operations; undertake counterintelligence operations to confuse perpetrators; assess the impact upon them of countermeasures; and insulate responsible officials from criminal influence.

Use preventative rather than reactive responses by (1) a unilateral internal thrust to safeguard one's national borders and (2) a multilateral external thrust to assist foreign states to nip their own criminal problems and criminal safe havens in the bud.

For violence minimization, reduce criminals' zero-sum competitive situational perceptions, dampen criminals' extreme desperate or arrogant emotions, and strengthen well-trained armed forces and police officers to promote safety.

For corruption minimization, apply external pressure or assistance to reduce holes in law enforcement within countries beset by criminal activity and to break up collusive relationships between criminals and national government officials.

For individual/human security maximization, increase local accountability and vigilance (of a "neighborhood watch" variety) to nip criminal problems in the bud because national governments alone cannot manage ensuing dangers.

For national/state security maximization, safeguard more carefully the integrity of democratic processes within criminally infested states through transparency, meaningful checks and balances, and policy harmonization.

Employ a wider range of creative and persuasive positive and negative incentives to get government officials and members of societies to change specific behavior—stimulated by dysfunctional cultural norms—that facilitate transnational criminal activities.

Undertake a target-centered threat management approach incorporating the combined use of defense and law enforcement resources to increase protection of the most vulnerable individuals and institutions.

much better specific knowledge about the strength of the perpetrators; their goals, plans, and intentions; and the actual impact of the implemented countermeasures on them.[48] To accomplish these information acquisition tasks, cross-national intelligence sharing is essential, and to facilitate this end, the barriers caused by distrust (such as in dealing with Mexican drug cartels) must be overcome. For this purpose, human intelligence (rather than technical intelligence gathered through electronic means) is most vital,[49] as the concealed nature of transnational criminal activities makes them difficult to discern even at close range using advanced technology. There also needs to be careful tracking of rapidly changing new technologies useful to transnational organized crime to facilitate, distort, or conceal their illicit cross-border transfers. Furthermore, secure sharing of intelligence among relevant agencies both within and across states is essential to track these elusive transactions.

A far more concerted focus of this intelligence collection needs to be on the tactics of corruption and violence used by transnational organized crime and on the individual and state security impacts of these criminal tactics. In tracking these tactics and impacts, there needs to be a move away from a focus on the short term toward inclusion of long-term intelligence collection and analysis goals that support the formulation and implementation of long-range countermeasures: "The sophisticated, complex, and transnational nature of organized crime groups and activities demands that a long-term policy and enforcement approach be undertaken," with responsible authorities relying less on small but immediate capture of lower-echelon criminals or seizures of illicit goods and relying more on intelligence surrounding "undercover operations or financial investigations that target upper-echelon members and seek to fully dismantle criminal organizations and operations."[50] The greater time span involved in this long-run focus could facilitate improved comprehension and prediction of changing patterns of transnational criminal adaptation.

Officials involved in collecting this intelligence need to be better insulated from penetration by transnational organized crime.[51] In many countries, appropriate intelligence collection goals may exist, but bribery or extortion threats may prevent them from being pursued effectively, for transnational criminals are experts at ferreting out key leverage points. In special circumstances, however, because transnational criminal organizations will do virtually anything for a profit, governments may sometimes wish to nurture a special relationship with members of these organizations to gather information on transnational terrorists with whom these criminals do illicit business.[52]

In addition to expanded and refocused intelligence collection, more proactively disruptive counterintelligence operations toward transnational organized crime may merit consideration. Even though such efforts could have devastating consequences if detected, there are special circumstances that might warrant their use. In particular, because transnational criminal organizations—whose successful operations often rest on a thin veneer of mutual respect and fear among participants—"are vulnerable to efforts designed to sow confusion and distrust," there could be more intense use against them of means such as "the strategic penetration of criminal groups, the application of disinformation through narrow channels to undermine confidence and trust among criminal leaders, and the employment of double agents and sting operations for long-term disruption."[53] Indeed, fluid covert deception—with the ultimate aim of stymieing or shrinking transnational criminal activities—may prove to be effective in this regard. Given (1) the involvement of transnational criminal organizations in so many facets of legitimate international businesses, (2) the number of strategic and tactical alliances among them, and (3) their highly covert relationships and transactions, these disorienting counterstrategies seem a lot more useful against transnational criminals than against many other disruptive nonstate groups, including transnational terrorists.

Substituting Preventative for Reactive Responses

Given how subtly entrenched transnational organized crime is within societies, it appears crucial to move from reactive to preventative countermeasures. This approach would carefully track illicit cross-border transactions, undertake precautionary policies to minimize criminal expansion, and specifically keep criminals and criminal activities away from vulnerable areas.[54] Underlying this strategy would be an emphasis on insulating countries from the entrance of transnational criminal activities rather than—as is often the case today—dealing with transnational crime after it has taken root inside a country. In addition, for certain kinds of transnational criminal activities—such as drug running—preventative steps might include education, treatment, and rehabilitation of those most susceptible to illicit drug addiction. Most generally, it appears important to find internationally acceptable ways to challenge and undermine norms that permit and promote the development of transnational organized crime.

For security-capable advanced industrial societies, there are two principal components to this preventative strategy. First, a largely unilateral internal thrust to safeguard one's own national borders against criminal intrusion seems essential. Second, a largely multilateral external thrust appears crucial to improve the defenses of other countries without strong security capabilities so that they can develop early warning systems, avoid becoming criminal safe havens, and nip their own criminal problems in the bud before they spread elsewhere. Although the first priority is protecting one's own borders, doing so without shoring up others' defenses against criminal intrusion would appear to be fruitless within a highly interdependent world.

Looking at the first strategy of safeguarding one's own borders, this unilateral strategy involves capable government law enforcement and defense agencies engaging in effective inspection, detection, and monitoring of everything that comes across their national boundaries.[55] An underlying goal would be to amplify the sense of insecurity among criminals and ultimately to deter criminal activity in the first place by altering the perceived positive cost-benefit ratio of entrance into a life of crime.[56] Improvements could include performing more cargo inspections closer to their point of origin; implementing new technologies to provide electronic border filtering discriminating between the legitimate and the illicit crossing of goods, services, and people; and identifying and facilitating low-risk frequent travelers.[57] Some coordination—though not always complete harmonization—should occur among neighboring states' unilateral safeguarding of national borders, particularly if a common transshipment state is right next to a primary receiving state (as with Canada and the United States) for illicit cross-border transactions.

Turning to the second strategy of improving the defenses of other countries, this multilateral approach involves having capable government law enforcement and defense agencies reach out to needy states to forestall the contagion into one's own country of criminals and criminal activities elsewhere. An initial step in this strategy would be to promote the development and refinement of early warning systems—based on information gathered and shared by numerous sources in numerous countries about suspicious travelers or packages about to arrive—to help other states improve their detection of criminals or criminal goods and services preparing to enter their societies. A second step would be denying transnational criminals safe havens in other countries by inducing cooperation with foreign law enforcement and defense agencies and negotiating credible extradition agreements.[58] A third step would be to assist directly these needy states, enhancing the ability of foreign governments to control their own crime problems before they seep abroad. Given that "police and judicial systems in many developing countries are ill-prepared to combat sophisticated criminal organizations because they lack adequate resources, have limited investigative authorities, or are plagued by corruption," capable countries like the United States would need to expand their foreign law enforcement and defense partners and help "by providing technical assistance and training to improve the criminal justice capacities of other governments, and helping their police forces, prosecutors, and judges become more effective crime fighters."[59] On occasion, even needy recipients may require convincing about the value of this external defensive assistance.

Implementing Distinctive Means to Contain Corruption and Violence

For corruption-oriented transnational criminal behavior, the usual recommendations are (1) to increase the exposure of corrupt acts and their perpetrators, (2) to increase the penalties for those convicted of corruption, and (3) to sign international agreements banning corruption. Transparency and accountability are indeed essential to reduce crimes of greed,[60] and certainly new more creative and culturally sensitive ways could be developed to promote these two values within countries lacking such an emphasis. In a parallel fashion, penalties for corruption could be more finely tuned for maximum impact, and international agreements could be publicized and monitored in such a way so as to benefit the promotion of enlightened international norms.

The first recommendation is problematic, however, because often within governments one convicted corrupt official is simply replaced by another who may have learned lessons from a predecessor and be more clever at not getting caught. Similarly, the second recommendation is weak because the monetary rewards from corruption are so large that they may eclipse the pain associated with any possible penalty. Finally, the third recommendation may achieve little positive change in transnational criminal behavior: for example, the United Nations Convention against Corruption—developed in 2003, entered into force in 2005, and ratified by more than 120 countries—has yet to reduce substantially global criminally induced corruption because, as the United Nations itself admits, "efforts have fallen short of potentials when it comes to concrete actions."[61]

So although these three common thrusts are important, to contain corruption, a need exists to go well beyond them to apply external pressure or assistance so as to (1) to reduce holes in law enforcement within countries beset by criminal corruption and (2) to break up collusive relationships between criminals and national government officials. Critical to this effort are anticipating the probability of emerging corruption in response to existing regulation[62] and shoring up credible well-functioning authoritative infrastructures. It is vital to have more coherent efforts by (1) Western states to provide economic assistance to weak or failing states to help with internal law enforcement and "to ease the domestic impact associated with the loss of illicit source of foreign exchange in weak states,"[63] and (2) international organizations such as the World Bank to ban state ties to criminal organizations as a prerequisite for receipt of financial benefits.

In addition, harsher negative sanctions and stronger positive incentives need to be applied vis-à-vis societies whose cultural norms support widespread corruption in a manner facilitating transnational organized crime. As long as corruption is accepted as standard business practice in parts of the world, criminal elements will thrive there. As a part of this process, societies need to discuss and clarify what kinds of personal behavior and transactions they find absolutely unacceptable. Key officials vulnerable to bribery—particularly underpaid low-ranking ones—need more training to cause them to see any money-generating collusion with transnational criminals as zero-sum with both their own interests and their state's interests. In many ways, sustained efforts promoting a "culture of lawfulness"—involving schools, religious institutions, and the mass media—are at the core of undercutting "the political-criminal nexus" and reducing corruption.[64] Moreover, societies exhibiting privileged inequality rather than merit-based opportunity may need incentives to promote change. In both of these cases, the prevailing current global attitude is tolerance of cultural self-determination—regardless of cultural values—but this may ultimately prove to be an unaffordable luxury if integrity is to be restored.

Turning to violence-oriented transnational criminal behavior, the usual responses are (1) to beef up law enforcement's ability to confront the perpetrators of violence, (2) to increase monitoring and vigilance regarding violent activities, and (3) to increase penalties, especially for the most severe acts of violence. Certainly, "strengthening the armed forces and the police further is an essential part of restoring citizens' lives to safety" in the face of the dangers posed by transnational organized crime.[65] Especially within states where transnational criminals possess more coercive power than government authorities, this action seems to be an essential first step. It seems pivotal that this "law-and-order" solution be done in a way that has maximum visibility to potentially disruptive criminal forces.

It would appear to be foolhardy, however, to address criminal violence through force alone, as this thrust could easily (as mentioned earlier in this chapter) lead to a spiraling bloody action-reaction cycle and to neglect of needed accompanying social measures and justice reform.[66] Particularly within transitional developing societies, a danger exists that responses to crime could become overly militarized—reversing any progress toward civil society—because of intense pressures (1) from the government security establishment itself to use its capabilities in a familiar and traditional way and (2) from the public for immediate decisive government action against lawlessness.[67]

One short-term fix for criminal violence could involve relaxing domestic gun control when criminals possess a significant coercive advantage over defenseless targets (vulnerable individuals and groups), along with tightening domestic gun control when tracking is low of who owns what arms and even the most dangerous elements within a society find easy access to powerful weapons. Enhanced protection of probable high-profile targets of criminal violence seems especially important. On a more fundamental level, it is useful where possible as part of a long-run strategy to begin to identify and mitigate the root causes of societal violence.

Furthermore, in addressing criminal violence, there is also a crucial need to address transnational criminals' perceptions of—and emotional responses to—the predicaments they encounter. In particular, there is a need to work on reducing criminals' zero-sum competitive perceptions of a contentious confrontational situation between two sides, which can be successful "when they decide that cooperation yields vastly greater benefits to both than antagonism."[68] Having transnational criminals reach this particular conclusion may require that outsiders, including government, media, and business contacts, help them frame the ongoing predicament in a particular manner. At the same time, it seems important to try to minimize criminals' dangerous extreme crisis emotions of "back-to-the-wall" desperation or smug arrogance. Because the emotions surrounding violence—and the recruitment of new personnel for violent transnational criminal organizations—are often associated with human rights abuses, demonization of enemies, severe unemployment, and easy weapons access, a greater effort is needed to reduce the presence of these conducive conditions. Cross-national positive and negative incentives can help in this regard. As with corruption, what needs to be avoided is a passive fatalistic acceptance of the global inevitability of violence.

Implementing Distinctive Means to Protect Individual and State Security

Looking first at national/state security, compared to individual/human security, this thrust has been more widely discussed and better documented. The usual approach heavily emphasizes increasing military expenditures on personnel, equipment, and training to physically protect the state from coercive foreign intrusion. Unfortunately, when it comes to the transnational criminal threat, this type of coercion seems to be relatively useless in interdicting the dangers to the state because transnational criminals do not enter countries by force and instead often set up shop when their services are most needed or desired by both government officials and private citizens.

Showing more promise in protecting state security from the transnational criminal threat might be to find new ways, including increased regime transparency, to strengthen the legitimacy of the state government. Public relations campaigns could occur to increase public confidence in the government and increase public distrust of the purveyors of illicit goods and services. Safeguarding more carefully the integrity of democratic processes within criminally infested states is important through meaningful checks and balances to restrain the emergence of extortion and fraud. This approach may involve the creation of independent watchdog agencies or of incentives for "whistle-blowing" when problems surface. Such responses appear to warrant specific application to the transnational criminal threat because the potential for government infiltration appears to be highest.

In addition, highly centralized secret contingency plans may need to be in place to protect key government leaders and government structures from any disruptive action by transnational criminal organizations or other globally unruly forces. Any state funding ending up in the hands of subversive non-state groups should end, and those political groups opposed to transnational organized crime should be empowered. Covert containment of criminal elements may be useful to keep them far from administrative structures.

From a multilateral standpoint, accelerating efforts among governments to coordinate and harmonize their policies toward transnational organized crime appear essential to improve global monitoring and enforcement and to reduce the availability of safe havens and places where prosecution of transnational criminal activities is less certain or less severe. In addition, governments, financial institutions, and nongovernmental organizations need to face stiffer penalties if they partner up with transnational criminal organizations. Sharp differences among proximate states—in terms of what kind of criminal activity is tolerated, how vigorous monitoring and apprehension of criminals is, and how severe the penalties are for those apprehended—can lead to contagion of criminal threats among neighboring states, inevitably creating friction and finger-pointing by those involved. Of vital importance are cross-national sharing of information, extradition of criminals who have fled abroad, and acceptance of neutral sites for any needed criminal trials. The best way to implement effectively these ideas promoting state security would not be through signing international agreements, which generally have proven to be "toothless" when dealing with transnational organized crime, but rather through the use of enforceable tangible incentives and disincentives promoting policy change. Ideally, this incentive-based system would incorporate aid to willing states to help develop the necessary infrastructure to engage in successful countermeasures to deal with the threat.

Within this implementation of means to promote national/state security, a new balance may need to emerge between the rights of individual citizens to privacy and the protection from criminal intrusion of national interest and the national strategic infrastructure. The clandestine nature of transnational criminal activity—and its seamless blending in with legitimate commerce—means that, without some form of government eavesdropping or wiretapping, the ability to apprehend and prosecute successfully transnational criminals may be extremely low. Together the citizens and national government officials of affected countries need to decide where the appropriate balance lies and if it differs substantially from the existing status quo.

Turning to individual/human security, progress has been relatively slow because of confusion and disagreement about the most vital defense needs. The normal approach involves the use of an increased domestic police presence to protect individual citizens within the context of a tight "law-and-order" system to ensure preservation of the societal way of life. Unfortunately, such an approach does not work well against a subtle threat such as transnational crime that can blend in invisibly with law-abiding economic, social, and political institutions to conceal the illicit nature of its activities.

Improving individual/human security requires a change in the local law enforcement and defense focus. There is a need to integrate law enforcement and defense authorities in addressing the transnational criminal threat, incorporating a comprehensive "whole-of-government" approach. Rather than simply protecting individual citizens and maintaining law and order, there is a need to emphasize early detection and interdiction of unlawful transnational criminal activities so as to make areas less attractive to criminals and to stop those criminals who enter before they can take control of a particular community. This approach includes enhancing the information-gathering capabilities of local police, who know their territory, may be ethnically closer to the communities served, are more aware of local changes, and are usually more acceptable to local community leaders.[69] Within transitional developing countries fighting transnational organized crime, a "key to building the legitimacy of the police is to ensure effective forms of local control and accountability—in effect, to make citizens believe that the police are responsive to their needs, and not those of some bureaucrat in a distant capital."[70]

Having transnational organized crime so deeply linked to the global activities of multinational corporations opens the door to an anticrime individual security thrust involving the private sector, including not just business but the full range of nongovernmental organizations. The most effective global responses to transnational organized crime require creative input from the private sector, public-private partnerships, and community education:[71] "In today's globalized world, where illicit criminal activities and their actors threaten both our international security and private sector interests, public and private non-governmental entities can be crucial allies," and "greater cooperation and coordination with non-governmental groups can serve as a force multiplier in our war against international crime."[72] The result can be improving fragmented societies' sense of cohesion and resiliency.

Education programs sponsored by the government and private media could expose transnational criminal activities and teach citizens about the nature of the threat and how to prepare for it. One challenge is to get private citizens, through increased visibility of negative spillover effects, to become more fully aware of the broader long-term ripple effect of engaging in unsanctioned criminal transactions on the rest of the community. A joint need exists to reduce cultural acceptance of human rights violations undertaken by lawless criminals while at the same time increasing cultural tolerance of different values among law-abiding social groups.

Furthermore, enhancing bottom-up local responsibility seems essential to provide protection against the individual/human security dangers associated with transnational organized crime. Such preparedness works best with "a population that acknowledges that security must become everyone's business."[73] There is a need for more local accountability, preparedness, and vigilance, often of a "neighborhood watch" variety, to help with monitoring and enforcement, for the scope of the threat is beyond the capacity of any national government alone—no matter what the size and strength of its police force—to manage. Specifically, "if local communities can be convinced to turn against those who perpetrate barbaric acts of violence," then the chances increase that citizens who work with or support criminals can be identified and rooted out.[74] Central to this effort is government promotion of civic engagement and civil society, encouraging the sometimes unintended consequences of nongovernmental organization efforts involving "the construction of civil society buffers against the intrusion of transnational organized crime."[75]

National governments need to be careful about how they attempt to stimulate this local responsibility, as community crime prevention may seem on the surface "to increase the scope for voluntary and citizen participation in the local governance of crime" but underneath may be "constrained and weighted down with central government performance targets such that local agendas and community needs are marginalised."[76] To be most effective, local responsibility should be decentralized and vary according to distinctive cultural norms embodying differing levels of tolerance for corruption and violence. Local municipal responsibility for civil defense, however, can potentially create a large differential between the best and worst protected areas—often corresponding to socioeconomic disparities—so a central authority would need to set universal minimally acceptable levels of protection.

Undertaking Target-Centered Threat Management

Given the largely covert nature of transnational organized crime, concentrating on isolating the culprit for each global case of illicit activity is likely to prove futile. For that reason, security analysis needs to move away from its traditional focus on identifying criminal initiators and to move toward—incorporating the combined use of defense and law enforcement resources—a target-centered threat management approach[77] emphasizing victim needs designed to increase protection of vulnerable individuals and institutions. For dealing with the transnational criminal threat, this target-centered approach encompasses vital interests/protection priorities, involving assets within targets at risk for criminal disruption; vulnerability to damage/loss, involving threat targets' anticipation and preparation for the risk of criminal intrusion; and the probability and magnitude of damage/loss, involving the chances of the risks occurring and the impact of these risk if they did occur on targets. This target-centered approach would focus on high-risk groups, including those most exposed and susceptible to the criminal threat; volatile geographic areas such as large cities, border regions, source and transit countries, and smuggling routes; ominous emerging crime trends such as those involving cybercrime; and vulnerable economic sectors and markets such as financial services and marine ports.[78] By emphasizing more what a threat target cares and can do something about, its security regarding incoming criminal dangers could be improved.

Target-centered management of transnational organized crime would involve critical application of "target-hardening" techniques, determining "what is it that makes certain enterprises—such as banking, aluminum and the telecommunication industries—particularly vulnerable to organized crime" and then developing policies to reduce this vulnerability.[79] Looking first at vital interests or protection priorities, to address the importance of risked assets within a threat target, the target should carefully identify and shield critical facilities and leaders from transnational criminal disruption. Turning to dangerous instigators or harmful events, to address the disruptive capacity of risk sources, a threat target should attempt to isolate transnational criminal organizations diplomatically, militarily, or economically through a variety of multilaterally applied positive and negative sanctions,[80] and build where possible a coalition of those opposed to these criminal groups and supportive of the threat targets. As to vulnerability to damage or loss, to address a threat target's risk anticipation and preparation, the target should develop sensitive and accurate early warning systems with well-established follow-up procedures for dealing with the entrance of new transnational criminal groups or the expansion/modification of activities of existing criminal groups. Moving to the probability of damage or loss, to address the likelihood of risks occurring within a threat target, the target should dissuade transnational criminal organizations from carrying out expressed threats by finding ways to show them that their actions would be futile or would backfire and by making clear to them the negative consequences if they decided to go through with their threats. Concluding with the magnitude of damage or loss, to address the impact of actualized risks on a threat target, the target should prepare its population psychologically for the scope of possible negative consequences of transnational criminal activity and formulate realistic recovery plans.

POLICY EFFECTIVENESS VERSUS VALUE MAINTENANCE

Transnational organized crime has placed national governments in a real international relations bind. Illicit cross-border activities tend to bring to the surface basic value clashes—summarized in figure 8.4—between individual freedom and collective order, between economic profit and political security, and between civil openness and societal protection. These clashes, which reflect contradictions among the fundamental norms widely accepted in today's world, can paralyze policy-making initiatives until or unless a government and its citizens begin to grapple directly with the contradictions involved. The United States, in particular, has been handicapped in its response

Figure 8.4. Value clashes fostered by combating transnational organized crime

Effective restraint of transnational organized crime seems impeded less by the defensive abilities of criminal organizations and more by the self-imposed constraints on Western states' security operations, such as domestic and international law, respect for privacy, and an aversion to harming innocent people and property.

Individual Freedom versus Collective Order
Linked to the tradeoff between pursuing justice/fairness and pursuing stability/peace.

As the threat from transnational criminal activity increases, the pressures within states intensify to downplay justice in order to achieve stability.

Economic Profit versus Political Security
Linked to the tradeoff between gaining narrow material benefits for oneself and contributing broad benefits to the greater community.

Many blithely assume that the pursuit of profit through the facilitation of all kinds of cross-national transactions, including illicit ones, is perfectly harmonious with improving security.

Civil Openness versus Societal Protection
Linked to the tradeoff between the efficiency of the free flow of goods and services across national borders and the inescapable vulnerability to disruption deriving from criminal involvement in that flow.

Built-in limits exist on states' abilities to deter illicit cross-border transactions if they wish to maintain open societies, and open free-market system benefits contrast sharply with criminally controlled transfer costs.

Critical value clashes within affected areas are perhaps more important than any other impediment in paralyzing Western societies and preventing them from taking effective security action to constrain transnational organized crime.

to transnational organized crime by these pivotal value controversies. As seen earlier, however, a widespread lack of political courage has, up until this point, largely prevented those responsible from confronting these deeply divisive issues directly, as neither private citizens nor government officials are in agreement about the countermeasures and sacrifices needed to constrain the criminal threat.

The tensions between individual freedom and collective order connect to the tradeoffs involved in the choice between pursuing justice/fairness and pursuing stability/peace. As the threat from transnational criminal activity increases, the pressures within states intensify to downplay justice in order to achieve stability because of the ambiguities surrounding globally accepted notions of fair play. This emphasis on stability, preserving existing authority structures and the integrity of national boundaries in the face of disruptive turmoil generated by transnational organized crime, can be intrinsically problematic in a rapidly changing world: the legitimacy of these structures and boundaries can be quite arbitrary when looked at in broad historical perspective,[81] and a focus on stability can lead to disappointment because of readily recognizable needs for continuing adaptation and movement.[82] Yet if one considers the alternative emphasis on justice, promoting the rights of individuals and groups, then the specter emerges of inadvertently facilitating violent chaos as a result of the many changes necessitated especially within dysfunctional states.

The tensions between profit and security relate directly to the need for recognition of the tradeoffs in today's world between gaining narrow material benefits for oneself and contributing broad benefits to the greater community. In this regard, many blithely assume that the pursuit of profit through the facilitation of all kinds of cross-national transactions, including illicit ones, is perfectly harmonious with improving national security. Although the economic "invisible hand" can indeed maximize national security, transnational organized crime can easily mutate the principles of free-market exchange so that the money goes to a few who do not operate in an open competitive environment and so that broader societal and security benefits do not occur.

Finally, the tensions between openness and protection reflect a fundamental tradeoff in today's highly interdependent world—between the efficiency of the free global flow of goods and services and the inescapable vulnerability to disruption deriving from criminal involvement in that flow. Built-in limits exist on states' abilities to deter illicit cross-border transactions "if they wish to maintain open societies and keep their borders open to high volumes of legitimate cross-border exchange."[83] Indeed, "the inescapable predicament facing border control strategists is that the massive volume of cross-border trade and travel requires that borders function not simply as barriers against CTAs [clandestine transnational actors], but as filters that do not impede legitimate border crossings."[84] Open free-market system benefits contrast sharply with criminally controlled transfer costs. Although free-market advocates might object that the free-market principles do not apply to inherently harmful flows, criminal traffickers of illicit arms, drugs, and humans would respond by arguing that demand is high within so-called enlightened societies for what they have to offer, and that, in the end, their illicit activity "is like any other business, entailing no special moral responsibility."[85]

Perhaps the fundamental policy challenge within Western states is how to address transnational organized crime effectively while at the same time not sacrificing cherished enlightened societal values. If willingness existed to forgo democratic processes and cross-border openness, along with broader liberal internationalist principles, then the solution would be a lot simpler. Effective restraint of transnational organized crime seems impeded less by the defensive abilities of criminal organizations and more by the self-imposed constraints under which Western states operate, such as domestic and international law, respect for privacy, and an aversion against harming innocent people and property (collateral damage). Because of these constraints, the potentially most effective countermeasure—utterly intrusive surveillance combined with utterly ruthless security forces—is decidedly off-limits.

Maintaining cherished open societal values while reining in disruptive unruly activity appears to be even more difficult when confronting transnational organized crime than it is when confronting transnational terrorism. When the hue and cry emerged in the United States after the passage of the Patriot Act—which may have moved the country in an Orwellian direction by allowing the government greater ability to monitor and restrict citizens' activities so as to increase the chances of apprehending terrorists—at least the vast majority of those affected had no connection to or sympathy for the terrorist cause. In contrast, when calculating the number of citizens who directly or indirectly encourage the entrance of illegal migrants, take advantage of sex tourism, imbibe in illicit drugs obtained covertly from abroad, purchase illegal arms smuggled into the country, or distribute or purchase a host of other unsanctioned foreign contraband items, it is readily evident that—should such restrictive legislation be passed—the level of resentment, outrage, and demand for a return to a more open society would be even more fervent. Over time, transnational organized crime has constructed an intrusive web within and across Western democratic societies from which meaningful extrication on the part of knowingly or unknowingly ensnared parties is quite difficult.

CONCLUDING THOUGHTS

Given the persistence of the transnational criminal threat in international relations, there is no way for those tasked with protection to duck the challenge. They need to prioritize emerging dangers when the criminal tactics and the state and individual security impacts are deemed to be most dangerous. The responsible parties ought nimbly to find ways to discern and defuse ominous criminal dangers before they materialize, promote flexibility in modifying responses as criminals themselves adapt to differing countermeasures, and carefully monitor the success of efforts to constrain these illicit global transactions. Undertaking strong countermeasures against transnational criminals is not "a matter of grace, charity or patronizing kindness" but rather "a matter of intense national and global self-interest."[86]

Left inappropriately unattended to, transnational organized crime could become so pervasive that national governments might lose their sense of noble purpose, civil society bonds might lose all sense of coherence, and private citizens might lose any ability to differentiate between legitimate and illegitimate activity. A truly nightmare future scenario might involve a complete global descent into chaotic anarchy:

> The worst case scenario is that TOC [transnational organized crime] will slowly corrupt and undermine effective governance at all levels, from the local to the state to the global, corroding global weapons, environmental and health control regimes and fueling armed conflict. In some areas of the globe where state control is weakest, predatory warlords, kingpins and gang-leaders financed by participation in TOC may wrest control of large segments of territory, markets or population away from governments. Powerful states would likely respond by adopting a highly defensive and confrontational strategy, raising significant barriers both within and at their borders to the penetration of OC [organized crime] and terror groups. International relations would be increasingly "criminalized," with powerful states seeking to use all the tools at their disposal—ranging from military force to UN Security Council Resolutions—to

control "rogue," "outlaw" or criminalized states, and non-state actors. In this atmosphere of permanent confrontation, crisis would become endemic, and respect for human rights standards would gradually erode. Slowly, but surely, TOC would strangle effective public governance, with catastrophic effects.[87]

Once such an ominous criminally induced scenario is fully set in motion, little could be done to stop it and pull the world out of its downward spiral.

If, in contrast, those responsible are willing early on to consider unorthodox countermeasures—including redirecting intelligence and counterintelligence, substituting preventative for reactive responses, implementing distinctive means to contain corruption and violence and to protect individual and state security, and undertaking target-centered threat management—then the possibility exists to reverse course and to prevent this dire outcome. Transnational criminals usually anticipate that anyone attempting to restrain them is mired in bureaucratic inertia and unable to make timely and effective adjustments to their subtle fluid changes in tactics and societal disruptions. The options presented here provide a chance to violate these expectations, surprise transnational criminals, and gain, at least temporarily, the upper hand in the battle for global order.

NOTES

Chapter 1

1. Raine and Cilluffo, *Global Organized Crime*, p. ix.

2. Even a recent major publication that promisingly claims "to understand the havoc wrought by the corruption and violence of the world's economic gangsters" falls into this trap by omitting conditional analysis of these two tactics. See Fisman and Miguel, *Economic Gangsters*, p. 7.

3. Godson and Williams, "Strengthening Cooperation against Transsovereign Crime: A New Security Imperative," in Cusimano, *Beyond Sovereignty*, p. 114.

4. Ibid., p. 117.

5. Passas, "Cross-Border Crime and the Interface between Legal and Illegal Actors," in van Duyne, von Lampe, and Passas, *Upperworld and Underworld in Cross-Border Crime*, p. 11.

6. Kelly, "Criminal Underworlds: Looking Down on Society from Below," in Kelly, *Organized Crime*, p. 11.

7. von Lampe, "Organized Crime Research in Perspective," in van Duyne, von Lampe, and Passas, *Upperworld and Underworld in Cross-Border Crime*, p. 191.

8. Woodiwiss, "Transnational Organized Crime: The Strange Career of an American Concept," in Beare, *Critical Reflections on Transnational Organized Crime, Money Laundering, and Corruption*, p. 3.

9. See, as just one prominent example of the myriad discussions of definitional issues, Mueller, "Transnational Crime," pp. 13–21; and Reuter and Petrie, *Transnational Organized Crime*, pp. 7–8.

10. Reuter and Petrie, *Transnational Organized Crime*, p. 8.

11. Ibid.

12. Williams, "Organizing Transnational Crime: Networks, Markets and Hierarchies," in Williams and Vlassis, *Combating Transnational Crime*, pp. 61–62.

13. Thachuk, "An Introduction to Transnational Threats," in Thachuk, *Transnational Threats*, p. 4.

14. Berdal and Serrano, *Transnational Organized Crime and International Security*, p. 7.

15. U.S. Department of Justice, *Overview of the Law Enforcement Strategy to Combat International Organized Crime*, p. 10.

16. Reuter and Petrie, *Transnational Organized Crime*, p. 16.

17. Naim, *Illicit*, pp. 2, 8.

18. Edwards and Gill, "After Transnational Organized Crime? The Politics of Public Safety," in Edwards and Gill, *Transnational Organized Crime*, pp. 273–74.

19. Mair, "The New World of Privatized Violence," in Pfaller and Lerch, *Challenges of Globalization*, p. 56.

20. Galeotti, "Transnational Organized Crime: Law Enforcement as a Global Battlespace," in Bunker, *Non-State Threats and Future Wars*, p. 36.

21. Findlay, *The Globalisation of Crime*, p. 127.

22. Mueller, "Transnational Crime," p. 15.

23. Kerry, *The New War*, p. 21; Naim, *Illicit*, p. 88; and Castle, "Transnational Organized Crime and International Security," p. 12.

24. Picarelli, "Transnational Organized Crime," in Williams, *Security Studies*, p. 456.

25. Burgess, "Non-Military Security Challenges," in Snyder, *Contemporary Security and Strategy*; and Caldwell and Williams, *Seeking Security in an Insecure World*, p. 106.

Chapter 2

1. Cooper, "The War Next Door: Homeland Security Secretary Says Every American Has a Stake in Mexico's War against Murderous Gangs.

2. Ibid.

3. Felbab-Brown, "The Violent Drug Market in Mexico and Lessons from Colombia," p. 1.

4. Ibid., p. 6.

5. MacAskill, "FBI Deployed by US to Fight Mexican Drug Lords," p. 18.

6. Boot, "Pirates, Then and Now: How Piracy Was Defeated in the Past and Can Be Again," p. 94.

7. Hanson, "Combating Maritime Piracy."

8. Hunter, "Somali Pirates Living the High Life."

9. Boot, "Pirates, Then and Now: How Piracy Was Defeated in the Past and Can Be Again," p. 103.

10. Picarelli, "Transnational Organized Crime," in Williams, *Security Studies*, pp. 454–55.

11. Richards, *Transnational Criminal Organizations, Cybercrime, and Money Laundering*, p. iii; and Williams, "Strategy for a New World: Combating Terrorism and Transnational Organized Crime," in Baylis et al., *Strategy in the Contemporary World*, p. 198.

12. United Nations Office on Drugs and Crime, "Effective Measures to Combat Transnational Organized Crime," p. 1.

13. For varying estimates, see Berdal and Serrano, *Transnational Organized Crime and International Security*, p. 2; Picarelli, "Transnational Organized Crime," in Williams, *Security Studies*, p. 456; and Mair, "The New World of Privatized Violence," in Pfaller and Lerch, *Challenges of Globalization*, p. 54.

14. van Dijk, *The World of Crime*, pp. 164–67.

15. Williams, "Organizing Transnational Crime: Networks, Markets and Hierarchies," p. 59.

16. Naylor, *Wages of Crime*, p. 15; see also Schelling, *Choice and Consequence*, p. 180.

17. Lea and Stenson, "Security, Sovereignty, and Non-State Governance 'From Below,'" pp. 18–19.

18. Mandel, *The Changing Face of National Security*, p. 30, for an astute early formulation of this trend, see Scott, *The Revolution in Statecraft*.

19. Godson and Olson, "International Organized Crime," p. 22.

20. Friman and Andreas, *The Illicit Global Economy and State Power*, p. 2.

21. Mandel, *Global Threat*, chapter 2.

22. Naim, *Illicit*, p. 7; Williams, "Organizing Transnational Crime: Networks, Markets and Hierarchies"; Reuter and Petrie, *Transnational Organized Crime*, p. 10; and U.S. Department of Justice, *Overview of the Law Enforcement Strategy to Combat International Organized Crime*, p. 10.

23. Mair, "The New World of Privatized Violence," in Pfaller and Lerch, *Challenges of Globalization*, p. 54.

24. Chatterjee, *The Changing Structure of Organized Crime Groups*, p. 2.

25. Godson and Olson, *International Organized Crime*.

26. Williams, "New Context, Smart Enemies," in Bunker, *Non-State Threats and Future Wars*, p. x.

27. Kraska, "Militarization and Policing—Its Relevance to 21st Century Police," p. 1. See also Lutterbeck, "Blurring the Dividing Line: The Convergence of Internal and External Security in Western Europe," pp. 231–53; and Bigo, "When Two Become One: Internal and External Securitisations in Europe," in Kelstrup and Williams, *International Relations Theory and the Politics of European Integration, Power, Security and Community*, pp. 171–205.

28. Lutterbeck, "Between Police and Military: The New Security Agenda and the Rise of the Gendarmeries"; Kraska, "Militarization and Policing—Its Relevance to 21st Century Police," p. 2; and Andreas and Price, "From War Fighting to Crime Fighting: Transforming the American National Security State," pp. 31, 52.

29. Lutterbeck, "Between Police and Military: The New Security Agenda and the Rise of the Gendarmeries," pp. 45–46.

30. U.S. Department of Justice, *Overview of the Law Enforcement Strategy to Combat International Organized Crime*, p. 1.

31. Lutterbeck, "Blurring the Dividing Line: The Convergence of Internal and External Security in Western Europe," p. 232.

32. See Mandel, *Deadly Transfers and the Global Playground*.

33. Godson, "The Political-Criminal Nexus and Global Security," in Godson, *Menace to Society*, p. 9.

34. Nadelmann, "Global Prohibition Regimes: The Evolution of Norms in International Society," pp. 479–526; and Andreas, "Transnational Crime and Economic Globalization," in Berdal and Serrano, *Transnational Organized Crime and International Security*, p. 39.

35. Hill, *The Japanese Mafia*, p. 15.

36. Naim, *Illicit*, p. 4.

37. Shelley, "Transnational Organized Crime: An Imminent Threat to the Nation-State?" p. 465.

38. Finckenauer, "Meeting the Challenge of Transnational Crime," p. 3.

39. Shelley, "Transnational Organized Crime: An Imminent Threat to the Nation-State?" p. 466.

40. Kerry, *The New War*, p. 20.

41. Findlay, *The Globalisation of Crime*, p. 2.

42. Dobriansky, "The Explosive Growth of Globalized Crime," p. 5.

43. Serrano, "Transnational Organized Crime and International Security: Business as Usual?" in Berdal and Serrano, *Transnational Organized Crime and International Security*, p. 26; and Williams, "Strategy for a New World: Combating Terrorism and Transnational Organized Crime," in Baylis et al., *Strategy in the Contemporary World*, p. 194.

44. Glenny, *McMafia*, p. 345.

45. Andreas, "Transnational Crime and Economic Globalization," in Berdal and Serrano, *Transnational Organized Crime and International Security*, p. 39.

46. Schelling, *Choice and Consequence*, p. 186.

47. Wagley, "Transnational Organized Crime: Principal Threats and U.S. Responses," p. 1.

48. United Nations Office on Drugs and Crime, "Effective Measures to Combat Transnational Organized Crime," p. 1.

49. Findlay, *The Globalisation of Crime*, p. 150.

50. Manwaring, "The New Global Security Landscape: The Road Ahead," in Bunker, *Networks, Terrorism and Global Insurgency*, pp. 24–26.

51. Thomas, Kiser, and Casebeer, *Warlords Rising*, p. 55.

52. Manwaring, "The New Global Security Landscape: The Road Ahead," in Bunker, *Networks, Terrorism and Global Insurgency*, p. 21.

53. Godson, "The Political-Criminal Nexus and Global Security," in Godson, *Menace to Society*, pp. 9–10, 14.

54. Serrano, "Transnational Organized Crime and International Security: Business as Usual?" in Berdal and Serrano, *Transnational Organized Crime and International Security*, p. 29.

55. Manwaring, *A Contemporary Challenge to State Sovereignty*, p. 9; Kay, *Global Security in the Twenty-first Century*, pp. 241–42; and Patrick, "Weak States and Global Threats: Fact or Fiction?" pp. 38–39.

56. Thachuk, "An Introduction to Transnational Threats," in Thachuk, *Transnational Threats*, p. 9.

57. Berry and et al., "Nations Hospitable to Organized Crime and Terrorism," p. 1.

58. Williams and Picarelli, "Combating Organized Crime in Armed Conflict," in Ballentine and Nitzschke, *Profiting from Peace*, p. 124.

59. Lutterbeck, "The New Security Agenda: Transnational Organized Crime and International Security."

60. Shelley, "The Unholy Trinity: Transnational Crime, Corruption, and Terrorism," p. 104.

61. Naylor, "The Insurgent Economy: Black Market Operations of Guerrilla Organizations," p. 47.

62. Harvey, *Global Disorder*, p. 196.

63. Reinares and Resa, "Transnational Organized Crime as an Increasing Threat to the National Security of Democratic Regimes: Assessing Political Impacts and Evaluating State Responses," p. 14.

64. Naim, *Illicit*, p. 4.

65. Picarelli, "Transnational Organized Crime," p. 455.

66. United Nations Office on Drugs and Crime, "Effective Measures to Combat Transnational Organized Crime," p. 1.

67. Williams, "Strategy for a New World: Combating Terrorism and Transnational Organized Crime," in Baylis et al., *Strategy in the Contemporary World*, p. 194.

68. Reuter and Petrie, *Transnational Organized Crime*, pp. 1–2.

69. Levi, "Liberalization and Transnational Financial Crime," in Berdal and Serrano, *Transnational Organized Crime and International Security*, p. 64; and Kay, *Global Security in the Twenty-first Century*, pp. 239–40.

70. Negroponte, *Annual Threat Assessment of the Director of National Intelligence for the Senate Select Committee on Intelligence*, p. 10; and Naim, *Illicit*, p. 4.

71. Reinares and Resa, "Transnational Organized Crime as an Increasing Threat to the National Security of Democratic Regimes: Assessing Political Impacts and Evaluating State Responses," p. 10.

72. Levi, "Liberalization and Transnational Financial Crime," in Berdal and Serrano, *Transnational Organized Crime and International Security*, p. 65.

73. Lutterbeck, "The New Security Agenda: Transnational Organized Crime and International Security."

74. *National Security Strategy of the United States of America*, p. 3.

75. Manwaring, "The New Global Security Landscape: The Road Ahead," in Bunker, *Networks, Terrorism and Global Insurgency*, pp. 22–23.

76. Lake, *6 Nightmares*, pp. x–xi.

77. Findlay, *The Globalisation of Crime*, pp. 64–65.

78. U.S. Department of Justice, *Overview of the Law Enforcement Strategy to Combat International Organized Crime*, p. 1.

79. Jenkins, *Unconquerable Nation*, p. 151.

80. Zhang and Chin, "Characteristics of Chinese Human Smugglers," p. ii.

81. Hill, *The Japanese Mafia*, p. 30.

82. Godson, "The Political-Criminal Nexus and Global Security," in Godson, *Menace to Society*, p. 5.

83. Lea and Stenson, "Security, Sovereignty, and Non-State Governance 'From Below,'" p. 13.

84. Adamson, "Crossing Borders: International Migration and National Security," p. 194.

85. U.S. Department of Justice, *Overview of the Law Enforcement Strategy to Combat International Organized Crime*, pp. 2, 6.

86. Williams and Picarelli, "Combating Organized Crime in Armed Conflict," in Ballentine and Nitzschke, *Profiting from Peace*, pp. 124, 129.

87. Williams, "Human Commodity Trafficking: An Overview," in Williams, *Illegal Migration and Commercial Sex*, p. 1.

88. Lea and Stenson, "Security, Sovereignty, and Non-State Governance 'From Below,'" p. 23.

89. Robinson, *The Merger*, p. 17.

90. Andreas, "Transnational Crime and Economic Globalization," in Berdal and Serrano, *Transnational Organized Crime and International Security*, p. 43.

91. Shelley, "The Unholy Trinity: Transnational Crime, Corruption, and Terrorism," p. 103.

92. Lea and Stenson, "Security, Sovereignty, and Non-State Governance 'From Below,'" p. 23.

92. Renner, *Fighting for Survival*, p. 192.

94. Hari, "You Are Being Lied to About Pirates."

95. Friman and Andreas, *The Illicit Global Economy and State Power*, p. 2.

96. See, for example, Cockayne and Mikulaschek, "Transnational Security Challenges and the United Nations," p. 9.

97. Sterling, *Thieves' World*, p. 21.

98. Harris, *Political Corruption*, p. 168.

99. Ibid., p. 169.

100. Makarenko, "The Crime–Terror Continuum: Tracing the Interplay between Transnational Organised Crime and Terrorism," p. 138.

101. Lea and Stenson, "Security, Sovereignty, and Non-State Governance 'From Below,'" p. 18.

102. Harris, *Political Corruption*, p. 173.

103. Lea and Stenson, "Security, Sovereignty, and Non-State Governance 'From Below,'" p. 25.

104. Shelley et al., "Methods and Motives: Exploring Links between Transnational Organized Crime and International Terrorism," p. 60.

105. Felbab-Brown, "Drugs, Violence and Instability: A Global Perspective."

106. Galeotti, "Transnational Organized Crime: Law Enforcement as a Global Battlespace," in Bunker, *Non-State Threats and Future Wars*, pp. 34–35.

107. Robinson, *The Merger*, p. 19.

Chapter 3

1. Nordstrom, *Global Outlaws*, p. 140.

2. Robinson, *The Merger*, p. 20.

3. Viano, Magallanes, and Bridel, *Transnational Organized Crime*, p. 4.

4. Reinares and Resa, "Transnational Organized Crime as an Increasing Threat to the National Security of Democratic Regimes: Assessing Political Impacts and Evaluating State Responses," p. 4.

5. Naylor, *Wages of Crime*, p. 15.

6. Fisman and Miguel, *Economic Gangsters*, p. 18.

7. Bibes, "Transnational Organized Crime and Terrorism," pp. 250–51.

8. Thachuk, "Corruption and International Security," p. 145.

9. van Dijk, *The World of Crime*, p. 181.

10. See Moody-Stuart, *Grand Corruption in Third World Development*.

11. Holmes, "Some Concluding Observations: A Quadrumvirate in Future?" in Holmes, *Terrorism, Organised Crime and Corruption*, p. 239.

12. van Dijk, *The World of Crime*, p. 159.

13. Nadelmann, *Cops across Borders*, pp. 266–71.

14. Williams, "Strategy for a New World: Combating Terrorism and Transnational Organized Crime," in Baylis et al., *Strategy in the Contemporary World*, pp. 197–98.

15. Definition of corruption given on Transparency International's Web site: http://www.transparency.org/about_us.

16. Harris, *Political Corruption*, p. 14.

17. Rose-Ackerman, *Corruption and Government*, p. 23.

18. Picarelli, "Transnational Organized Crime," in Williams, *Security Studies*, p. 461.

19. U.S. Department of Justice, *Overview of the Law Enforcement Strategy to Combat International Organized Crime*, p. 8.

20. Newell and Bull, "Introduction," in Bull and Newell, *Corruption in Contemporary Politics*, p. 1.

21. Ibid.

22. Holmes, "Introduction," in Holmes, *Terrorism, Organised Crime and Corruption*, pp. 4–5.

23. Andreas and Nadelmann, *Policing the Globe*, p. 246.

24. Holmes, "Introduction," in Holmes, *Terrorism, Organised Crime and Corruption*, p. 2.

25. Harris, *Political Corruption*, p. 14.

26. Fisman and Miguel, *Economic Gangsters*, pp. 80–81.

27. Bull and Newell, "Conclusion: Political Corruption in Contemporary Democracies," in Bull and Newell, *Corruption in Contemporary Politics*, pp. 236–40.

28. Passas, "Globalization and Transnational Crime: Effects of Criminogenic Asymmetries," in Williams and Vlassis, *Combating Transnational Crime*, p. 27; and Serrano and Toro, "From Drug Trafficking to Transnational Organized Crime in Latin America," in Berdal and Serrano, *Transnational Organized Crime and International Security*, p. 170.

29. Thachuk, "Corruption and International Security," p. 146.

30. Cockayne, "Transnational Organized Crime: Multilateral Responses to a Rising Threat," p. 7.

31. U.S. Department of Justice, *Overview of the Law Enforcement Strategy to Combat International Organized Crime*, p. 8.

32. Shaw, "Crime, Police and Public in Transitional Societies," p. 12.

33. Taken from the section on "Why Does Fighting Corruption Matter?" on the Transparency International Web site: http://www.transparency.org/about_us.

34. Newell and Bull, "Introduction," in Bull and Newell, *Corruption in Contemporary Politics*, pp. 4–5; and Bull and Newell, "Conclusion: Political Corruption in Contemporary Democracies," in Bull and Newell, *Corruption in Contemporary Politics*, pp. 242–43.

35. Thachuk, "Corruption and International Security," p. 146.

36. Godson and Olson, "International Organized Crime," p. 21.

37. Reinares and Resa, "Transnational Organized Crime as an Increasing Threat

to the National Security of Democratic Regimes: Assessing Political Impacts and Evaluating State Responses," pp. 20, 29.

38. Godson and Williams, "Strengthening Cooperation against Transsovereign Crime: A New Security Imperative," in Cusimano, *Beyond Sovereignty*, p. 114.

39. Fisman and Miguel, *Economic Gangsters*, pp. 49–50.

40. van Soest, *The Global Crisis of Violence*, p. 11.

41. Volkov, *Violent Entrepreneurs*, p. 27.

42 Fisman and Miguel, *Economic Gangsters*, pp. 114, 136.

43. van Creveld, *The Transformation of War*, p. 197.

44. Williams, "Strategy for a New World: Combating Terrorism and Transnational Organized Crime," in Baylis et al., *Strategy in the Contemporary World*, p. 193.

45. Smith, *The Penguin State of the World Atlas*, p. 60.

46. Smith, *The Penguin Atlas of War and Peace*, p. 38.

47. Findlay, *The Globalisation of Crime*, p. 105.

48. Luna, "Dismantling Illicit Networks and Corruption Nodes," p. 3.

49. van Dijk, *The World of Crime*, p. 157.

50. U.S. Department of Justice, *Overview of the Law Enforcement Strategy to Combat International Organized Crime*, p. 9.

51. van Dijk, *The World of Crime*, p. 157.

52. U.S. Department of Justice, *Overview of the Law Enforcement Strategy to Combat International Organized Crime*, pp. 8–9.

53. Friman and Andreas, *The Illicit Global Economy and State Power*, p. 13.

54. Findlay, *The Globalisation of Crime*, p. 104.

55. Williams, "Strategy for a New World: Combating Terrorism and Transnational Organized Crime," in Baylis et al., *Strategy in the Contemporary World*, p. 197.

56. Cockayne, "Transnational Organized Crime: Multilateral Responses to a Rising Threat," p. 6.

57. Tunstall, "Transnational Organized Crime and Conflict: Strategic Implications for the Military," p. 3.

58. Schelling, *Choice and Consequence*, pp. 182, 193.

59. Williams, "Cooperation among Criminal Organizations," in Berdal and Serrano, *Transnational Organized Crime and International Security*, p. 67.

60. Sullivan and Bunker, "Drug Cartels, Street Gangs, and Warlords," in Bunker, *Non-State Threats and Future Wars*, pp. 42–48.

61. Dishman, "Terrorism, Crime and Transformation," p. 45; and Makarenko, "'The Ties That Bind': Uncovering the Relationship between Organised Crime and Terrorism," in Siegal, van de Bunt, and Zaitch, *Global Organized Crime*, pp. 166–67.

62. Godson and Olson, "International Organized Crime," p. 21.

63. Williams, "Strategy for a New World: Combating Terrorism and Transnational Organized Crime," in Baylis et al., *Strategy in the Contemporary World*, p. 197.

64. Williams, "Transnational Criminal Organisations and International Security," p. 107.

65. Paris, "Human Security: Paradigm Shift or Hot Air?" p. 87.

66. Williams, Transnational Criminal Organisations and International Security," p. 107.

67. Picarelli, "Transnational Organized Crime," in Williams, *Security Studies*, p. 162.

68. Godson and Olson, "International Organized Crime," p. 21.

69. Reinares and Resa, "Transnational Organized Crime as an Increasing Threat to the National Security of Democratic Regimes: Assessing Political Impacts and Evaluating State Responses," p. 11.

70. Stanislawski, "Transnational 'Bads' in the Globalized World: The Case of Transnational Organized Crime," p. 160; and Thachuk, "An Introduction to Transnational Threats," in Thachuk, *Transnational Threats*, p. 10.

71. United Nations Office on Drugs and Crime, "Organized Crime and Its Threat to Security: Tackling a Disturbing Consequence of Drug Control," p. 4.

72. Mittleman and Johnston, "Global Organized Crime," in Mittleman, *The Globalization Syndrome*, p. 210.

73. Reuter and Petrie, *Transnational Organized Crime*, pp. 1–2; and Williams, "Strategy for a New World: Combating Terrorism and Transnational Organized Crime," in Baylis et al., *Strategy in the Contemporary World*, p. 200.

74. Williams, "Strategy for a New World: Combating Terrorism and Transnational Organized Crime," in Baylis et al., *Strategy in the Contemporary World*, p. 200.

75. Adamson, "Crossing Borders: International Migration and National Security," p. 191.

76. Picarelli, "Transnational Organized Crime," in Williams, *Security Studies*, p. 462.

77. Reinares and Resa, "Transnational Organized Crime as an Increasing Threat to the National Security of Democratic Regimes: Assessing Political Impacts and Evaluating State Responses," p. 69.

78. Dupont, "Transnational Crime, Drugs, and Security in East Asia," p. 436.

79. Cirincione, Wolfsthal, and Rajkumar, *Deadly Arsenals*, p. 3; Sullivan, "International Organized Crime: A Growing National Security Threat," pp. 1–2; and Thornton, *Asymmetric Warfare*, pp. 14–16.

80. Naim, *Illicit*, p. 5.

81. MacDonald, "The New 'Bad Guys': Exploring the Parameters of the Violent New World Order," in Manwaring, *Gray Area Phenomena*, pp. 41–42.

82. Edwards and Gill, "After Transnational Organized Crime? The Politics of Public Safety," in Edwards and Gill, *Transnational Organized Crime*, p. 267.

83. Viano, *Global Organized Crime and International Security*, p. xi; see also Shel-

ley, "Transnational Organized Crime: An Imminent Threat to the Nation-State?" pp. 488–89.

84. Reinares and Resa, "Transnational Organized Crime as an Increasing Threat to the National Security of Democratic Regimes: Assessing Political Impacts and Evaluating State Responses," p. 10.

85. Dupont, "Transnational Crime, Drugs, and Security in East Asia," p. 436; and Picarelli, "Transnational Organized Crime," in Williams, *Security Studies*, p. 162.

86. Mittleman and Johnston, "Global Organized Crime," in Mittleman, *The Globalization Syndrome*, p. 218.

87. Manwaring, "Gangs and Other Transnational Criminal Organizations (TCOs) as Transnational Threats to National Security and Sovereignty," p. 8.

Chapter 4

1. van Dijk, *The World of Crime*, p. 148.

2. Booth, *The Triads*, pp. 124–26.

3. Schloss, "Fears Triads Stepping Up Japan Role," p. 3.

4. Booth, *The Dragon Syndicates*, p. 322.

5. Ibid., pp. 317–18.

6. Robinson, *The Merger*, pp. 171–72; and Shanty, *Organized Crime*, p. 59.

7. Dovkants, "The London Connection," p. 22.

8. Picarelli, "Transnational Organized Crime," in Williams, *Security Studies*, p. 456.

9. For a general discussion of this issue, without reference to particular transnational criminal organizations, see Lea and Stenson, "Security, Sovereignty, and Non-State Governance 'From Below,'" pp. 24–25.

10. Allum and Sands, "Explaining Organized Crime in Europe: Are Economists Always Right?" p. 138.

11. Ibid.

12. Zhang and Chin, "Characteristics of Chinese Human Smugglers," pp. 10–11.

13. Hays, "Triads and Organized Crime in China."

14. Booth, *The Dragon Syndicates*, p. 3.

15. Chu, *The Triads as Business*, p. xi.

16. Chin, Zhang, and Kelly, "Transnational Chinese Organized Crime Activities: Patterns and Emerging Trends," pp. 127–54.

17. Wong, "Chinese Crime Organizations as Transnational Enterprises," in Thachuk, *Transnational Threats*, p. 133; and BBC News, "Terror of the Triads."

18. Miller, "The Threat of Transnational Crime in East Asia," p. 10.

19. Chu, *The Triads as Business*, p. 39.

20. Xia, "Organizational Formations of Organized Crime in China: Perspectives from the State, Markets, and Networks," p. 10.

21. Curtis et al., "Transnational Activities of Chinese Crime Organizations," p. 3.

22. Xia, "Organizational Formations of Organized Crime in China: Perspectives from the State, Markets, and Networks," pp. 2–3.

23. Wang, "Forget Riots, Collusion between Officials and Triads Is a Bigger Danger," p. 6.

24. Gong, "Dangerous Collusions: Corruption as a Collective Venture in Contemporary China," pp. 86–87.

25. Williams, "Transnational Criminal Organisations and International Security," p. 103.

26. Kumbon, "Asian Mafia Has Grip on PNG," p. 12.

27. Hays, "Triads and Organized Crime in China."

28. Chu, "Hong Kong Triads after 1997," p. 6.

29. Mulholland, "Ferris versus the Triads," p. 36.

30. Wong, "Chinese Crime Organizations as Transnational Enterprises," in Thachuk, *Transnational Threats*, p. 138.

31. Kerry, *The New War*, pp. 59–60.

32. Wong, "Chinese Crime Organizations as Transnational Enterprises," in Thachuk, *Transnational Threats*, pp. 137, 139.

33. Curtis et al., "Transnational Activities of Chinese Crime Organizations," p. 47.

34. Miller, "The Threat of Transnational Crime in East Asia," p. 10.

35. Emmers, "Globalization and Non-Traditional Security Issues: A Study of Human and Drug Trafficking in East Asia," p. 7.

36. Szubin, "Impact Report: Economic Sanctions against Colombian Drug Cartels," p. 15.

37. Ibid., p. 41.

38. MacDonald, *Dancing on a Volcano*, pp. 28–29.

39. Naim, *Illicit*, p. 70.

40. Kerry, *The New War*, p. 71.

41. Chabat, "Networks of Corruption and Violence."

42. Forero, "Venezuela Increasingly a Conduit for Cocaine: Smugglers Exploit Graft, Icy Relations with U.S.," p. A1.

43. "Colombia: The Cartels Reorganize."

44. Lois, "Madrid: European Capital of Cocaine," pp. T12, 11Z.

45. Kraul, "New Colombia Drug Gangs Wreak Havoc: The Killing of a Farm Leader Suggests the Rise of Former Right-Wing Paramilitary Fighters," p. 8.

46. Lee and Thoumi, "Drugs and Democracy in Colombia," in Godson, *Menace to Society*, pp. 79–83.

47. Garcés, "Colombia: The Link between Drugs and Terror," p. 96.

48. McLean, "Colombia: Failed, Failing, or Just Weak?" p. 127.

49. Harman, "The War on Drugs: Ambushed in Jamundi—Why the Massacre of

an Elite US-Trained Colombian Police Team Prompted Congress to Freeze Drug-War Funding," p. 1.

50. Kerry, *The New War*, p. 76.

51. MacDonald, *Dancing on a Volcano*, p. 27.

52. Garcés, "Colombia: The Link between Drugs and Terror," pp. 94–95.

53. Sanín, "Internal Conflict, Terrorism and Crime in Colombia," p. 141.

54. Kraul, "Colombian Drug Lord Killed: Cartel Leader, Indicted by U.S., Is Found Shot to Death in Venezuela," p. 3.

55. Sanín, "Internal Conflict, Terrorism and Crime in Colombia," p. 141.

56. McLean, "Colombia: Failed, Failing, or Just Weak?" pp. 126, 132.

57. Ibid., pp. 124, 131.

58. Millett, "Weak States and Porous Borders: Smuggling along the Andean Ridge," in Thachuk, *Transnational Threats*, p. 169.

59. Sweeney, "Colombia's Narco-Democracy Threatens Hemispheric Security."

60. MacDonald, *Dancing on a Volcano*, pp. 124–34.

61. Paoli, "Mafia and Organized Crime in Italy: The Unacknowledged Success of Law Enforcement," p. 856.

62. Hess, "The Traditional Sicilian Mafia: Organized Crime and Repressive Crime," in Kelly, *Organized Crime*, pp. 114–16.

63. Lea and Stenson, "Security, Sovereignty, and Non-State Governance 'From Below,'" p. 19.

64. Dickie, *Cosa Nostra*, p. 21.

65. Jamieson, "Transnational Organized Crime—A European Perspective: Trends in Transnational Crime during the 1990s," p. 381.

66. Saija and Irrera, "Institutions and Mafia in Italy: The Case of Messina," pp. 394–95.

67. Kerry, *The New War*, p. 91.

68. Harris, *Political Corruption*, p. 165.

69. Ellison, "New York Arrests Signal Resurgence of Mafia," p. 21.

70. Harwood, "Italian Mafia Is Europe's Number One Business."

71. Popham, "Has the Italian Mafia Spread Its Tentacles throughout Europe? The Big Question," p. 38.

72. Paoli, "Italian Organised Crime: Mafia Associations and Criminal Enterprises," p. 26.

73. See Longrigg, "How to Do Business Like the Mafia," p. 12.

74. Paoli, "Mafia and Organized Crime in Italy: The Unacknowledged Success of Law Enforcement," p. 859.

75. Paoli, "Broken Bonds: Mafia and Politics in Sicily," in Godson, *Menace to Society*, pp. 57–58.

76. Kreyenbuhl, "The Mafia and Italian Politics," p. 27.

77. Paoli, "Crime, Italian Style," p. 164.

78. Dickie, *Cosa Nostra*, p. 22.

79. Kreyenbuhl, "The Mafia and Italian Politics," p. 27.

80. Seindal, *Mafia*, p. 100.

81. Owen, "Death Threats and Arson Fail to Halt Businessmen's Anti-Mafia Fight," p. 36.

82. Gambetta, *The Sicilian Mafia*, pp. 40–43.

83. Paoli, *Mafia Brotherhoods*, p. 102.

84. Popham, "Has the Italian Mafia Spread Its Tentacles throughout Europe?" p. 38.

85. Allum and Siebert, *Organized Crime and the Challenge to Democracy*, p. 149.

86. Dickie, *Cosa Nostra*, p. 22.

87. Hooper, "Death and Dirt Collide in Mafia Violence."

88. Hooper, "Move Over, Cosa Nostra," p. 6.

89. Paoli, "The Illegal Drugs Market," pp. 189, 195–96.

90. Bacon, "Balkan Trafficking in Historical Perspective," in Thachuk, *Transnational Threats*, p. 88.

91. Seindal, *Mafia*, p. 92.

92. Dickie, *Cosa Nostra*, p. 22.

93. Kreyenbuhl, "The Mafia and Italian Politics," p. 26; and Kerry, *The New War*, p. 91.

94. Hill, *The Japanese Mafia*, p. 65.

95. Delfs, "Clash of Loyalties," pp. 30, 34.

96. Kerry, *The New War*, p. 22.

97. Kaplan and Dubro, *Yakuza*, p. 265; and Fackler, "Mayor's Death Forces Japan's Crime Rings into the Light," p. 3.

98. Hill, *The Japanese Mafia*, p. 37; Kaplan and Dubro, *Yakuza*, pp. 150, 157–58, 178, 180–83, 238, 244; and Lal, "Japanese Trafficking and Smuggling," in Thachuk, *Transnational Threats*, p. 147.

99. Kaplan and Dubro, *Yakuza*, pp. 227–28, 243.

100. Hill, *The Japanese Mafia*, p. 265.

101. Adelstein, "This Mob Is Big in Japan," p. B2.

102. Johnston, "Yakuza in Japan: From Rackets to Real Estate, Yakuza Multifaceted."

103. Hill, *The Japanese Mafia*, p. 274.

104. Treverton et al., *Film Piracy, Organized Crime, and Terrorism*, pp. 113–18.

105. Friman, "Obstructing Markets: Organized Crime Networks and Drug Control in Japan," in Friman and Andreas, *The Illicit Global Economy and State Power*, p. 189.

106. Hill, *The Japanese Mafia*, pp. 63–64.

107. Miller, "The Threat of Transnational Crime in East Asia," p. 12.

108. Kaplan and Dubro, *Yakuza*, pp. 150–51.

109. McFarlane, "Transnational Crime and Asia-Pacific Security," in Simon, *The Many Faces of Asian Security*, p. 204.

110. Hill, *The Japanese Mafia*, p. 64.

111. Chemko, "The Japanese Yakuza: Influence on Japan's International Relations and Regional Politics (East Asia and Latin America)."

112. Ibid.

113. Miller, "The Threat of Transnational Crime in East Asia," p. 11.

114. Kaplan and Dubro, *Yakuza*, pp. 157, 178.

115. Adelstein, "This Mob Is Big in Japan," p. B2; and Kaplan and Dubro, *Yakuza*, pp. 199, 216–17.

116. Kaplan and Dubro, *Yakuza*, p. 155.

117. Reinares and Resa, "Transnational Organized Crime as an Increasing Threat to the National Security of Democratic Regimes: Assessing Political Impacts and Evaluating State Responses," pp. 71–72.

118. Lal, "Japanese Trafficking and Smuggling," in Thachuk, *Transnational Threats*, p. 148.

119. Ibid., p. 143.

120. Miller, "The Threat of Transnational Crime in East Asia," p. 11.

121. Kaplan and Dubro, *Yakuza*, pp. 150–51, 333.

122. Paoli, "Italian Organised Crime: Mafia Associations and Criminal Enterprises," pp. 21–22.

123. Reinares and Resa, "Transnational Organized Crime as an Increasing Threat to the National Security of Democratic Regimes: Assessing Political Impacts and Evaluating State Responses," pp. 71–72.

124. Kattoulas, "Taking Care of Business," p. 93.

125. Webster et al., *Russian Organized Crime*, p. 17.

126. Boskholov, "Organized Crime and Corruption in Russia," p. 270.

127. "Organized Crime in Russia."

128. Volkov, *Violent Entrepreneurs*, p. 2.

129. Sterling, *Thieves' World*, p. 90.

130. Sullivan, "International Organized Crime: A Growing National Security Threat," p. 1.

131. Kerry, *The New War*, pp. 22, 34–35.

132. Robinson, *The Merger*, p. 17.

133. McFarlane, "Transnational Crime and Asia-Pacific Security," in Simon, *The Many Faces of Asian Security*, p. 208.

134. Ibid., pp. 207–8.

135. "Organized Crime in Russia."

136. Finckenauer and Waring, *Russian Mafia in America*, pp. 123–24.

137. Cheloukhine, "The Roots of Russian Organized Crime: From Old-Fashioned Professionals to the Organized Criminal Groups of Today," p. 367.

138. Kerry, *The New War*, pp. 22, 34–35.

139. Harris, *Political Corruption*, p. 165.

140. Sokolov, "From Guns to Briefcases: The Evolution of Russian Organized Crime," p. 68.

141. Caldwell et al., "Capitalizing on Transition Economies: The Role of the Russian Mafiya in Trafficking Women for Forced Prostitution," in Williams, *Illegal Migration and Commercial Sex*, pp. 50–51.

142. Bagley, *Globalization and Transnational Organized Crime*, p. 10.

143. Boskholov, "Organized Crime and Corruption in Russia," p. 273.

144. Cheloukhine and King, "Corruption Networks as a Sphere of Investment Activities in Modern Russia," pp. 117, 121–22.

145. Cheloukhine, "The Roots of Russian Organized Crime: From Old-Fashioned Professionals to the Organized Criminal Groups of Today," p. 374.

146. Cheloukhine and King, "Corruption Networks as a Sphere of Investment Activities in Modern Russia," p. 109.

147. Finckenauer and Voronin, "The Threat of Russian Organized Crime," p. 23.

148. Shelley, "Russia and Ukraine: Transition or Tragedy?" in Godson, *Menace to Society*, p. 204.

149. Tsyganov, "The State, Business and Corruption in Russia," in Holmes, *Terrorism, Organised Crime and Corruption*, p. 148.

150. Cheloukhine and King, "Corruption Networks as a Sphere of Investment Activities in Modern Russia," pp. 111–12.

151. Shvarts, "The Russian Mafia: Expulsion of Law," pp. 373–74.

152. Varese, *The Russian Mafia*, p. 189.

153. "Organized Crime in Russia."

154. Webster et al., *Russian Organized Crime*, pp. 40–41.

155. Finckenauer and Waring, *Russian Mafia in America*, pp. 158–59.

156. Allum and Sands. "Explaining Organized Crime in Europe: Are Economists Always Right?" p. 144.

157. Finckenauer and Waring, *Russian Mafia in America*, p. 134.

158. Finckenauer and Voronin, "The Threat of Russian Organized Crime," p. 15.

159. "Organized Crime in Russia."

160. Abramova, "The Funding of Traditional Organised Crime in Russia," pp. 18–21.

161. Blomfield, "Russian Mafia Killings Threaten Putin Legacy."

162. Handelman, "The Russian 'Mafiya,'" pp. 91–92.

163. Boskholov, "Organized Crime and Corruption in Russia," p. 271.

164. Kerry, *The New War*, p. 35.

165. Granville, "Crime That Pays: The Global Spread of the Russian Mafia," p. 447.

166. Ferguson, "On the Loose: The Market for Nuclear Weapons," p. 54.

167. Webster et al., *Russian Organized Crime*, p. 17.

168. Cheloukhine and King, "Corruption Networks as a Sphere of Investment Activities in Modern Russia," p. 109.

169. Finckenauer, "The Russian 'Mafia,'" p. 62.

Chapter 5

1. Miko, "International Human Trafficking," in Thachuk, *Transnational Threats*, p. 36.

2. MacDonald, *Dancing on a Volcano*, p. 5.

3. Zaitseva, "Organized Crime, Terrorism and Nuclear Trafficking," p. 9.

4. "Drug Smuggling: Stairway to Heaven."

5. Thompson, "The Changing Face of Gangland Crime," p. 1.

6. Williams, "Drugs and Guns," p. 46.

7. McMahon, "Afghanistan: UN Official Describes Effort to Track Al-Qaeda."

8. Curtis and Karacan, *The Nexus among Terrorists, Narcotics Traffickers, Weapons Proliferators, and Organized Crime Networks in Western Europe*, p. 21.

9. Harris, *Political Corruption*, pp. 192–93.

10. Murunga, "Conflict in Somalia and Crime in Kenya: Understanding the Trans-Territoriality of Crime," p. 149.

11. Lumpe, Meek, and Naylor, "Introduction to Gun-Running," in Lumpe, *Running Guns*, p. 1.

12. Abel, "Manufacturing Trends—Globalising the Source," in Lumpe, *Running Guns*, p. 81.

13. Mandel, "Exploding Myths about Global Arms Transfers," p. 47.

14. Laurance, Political Implications of Illegal Arms Exports from the United States," p. 525.

15. Naim, *Illicit*, pp. 41, 61.

16. Martin and Romano, *Multinational Crime*, p. 69; and Cukier and Sidel, *The Global Gun Epidemic*, p. 88.

17. Lee, "Nuclear Smuggling: Patterns and Responses," pp. 97–98.

18. Snyder, "Disrupting Illicit Small Arms Trafficking in the Middle East," p. 51.

19. Cukier and Shropshire, "Domestic Gun Markets: The Licit-Illicit Links," in Lumpe, *Running Guns*, p. 156.

20. Cukier and Sidel, *The Global Gun Epidemic*, p. 91.

21. Nordstrom, *Global Outlaws*, pp. 177–78.

22. Naylor, "Gunsmoke and Mirrors: Financing the Illegal Trade," in Lumpe, *Running Guns*, p. 172.

23. Picarelli, "Transnational Organized Crime," in Williams, *Security Studies*, pp. 458–59.

24. Naylor, "Gunsmoke and Mirrors: Financing the Illegal Trade," in Lumpe, *Running Guns*, p. 173.

25. Lee, *Smuggling Armageddon*, p. 64.

26. Lee, "Nuclear Smuggling: Patterns and Responses," p. 101.

27. Smigielski, "Addressing the Nuclear Smuggling Threat," in Thachuk, *Transnational Threats*, p. 53.

28. Lee and Ford, "Nuclear Smuggling," in Cusimano, *Beyond Sovereignty*, p. 70.

29. Calvani, "Transnational Organized Crime: Emerging Trends of Global Concern," p. 8.

30. Zaitseva and Hand, "Nuclear Smuggling Chains: Suppliers, Intermediaries, and End-Users," pp. 831–32.

31. Smigielski, "Addressing the Nuclear Smuggling Threat," in Thachuk, *Transnational Threats*, p. 55.

32. Brown et al., *State of the World 1998*, p. 140.

33. Handelman, *Comrade Criminal*, p. 234.

34. Brown et al., *State of the World 1998*, p. 131.

35. Naim, *Illicit*, p. 41.

36. Klare, "Secret Operatives, Clandestine Trades: The Thriving Black Market for Weapons," pp. 18–20; and Cukier and Sidel, *The Global Gun Epidemic*, p. 9.

37. Williams, "Terrorism, Organized Crime, and WMD Smuggling: Challenge and Response," p. 9.

38. "The Covert Arms Trade: The Second-Oldest Profession," p. 21.

39. "The Covert Arms Trade: The Second-Oldest Profession," p. 21; and Caldwell and Williams, *Seeking Security in an Insecure World*, p. 111.

40. Grant, "Smuggling and Trafficking in Africa," in Thachuk, *Transnational Threats*, p. 120.

41. Marsh, "Two Sides of the Same Coin? The Legal and Illegal Trade in Small Arms," p. 220.

42. Curtis and Karacan, *The Nexus among Terrorists, Narcotics Traffickers, Weapons Proliferators, and Organized Crime Networks in Western Europe*, p. 1; and Harris, *Political Corruption*, pp. 192–93.

43. Handelman, *Comrade Criminal*, p. 229.

44. Naylor, "Gunsmoke and Mirrors: Financing the Illegal Trade," in Lumpe, *Running Guns*, p. 156.

45. Leggett, "Law Enforcement and International Gun Trafficking," in Lumpe, *Running Guns*, p. 211.

46. Cukier and Sidel, *The Global Gun Epidemic*, p. 98.

47. Orogun, "Plunder, Predation and Profiteering: The Political Economy of Armed Conflicts and Economic Violence in Modern Africa," p. 301.

48. Cukier and Sidel, *The Global Gun Epidemic*, p. 101.

49. Lee, *Smuggling Armageddon*, p. 65.

50. Harris, *Political Corruption*, p. 194.

51. Lee, *Smuggling Armageddon*, p. 65.

52. Caldwell and Williams, *Seeking Security in an Insecure World*, p. 111.

53. Williams, *Violent Non-State Actors and National and International Security*, p. 7; and Berry et al., *Nations Hospitable to Organized Crime and Terrorism*, p. 127.

54. Snyder, *Disrupting Illicit Small Arms Trafficking in the Middle East*, p. 3.

55. Vermonte, *Small Is (Not) Beautiful*, pp. 3–6.

56. Lee, "Nuclear Smuggling: Patterns and Responses," p. 95.

57. Brown et al., *State of the World 1998*, p. 131.

58. Krause, *Arms and the State*, p. 195.

59. Pearson, *The Global Spread of Arms*, p. 106.

60. Krause, *Arms and the State*, pp. 196–97.

61. Pearson, *The Global Spread of Arms*, pp. 60–61.

62. "The Covert Arms Trade: The Second-Oldest Profession," p. 21; and Karp, "The Rise of Black and Gray Markets," 183–84.

63. Mandel, "Exploding Myths about Global Arms Transfers."

64. Laurance, "The New Gunrunning," pp. 232–35.

65. Saavedra, "Transnational Crime and Small Arms Trafficking and Proliferation," in Thachuk, *Transnational Threats*, p. 75.

66. Cukier and Sidel, *The Global Gun Epidemic*, p. 9.

67. Lumpe, Meek, and Naylor, "Introduction to Gun-Running," in Lumpe, *Running Guns*, p. 2.

68. Vermonte, *Small Is (Not) Beautiful*, p. 5.

69. Naylor, "The Structure and Operation of the Modern Arms Black Market," in Boutwell, Klare, and Reed, *Lethal Commerce*, pp. 52–53.

70. Williams, "Drugs and Guns," pp. 46–48.

71. Mandel, "Exploding Myths about Global Arms Transfers."

72. Cukier and Sidel, *The Global Gun Epidemic*, p. 9.

73. Sorokin, "Arms, Alliances, and Security Tradeoffs in Enduring Rivalries," p. 192.

74. Flynn, "The Global Drug Trade versus the Nation-State: Why the Thugs Are Winning," in Cusimano, *Beyond Sovereignty*, pp. 46–47.

75. Nadelmann, "Global Prohibition Regimes: The Evolution of Norms in International Society," pp. 502–3.

76. Ibid., pp. 479–526.

77. Kerry, *The New War*, p. 106.

78. Ibid., p. 87; and Picarelli, "Transnational Organized Crime," in Williams, *Security Studies*, p. 457.

79. Shelley, "The Rise and Diversification of Human Smuggling and Trafficking into the United States," in Thachuk, *Transnational Threats*, p. 197; and United Nations

Office on Drugs and Crime, "Organized Crime and Its Threat to Security: Tackling a Disturbing Consequence of Drug Control," p. 3.

80. Caldwell and Williams, *Seeking Security in an Insecure World*, p. 108.

81. Romm, *Defining National Security*, 9; and Naim, *Illicit*, p. 71.

82. Naim, *Illicit*, p. 71; and Harris, *Political Corruption*, p. 177.

83. Kidron and Segal, *The State of the World Atlas*, pp. 72–73.

84. Naim, *Illicit*, p. 72.

85. Kidron and Segal, *The State of the World Atlas*, pp. 72–73.

86. Renner, *Fighting for Survival*, p. 192.

87. Nadelmann, *Cops across Borders*, p. 255.

88. "Colombia's Drug Business: The Wages of Prohibition," p. 22.

89. Kerry, *The New War*, p. 88.

90. MacDonald, *Dancing on a Volcano*, pp. 7–8.

91. Romm, *Defining National Security*, pp. 9–10.

92. "Colombia's Drug Business: The Wages of Prohibition," p. 21.

93. Andreas and Nadelmann, *Policing the Globe*, p. 251.

94. Harris, *Political Corruption*, p. 179.

95. Desroches, *The Crime That Pays*, p. 149.

96. Ford, "U.S. Assistance Has Helped Mexican Counternarcotics Efforts, but the Flow of Illicit Drugs into the United States Remains High," p. 3.

97. Kidron and Segal, *The State of the World Atlas*, p. 144.

98. Fukumi, "Drug-Trafficking and the State: The Case of Colombia," in Allum and Siebert, *Organized Crime and the Challenge to Democracy*, pp. 95, 99.

99. Harris, *Political Corruption*, p. 177.

100. Flynn, "The Global Drug Trade versus the Nation-State: Why the Thugs Are Winning," in Cusimano, *Beyond Sovereignty*, p. 46.

101. Beare, *Critical Reflections on Transnational Organized Crime, Money Laundering, and Corruption*, p. 240.

102. Ibid., p. 247.

103. See, for example, Dupont, "Transnational Crime, Drugs, and Security in East Asia," p. 442.

104. Desroches, *The Crime That Pays*, pp. 131–32.

105. Siegel, van de Bunt, and Zaitch, *Global Organized Crime*, pp. 96–97.

106. Knipe, "British Police in Fight to Stop Mule Train," p. 2.

107. Fukumi, "Drug-Trafficking and the State: The Case of Colombia," in Allum and Siebert, *Organized Crime and the Challenge to Democracy*, pp. 96–97.

108. Beare, *Critical Reflections on Transnational Organized Crime, Money Laundering, and Corruption*, p. 249.

109. Felbab-Brown, "The Violent Drug Market in Mexico and Lessons from Colombia," p. 1.

110. Martin and Romano, *Multinational Crime*, p. 51.

111. Fukumi, "Drug-Trafficking and the State: The Case of Colombia," in Allum and Siebert, *Organized Crime and the Challenge to Democracy*, p. 95.

112. Desroches, *The Crime That Pays*, p. 121.

113. Martin and Romano, *Multinational Crime*, p. 62.

114. Beare, *Critical Reflections on Transnational Organized Crime, Money Laundering, and Corruption*, p. 252.

115. Martin and Romano, *Multinational Crime*, p. 63.

116. Harris, *Political Corruption*, p. 166.

117. Kerry, *The New War*, pp. 84–86.

118. Kidron and Segal, *The State of the World Atlas*, pp. 72–73.

119. Ibid., p. 144.

120. Moran, "International Economics and National Security," pp. 88–89.

121. Romm, *Defining National Security*, p. 13.

122. MacDonald, *Dancing on a Volcano*, pp. 7–8.

123. "Poison across the Rio Grande," p. 36.

124. Cooper, "The War Next Door: Homeland Security Secretary Says Every American Has a Stake in Mexico's War Against Murderous Gangs."

125. Williams, "Transnational Criminal Organisations and International Security," pp. 96–113; and Romm, *Defining National Security*, p. 9.

126. "Poison across the Rio Grande," p. 36.

127. Cockayne, "Transnational Organized Crime: Multilateral Responses to a Rising Threat," p. 10.

128. Flynn, "The Global Drug Trade versus the Nation-State: Why the Thugs Are Winning," in Cusimano, *Beyond Sovereignty*, p. 46.

129. Fukumi, "Drug-Trafficking and the State: The Case of Colombia," in Allum and Siebert, *Organized Crime and the Challenge to Democracy*, p. 97.

130. United Nations Office on Drugs and Crime, "Organized Crime and Its Threat to Security: Tackling a Disturbing Consequence of Drug Control," p. 4.

131. Perl, "United States Andean Drug Policy: Background and Issues for Decisionmakers," p. 29.

132. Grant, "Smuggling and Trafficking in Africa," in Thachuk, *Transnational Threats*, p. 119.

133. United Nations Office on Drugs and Crime, "Organized Crime and Its Threat to Security: Tackling a Disturbing Consequence of Drug Control," p. 3.

134. Flynn, "The Global Drug Trade versus the Nation-State: Why the Thugs Are Winning," in Cusimano, *Beyond Sovereignty*, p. 46.

135. Hardouin and Weichhardt, "Terrorist Fund Raising through Criminal Activities," pp. 303–8.

136. Hollis, "Narcoterrorism: A Definitional and Operational Transnational Challenge," in Thachuk, *Transnational Threats*, p. 23.

137. Sanderson, "Transnational Terror and Organized Crime: Blurring the Lines," p. 52.

138. Siers, "The Implications for U.S. National Security," in Thachuk, *Transnational Threats*, p. 215.

139. Kan, "Webs of Smoke: Drugs and Small Wars," p. 155.

140. Martin and Romano, *Multinational Crime*, pp. 64–65.

141. Harris, *Political Corruption*, p. 177.

142. United Nations Office on Drugs and Crime, "Organized Crime and Its Threat to Security: Tackling a Disturbing Consequence of Drug Control," p. 4.

143. Picarelli, "Transnational Organized Crime," in Williams, *Security Studies*, p. 458.

144. Kristof and Wudunn, *Half the Sky*, p. 10.

145. Gallagher, "Human Rights and the New UN Protocols on Trafficking and Migrant Smuggling: A Preliminary Analysis," p. 976.

146. Ibid., p. 1000.

147. Naim, *Illicit*, p. 89.

148. Williams, "Human Commodity Trafficking: An Overview," in Williams, *Illegal Migration and Commercial Sex*, p. 1.

149. Feingold, "Human Trafficking," p. 26.

150. Ibid., p. 28.

151. Greene, "U.S. and Multinational Coalition Disrupts Migrant Smuggling Operations," p. 12; and Finckenauer, "Russian Transnational Organized Crime and Human Trafficking," in Kyle and Koslowski, *Global Human Smuggling*, p. 172.

152. Adamson, "Crossing Borders: International Migration and National Security," p. 193.

153. Kyle and Dale, "Smuggling the State Back In: Agents of Human Smuggling Reconsidered," in Kyle and Koslowski, *Global Human Smuggling*, p. 30.

154. Miko, "International Human Trafficking," in Thachuk, *Transnational Threats*, p. 42.

155 Kerry, *The New War*, p. 136; and Feingold, "Human Trafficking," p. 28.

156. Picarelli, "Transnational Organized Crime," in Williams, *Security Studies*, p. 458.

157. Adamson, "Crossing Borders: International Migration and National Security," p. 193; and Greene, "U.S. and Multinational Coalition Disrupts Migrant Smuggling Operations," p. 12.

158. Kyle and Koslowski, *Global Human Smuggling*, p. 4; Naim, *Illicit*, pp. 88–89; and Caldwell and Williams, *Seeking Security in an Insecure World*, pp. 106, 207.

159. Weiner, *The Global Migration Crisis*, pp. 7–8.

160. Papademetriou, "Migration," p. 22.

161. Weiner, *The Global Migration Crisis*, pp. 5, 8.

162. Adamson, "Crossing Borders: International Migration and National Security," p. 193.

163. Williams, "Human Commodity Trafficking: An Overview," in Williams, *Illegal Migration and Commercial Sex*, p. 4.

164. Papademetriou, "Migration," p. 22.

165. Andreas and Nadelmann, *Policing the Globe*, p. 251.

166. Miller, "The Sanctioning of Unauthorized Migration and Alien Employment," in Kyle and Koslowski, *Global Human Smuggling*, p. 321.

167. "Smuggling Chinese: Heroin Substitute," p. 33; and "The New Trade in Humans," pp. 45–46.

168. Kerry, *The New War*, pp. 135–36.

169. Miko, "International Human Trafficking," in Thachuk, *Transnational Threats*, p. 39.

170. Chin, "The Social Organization of Chinese Human Smuggling," in Kyle and Koslowski, *Global Human Smuggling*, p. 221.

171. van Dijk, *The World of Crime*, p. 148.

172. Kerry, *The New War*, p. 145.

173. Naim, *Illicit*, p. 90.

174. Massey and Espinosa, "What Is Driving Mexico-U.S. Migration? A Theoretical, Empirical, and Policy Analysis," pp. 989–90.

175. Vagg, "Sometimes a Crime: Illegal Immigration and Hong Kong," p. 370; and Feingold, "Human Trafficking," p. 32.

176. Harris, *Political Corruption*, p. 192.

177. Koser, "The Smuggling of Asylum Seekers into Western Europe: Contradictions, Conundrums, and Dilemmas," in Kyle and Koslowski, *Global Human Smuggling*, p. 70.

178. Kyle and Koslowski, *Global Human Smuggling*, pp. 2–3.

179. Ibid., p. 8.

180. "Mexico's Northern Border: Dangerous Desert, Breached Border," p. 37; Nathan, "A Wall and Legalization: Coming Together and Defending U.S. Borders," p. A19; and Downes, "The Terrible, Horrible Urgent National Disaster That Immigration Isn't."

181. "Smuggling Chinese: Heroin Substitute," p. 33; and Kerry, *The New War*, pp. 136–38.

182. Weiner, *The Global Migration Crisis*, p. 8.

183. Nadelmann, "Global Prohibition Regimes: The Evolution of Norms in International Society," p. 491.

184. Jordan, "Trafficking in Human Beings: The Slavery That Surrounds Us," p. 15.

185. Kristof and Wudunn, *Half the Sky*, pp. 10–11.

186. Arlacchi, "Nations Build Alliances to Stop Organized Crime," p. 28.

187. Miko, "International Human Trafficking," in Thachuk, *Transnational Threats*, p. 38.

188. Kyle and Koslowski, *Global Human Smuggling*, p. 1.

189. Calvani, "Transnational Organized Crime: Emerging Trends of Global Concern," p. 11.

190. Ibid., pp. 10–11.

191. Miko, "International Human Trafficking," in Thachuk, *Transnational Threats*, p. 41.

192. Beare, "Illegal Migration: Personal Tragedies, Social Problems, or National Security Threats?" in Williams, *Illegal Migration and Commercial Sex*, p. 34.

193. Holmes, "Introduction," in Holmes, *Terrorism, Organised Crime and Corruption*, p. 2.

194. Kelly, "You Can Find Anything You Want: A Critical Reflection on Research on Trafficking in Persons within and into Europe," pp. 252–53.

195. Williams, "Human Commodity Trafficking: An Overview," in Williams, *Illegal Migration and Commercial Sex*, p. 4; and Beare, "Illegal Migration: Personal Tragedies, Social Problems, or National Security Threats?" in Williams, *Illegal Migration and Commercial Sex*, p. 35.

196. Wong, "The Rumor of Trafficking: Border Controls, Illegal Migration, and the Sovereignty of the Nation-State," in van Schendel and Abraham, *Illicit Flows and Criminal Things*, p. 86.

197. Hughes and Denisova, "The Transnational Political Criminal Nexus of Trafficking in Women from Ukraine," p. 57.

198. Feingold, "Human Trafficking," p. 26.

199. Gershuni, "Trafficking in Persons for the Purpose of Prostitution: The Israeli Experience," pp. 135–36; and King, *Woman, Child for Sale*, p. 210.

200. Hughes and Denisova, "The Transnational Political Criminal Nexus of Trafficking in Women from Ukraine," p. 43.

201. Shelley, *The Changing Position of Women*, p. 213.

202. Lee, "Human Security Aspects of International Migration: The Case of South Korea," p. 42.

203. Adamson, "Crossing Borders: International Migration and National Security," p. 194.

204. Kyle and Koslowski, *Global Human Smuggling*, p. 2.

205. Williams, "Human Commodity Trafficking: An Overview," in Williams, *Illegal Migration and Commercial Sex*, p. 1.

206. Henderson, "International Migration: Appraising Current Policies," 93–110.

207. Mandel, "Perceived Security Threat and the Global Refugee Crisis," pp. 77–78.

208. "The New Nativism," p. 5.

209. See Raspail, *The Camp of the Saints*, for a colorful and representative discussion of this fear of mass illegal immigration into Western Europe.

210. Adamson, "Crossing Borders: International Migration and National Security," pp. 165–66.

211. Mandel, *Deadly Transfers and the Global Playground*, chapter 5.

212. Zeskind, "The New Nativism: The Alarming Overlap between White Nationalists and Mainstream Anti-Immigrant Forces," p. A15.

213. Kerry, *The New War*, p. 148.

214. Papadopoulou, "Smuggling into Europe: Transit Migrants in Greece," p. 174.

215. Connelly and Kennedy, "Must It Be the Rest against the West?" p. 69.

216. Adamson, "Crossing Borders: International Migration and National Security," p. 194.

217. Weiner, *The Global Migration Crisis*, p. 3.

Chapter 6

1. van Dijk, *The World of Crime*, p. 145.

2. Manwaring, "Gangs and Other Transnational Criminal Organizations (TCOs) as Transnational Threats to National Security and Sovereignty," p. 1; and Stanislawski and Hermann, "Transnational Organized Crime, Terrorism, and WMD," p. 1.

3. van Dijk, "Mafia Markers: Assessing Organized Crime and Its Impact upon Societies," p. 46.

Chapter 7

1. See, for example, Thomas, Kiser, and Casebeer, *Warlords Rising*, pp. 121–56, for a discussion of the wide range of violent nonstate actors.

2. Williams, *Violent Non-State Actors and National and International Security*, p. 6.

3. Ibid., p. 4.

4. Cockayne and Mikulaschek, "Transnational Security Challenges and the United Nations: Overcoming Sovereign Walls and Institutional Silos," p. 2.

5. Mair, "The New World of Privatized Violence," in Pfaller and Lerch, *Challenges of Globalization*, p. 47.

6. Ibid., p. 48.

7. Lea and Stenson, "Security, Sovereignty, and Non-State Governance 'From Below,'" pp. 18–19; and Williams, *Violent Non-State Actors and National and International Security*, pp. 9, 12, and 15.

8. Williams, *Violent Non-State Actors and National and International Security*, pp. 9, 13–14, and 16.

9. Lea and Stenson, "Security, Sovereignty, and Non-State Governance 'From Below,'" p. 19; Mair, "The New World of Privatized Violence," in Pfaller and Lerch, *Challenges of Globalization*, p. 48; and Williams, *Violent Non-State Actors and National and International Security*, p. 16.

10. Mair, "The New World of Privatized Violence," in Pfaller and Lerch, *Challenges of Globalization*, p. 48.

11. Ibid., p. 48.

12. Kenney, *From Pablo to Osama*, p. 9.

13. Williams, *Violent Non-State Actors and National and International Security*, p. 4.

14. Mair, "The New World of Privatized Violence," in Pfaller and Lerch, *Challenges of Globalization*, p. 47.

15. Williams, *Violent Non-State Actors and National and International Security*, p. 17.

16. Kenney, *From Pablo to Osama*, p. 203.

17. Curtis and Karacan, *The Nexus among Terrorists, Narcotics Traffickers, Weapons Proliferators, and Organized Crime Networks in Western Europe*, pp. 3–4.

18. Williams, "Drugs and Guns," pp. 46–48; and Curtis and Karacan, *The Nexus among Terrorists, Narcotics Traffickers, Weapons Proliferators, and Organized Crime Networks in Western Europe*, p. 2.

19. Makarenko, "The Crime–Terror Continuum: Tracing the Interplay between Transnational Organised Crime and Terrorism," p. 130.

20. Reuter and Petrie, *Transnational Organized Crime*, pp. 5–6.

21. Schweitzer, *A Faceless Enemy*, p. 288.

22. Berdal and Serrano, "Transnational Organized Crime and International Security: The New Topography," in Berdal and Serrano, *Transnational Organized Crime and International Security*, p. 201.

23. Sanderson, "Transnational Terror and Organized Crime: Blurring the Lines," p. 53.

24. Kenney, *From Pablo to Osama*, p. 8.

25. Bovenkerk and Chakra, "Terrorism and Organised Crime," in Holmes, *Terrorism, Organised Crime and Corruption*, pp. 36, 38.

26. Williams, *Violent Non-State Actors and National and International Security*, p. 6.

27. Ibid., p. 17.

28. Bovenkerk and Chakra, "Terrorism and Organized Crime," in Holmes, *Terrorism, Organised Crime and Corruption*, p. 3.

29. Thachuk, *Transnational Threats*, p. ix.

30. Shelley, "Crime Victimizes Both Society and Democracy," p. 21.

31. Thachuk, "An Introduction to Transnational Threats," in Thachuk, *Transnational Threats*, p. 10.

32. Sanderson, "Transnational Terror and Organized Crime: Blurring the Lines," p. 55.

33. Berdal and Serrano, *Transnational Organized Crime and International Secu-*

rity, p. 8; and Sanderson, "Transnational Terror and Organized Crime: Blurring the Lines," p. 55.

34. Naim, *Illicit*, p. 3.

35. Bovenkerk and Chakra, "Terrorism and Organised Crime," in Holmes, *Terrorism, Organised Crime and Corruption*, p. 39.

36. Shelley, "The Unholy Trinity: Transnational Crime, Corruption, and Terrorism," p. 109.

37. O'Malley and Hutchinson, "Actual and Potential Links between Terrorism and Criminality," p. 2.

38. Makarenko, "'The Ties That Bind': Uncovering the Relationship between Organised Crime and Terrorism," in Siegal, van de Bunt, and Zaitch, *Global Organized Crime*, p. 159; Thachuk, *Transnational Threats*, p. ix; and Shelley et al., "Methods and Motives: Exploring Links between Transnational Organized Crime and International Terrorism," p. 76.

39. Williams, "Strategy for a New World: Combating Terrorism and Transnational Organized Crime," in Baylis et al., *Strategy in the Contemporary World*, p. 200.

40. See, for example, Garcés, "Colombia: The Link between Drugs and Terror," pp. 86–87.

41. Curtis and Karacan, *The Nexus among Terrorists, Narcotics Traffickers, Weapons Proliferators, and Organized Crime Networks in Western Europe*, p. 22.

42. Williams, "Strategy for a New World: Combating Terrorism and Transnational Organized Crime," in Baylis et al., *Strategy in the Contemporary World*, p. 200; and Sanderson, "Transnational Terror and Organized Crime: Blurring the Lines," pp. 50–51.

43. Björnehead, "Narco-Terrorism: The Merger of the War on Drugs and the War on Terror," p. 322.

44. Williams, *Violent Non-State Actors and National and International Security*, p. 15.

45. Shelley et al., "Methods and Motives: Exploring Links between Transnational Organized Crime and International Terrorism," p. 40.

46. Wagley, "Transnational Organized Crime: Principal Threats and U.S. Responses," p. 3.

47. Shelley et al., "Methods and Motives: Exploring Links between Transnational Organized Crime and International Terrorism," p. 53.

48. Bovenkerk and Chakra, "Terrorism and Organised Crime," in Holmes, *Terrorism, Organised Crime and Corruption*, pp. 35–36.

49. van Dijk, *The World of Crime*, p. 196.

50. Reinares and Resa, "Transnational Organized Crime as an Increasing Threat to the National Security of Democratic Regimes: Assessing Political Impacts and Evaluating State Responses," p. 43.

51. U.S. Department of Justice, *Overview of the Law Enforcement Strategy to Combat International Organized Crime*, p. 3.

52. Ibid.

53. Sanderson, "Transnational Terror and Organized Crime: Blurring the Lines," pp. 49–50; and O'Malley and Hutchinson, "Actual and Potential Links between Terrorism and Criminality," p. 2.

54. Sanderson, "Transnational Terror and Organized Crime: Blurring the Lines," p. 51.

55. Kerry, *The New War*, p. 187.

Chapter 8

1. Naim, *Illicit*, p. 220; and Sterling, *Thieves' World*, p. 244.

2. Williams and Picarelli, "Combating Organized Crime in Armed Conflict," in Ballentine and Nitzschke, *Profiting from Peace*, p. 136. See also Woolsey, "Global Organized Crime: Threats to U.S. and International Security," in Raine and Cilluffo, *Global Organized Crime*, p. 137.

3. Thachuk, *Transnational Threats*, p. viii.

4. Cusimano, *Beyond Sovereignty*, p. vii.

5. Thomas, Kiser, and Casebeer, *Warlords Rising*, pp. 186, 217.

6. Kenney, *From Pablo to Osama*, pp. 203–4.

7. Lumpe, Meek, and Naylor, "Introduction to Gun-Running," in Lumpe, *Running Guns*, pp. 5–7.

8. Nadelmann, *Cops across Borders*, p. 467; and Andreas and Nadelmann, *Policing the Globe*, p. 247.

9. Andreas and Nadelmann, *Policing the Globe*, pp. 245–46.

10. Findlay, *The Globalisation of Crime*, p. 127.

11. Thomas, Kiser, and Casebeer, *Warlords Rising*, p. 185.

12. Naim, *Illicit*, p. 8.

13. United Nations Office on Drugs and Crime, "Organized Crime and Its Threat to Security: Tackling a Disturbing Consequence of Drug Control," pp. 13–14. See also Shanty, *Organized Crime*, pp. 682–702.

14. Snyder, "Disrupting Illicit Small Arms Trafficking in the Middle East," pp. 6–7.

15. Pollard, "Globalization's Bastards: Illegitimate Non-State Actors in International Law," in Bunker, *Networks, Terrorism and Global Insurgency*, pp. 40–68.

16. Thachuk, *Transnational Threats*, p. viii.

17. Cockayne and Mikulaschek, "Transnational Security Challenges and the United Nations: Overcoming Sovereign Walls and Institutional Silos," p. 3.

18. Finckenauer, "Meeting the Challenge of Transnational Crime," p. 4.

19. For a discussion of the dynamics and dangers of this action-reaction cycle, see Mandel, *Global Threat*, pp. 108–10; and Ervin, *Open Target*, p. 210.

20. Kenney, *From Pablo to Osama*, p. 105.

21. Ibid., pp. 3–7.

22. Klare, *American Arms Supermarket*, p. 27.

23. Romm, *Defining National Security*, p. 9.

24. "Chinese Yearning to Work Free," p. 38; "The New Trade in Humans," pp. 45–46; and Vagg, "Sometimes a Crime: Illegal Immigration and Hong Kong," p. 372.

25. Andreas and Nadelmann, *Policing the Globe*, p. 251. See also Mandel, *Deadly Transfers and the Global Playground*, pp. 112–20.

26. Paoli, "The Paradoxes of Organized Crime," p. 52.

27. Thachuk, "An Introduction to Transnational Threats," in Thachuk, *Transnational Threats*, pp. 3, 4, 10, 15.

28. Holmes, "Introduction," in Holmes, *Terrorism, Organised Crime and Corruption*, pp. 15–16.

29. Shelley, "The Unholy Trinity: Transnational Crime, Corruption, and Terrorism," p. 105.

30. Thachuk, "An Introduction to Transnational Threats," in Thachuk, *Transnational Threats*, pp. 3, 15.

31. Glenny, *McMafia*, p. 343.

32. Schelling, *Choice and Consequence*, p. 191.

33. See, for example, Naim, *Illicit*, p. 239.

34. Sanderson, "Transnational Terror and Organized Crime: Blurring the Lines," p. 56.

35. Schneider, Beare, and Hill, "Alternative Approaches to Combating Transnational Crime," p. 6.

36. Ibid., pp. 57–136.

37. Kerry, *The New War*, p. 168.

38. Sterling, *Thieves' World*, p. 253.

39. See, for example, Mandel, *Deadly Transfers and the Global Playground*, chapter 12; and Naim, *Illicit*, pp. 241–42.

40. Schneider, Beare, and Hill, "Alternative Approaches to Combating Transnational Crime," p. 184.

41. U.S. Department of Justice, *Overview of the Law Enforcement Strategy to Combat International Organized Crime*, p. 1.

42. "Organized Crime in Russia."

43. Luna, "Dismantling Illicit Networks and Corruption Nodes," p. 7.

44. Nadelmann, *Cops across Borders*, pp. 475–76.

45. U.S. Department of Justice, *Overview of the Law Enforcement Strategy to Combat International Organized Crime*, p. 10.

46. Kerry, *The New War*, p. 190.

47. Ibid., p. 171.

48. Mandel, "Distortions in the Intelligence Decision-Making Process," in Cimbala, *Intelligence and Intelligence Policy in a Democratic Society*, p. 79.

49. Motley, "Coping with the Terrorist Threat: The U.S. Intelligence Dilemma," in Cimbala, *Intelligence and Intelligence Policy in a Democratic Society*, p. 169.

50. Schneider, Beare, and Hill, "Alternative Approaches to Combating Transnational Crime," p. 183.

51. Felbab-Brown, "The Violent Drug Market in Mexico and Lessons from Colombia," p. 25.

52. For elaboration on this idea, see Mandel, "Fighting Fire with Fire: Privatizing Counterterrorism," in Howard and Sawyer, *Defeating Terrorism*, pp. 62–73.

53. Godson and Williams, "Strengthening Cooperation against Transsovereign Crime: A New Security Imperative," in Cusimano, *Beyond Sovereignty*, p. 141.

54. Schneider, Beare, and Hill, "Alternative Approaches to Combating Transnational Crime," p. 185.

55. Dobriansky, "The Explosive Growth of Globalized Crime," p. 6.

56. Godson, "The Political-Criminal Nexus and Global Security," in Godson, *Menace to Society*, p. 19.

57. Andreas, "Redrawing the Line: Borders and Security in the Twenty-first Century," pp. 95–99.

58. Dobriansky, "The Explosive Growth of Globalized Crime," p. 6.

59. Swartz, "Helping the World Combat International Crime," p. 9.

60. Arlacchi, "Nations Build Alliances to Stop Organized Crime," p. 28.

61. United Nations Office on Drugs and Crime, "Organized Crime and Its Threat to Security: Tackling a Disturbing Consequence of Drug Control," p. 14.

62. Schneider, Beare, and Hill, "Alternative Approaches to Combating Transnational Crime," p. 190.

63. Siers, "The Implications for U.S. National Security," in Thachuk, *Transnational Threats*, p. 219.

64. Godson, "The Political-Criminal Nexus and Global Security," in Godson, *Menace to Society*, p. 19.

65. McLean, "Colombia: Failed, Failing, or Just Weak?" p. 133.

66. Ibid.

67. Shaw, "Crime, Police and Public in Transitional Societies," pp. 14–15.

68. Frank and Melville, "The Image of the Enemy and the Process of Change," in Gromyko and Hellman, *Breakthrough—Emerging New Thinking*, pp. 203–4.

69. Jenkins, *Unconquerable Nation*, p. 166.

70. Shaw, "Crime, Police and Public in Transitional Societies," p. 13.

71. Godson and Williams, "Strengthening Cooperation against Transsovereign Crime: A New Security Imperative," in Cusimano, *Beyond Sovereignty*, p. 142.

72. Luna, "Dismantling Illicit Networks and Corruption Nodes," p. 8.

73. See Flynn, "The Brittle Superpower," in Auerswald et al., *Seeds of Disaster, Roots of Response*, p. 32.

74. See Kay, *Global Security in the Twenty-first Century*, p. 249.

75. Picarelli, "Transnational Organized Crime," in Williams, *Security Studies*, p. 466.

76. Lea and Stenson, "Security, Sovereignty, and Non-State Governance 'From Below,'" p. 21.

77. See Mandel, *Global Threat*, chapter 5. Target-centered threat management would require quite radical shifts from the standard threat assessment and management systems currently being used in most countries.

78. Schneider, Beare, and Hill, "Alternative Approaches to Combating Transnational Crime," pp. 188–89.

79. Albini, "Organized Crime: The National Security Dimension," p. 10.

80. Perl, "International Terrorism: Threat, Policy, and Response," pp. 11–14.

81. Mandel, *The Changing Face of National Security*, p. 135.

82. Freedman, "Order and Disorder in the New World," p. 37.

83. Andreas and Nadelmann, *Policing the Globe*, p. 246.

84. Andreas, "Redrawing the Line: Borders and Security in the Twenty-first Century," pp. 95–96.

85. Sampson, *The Arms Bazaar*, pp. 329, 340.

86. Manwaring, "The New Global Security Landscape: The Road Ahead," in Bunker, *Networks, Terrorism and Global Insurgency*, p. 27.

87. Cockayne, "Transnational Organized Crime: Multilateral Responses to a Rising Threat," p. 17.

BIBLIOGRAPHY

Abel, Pete. "Manufacturing Trends—Globalising the Source." In *Running Guns: The Global Black Market in Small Arms*, edited by Lora Lumpe. London: Zed Books, 2000.

Abramova, Irina. "The Funding of Traditional Organised Crime in Russia." *Economic Affairs* 27 (March 2007): 18–21.

Adamson, Fiona B. "Crossing Borders: International Migration and National Security." *International Security* 31 (Summer 2006): 165–99.

Adelstein, Jake. "This Mob Is Big in Japan." *Washington Post*, May 11, 2008.

Albini, Joseph L. "Organized Crime: The National Security Dimension." Report of a conference held at the George C. Marshall European Center for Security Studies, Garmisch-Partenkirchen, Germany, August 29–September 2, 1999. http://www .marshallcenter.org/site-graphic/lang-en/page-pubs-conf-1/static/xdocs/conf/ static/reports/9909-report.pdf.

Allum, Felia, and Jennifer Sands. "Explaining Organized Crime in Europe: Are Economists Always Right?" *Crime, Law and Social Change* 41 (March 2004): 133–60.

Allum, Felia, and Renate Siebert, eds. *Organized Crime and the Challenge to Democracy.* New York: Routledge, 2003.

Andreas, Peter. "Redrawing the Line: Borders and Security in the Twenty-first Century." *International Security* 28 (Fall 2003): 78–111.

———. "Transnational Crime and Economic Globalization." In *Transnational Organized Crime and International Security: Business as Usual?* edited by Mats Berdal and Monica Serrano. Boulder, CO: Lynne Rienner, 2002.

Andreas, Peter, and Ethan Nadelmann. *Policing the Globe: Criminalization and Crime Control in International Relations.* Oxford: Oxford University Press, 2006.

Andreas, Peter, and Richard Price. "From War Fighting to Crime Fighting: Transforming the American National Security State." *International Studies Review* 3 (Autumn 2001): 31–52.

Arlacchi, Pino. "Nations Build Alliances to Stop Organized Crime." *Global Issues* 6 (August 2001): 27–30.

Bacon, Esther A. "Balkan Trafficking in Historical Perspective." In *Transnational Threats: Smuggling and Trafficking in Arms, Drugs, and Human Life*, edited by Kimberley L. Thachuk. Westport, CT: Praeger Security International, 2007.

Bagley, Bruce. *Globalization and Transnational Organized Crime: The Russian Mafia in Latin America and the Caribbean*. Coral Gables, FL: University of Miami Press, 2002.

BBC News. "Terror of the Triads." July 26, 1999. http://news.bbc.co.uk/2/hi/uk_news/404338.stm.

Beare, Margaret E., ed. *Critical Reflections on Transnational Organized Crime, Money Laundering, and Corruption*. Toronto: University of Toronto Press, 2003.

———. "Illegal Migration: Personal Tragedies, Social Problems, or National Security Threats?" In *Illegal Migration and Commercial Sex: The New Slave Trade*, edited by Phil Williams. London: Frank Cass, 1999.

Berdal, Mats, and Monica Serrano, eds. *Transnational Organized Crime and International Security: Business as Usual?* Boulder, CO: Lynne Rienner, 2002.

Berdal, Mats, and Monica Serrano. "Transnational Organized Crime and International Security: The New Topography." In *Transnational Organized Crime and International Security: Business as Usual?* edited by Mats Berdal and Monica Serrano. Boulder, CO: Lynne Rienner, 2002.

Berry, LaVerle, et al. "Nations Hospitable to Organized Crime and Terrorism." Federal Research Division, Library of Congress, Washington, DC, October 2003.

Bibes, Patricia. "Transnational Organized Crime and Terrorism." *Journal of Contemporary Criminal Justice* 17 (August 2001): 243–58.

Bigo, Didier. "When Two Become One: Internal and External Securitisations in Europe." In *International Relations Theory and the Politics of European Integration, Power, Security and Community*, edited by Morten Kelstrup and Michael C. Williams. London: Routledge, 2000.

Björnehead, Emma. "Narco-Terrorism: The Merger of the War on Drugs and the War on Terror." *Global Crime* 6 (August–November 2004).

Blomfield, Adrian. "Russian Mafia Killings Threaten Putin Legacy." *New Criminologist*, February 29, 2008. http://www.newcriminologist.com/article.asp?cid=153&nid=2042.

Boot, Max. "Pirates, Then and Now: How Piracy Was Defeated in the Past and Can Be Again." *Foreign Affairs* 88 (July–August 2009): 94–107.

Booth, Martin. *The Dragon Syndicates: The Global Phenomenon of the Triads*. New York: Carroll & Graf, 1999.

———. *The Triads*. London: Grafton, 1990.

Boskholov, Sergei. "Organized Crime and Corruption in Russia." March 2003. http://www.demokratizatsiya.org/Dem%20Archives/DEM%2003-03%20boskholov.pdf.

Bovenkerk, Frank, and Bashir Abou Chakra. "Terrorism and Organised Crime." In *Terrorism, Organised Crime and Corruption: Networks and Linkages*, edited by Leslie Holmes. Cheltenham, UK: Edward Elgar, 2007.

Brown, Lester R., et al. *State of the World 1998*. New York: Norton, 1998.

Bull, Martin J., and James L. Newell. "Conclusion: Political Corruption in Contemporary Democracies." In *Corruption in Contemporary Politics*, edited by Martin J. Bull and James L. Newell. London: Palgrave Macmillan, 2003.

Bunker, Robert J., ed. *Networks, Terrorism and Global Insurgency*. New York: Routledge, 2005.

———, ed. *Non-State Threats and Future Wars*. London: Frank Cass, 2003.

Burgess, J. Peter. "Non-Military Security Challenges." In *Contemporary Security and Strategy*, edited by Craig A. Snyder. London: Palgrave, 2007.

Caldwell, Dan, and Robert E. Williams Jr. *Seeking Security in an Insecure World*. New York: Rowman & Littlefield, 2006.

Caldwell, Gillian, Steve Galster, Jyothi Kanics, and Nadia Steinzor. "Capitalizing on Transition Economies: The Role of the Russian Mafiya in Trafficking Women for Forced Prostitution." In *Illegal Migration and Commercial Sex: The New Slave Trade*, edited by Phil Williams. London: Frank Cass, 1999.

Calvani, Sandro. "Transnational Organized Crime: Emerging Trends of Global Concern." NATO Defense College, Rome, November 16, 2009. http://www.sandrocalvani.it/docs/Speeches 091120.pdf.

Castle, Allan. "Transnational Organized Crime and International Security." Working Paper 19, Institute of International Relations, University of British Columbia, Vancouver, November 1997. http://www.iir.ubc.ca/site_template/workingpapers/webwp19.pdf.

Chabat, Jorge. "Networks of Corruption and Violence." BBC Radio World Service, November 2008. http://www.bbc.co.uk/worldservice/news/2008/11/081031_narcocorruption.shtml.

Chatterjee, Jharna. "The Changing Structure of Organized Crime Groups." Royal Canadian Mounted Police, Ottawa, 2005. http://dsp-psd.pwgsc.gc.ca/Collection/PS64-9-2005E.pdf.

Cheloukhine, Serguei. "The Roots of Russian Organized Crime: From Old-Fashioned Professionals to the Organized Criminal Groups of Today." *Crime, Law and Social Change* 50 (December 2008): 353–74.

Cheloukhine, Serguei, and Joseph King. "Corruption Networks as a Sphere of Investment Activities in Modern Russia." *Communist and Post-Communist Studies* 40 (March 2007): 107–22.

Chemko, Victoria. "The Japanese Yakuza: Influence on Japan's International Relations and Regional Politics (East Asia and Latin America)." http://www.conflicts.rem33.com/images/yett_secu/yakuza_chemko.htm.

"Chinese Yearning to Work Free." *Economist*, July 24, 1993.

Chin, Ko-Lin. "The Social Organization of Chinese Human Smuggling." In *Global Human Smuggling: Comparative Perspectives*, edited by David Kyle and Rey Koslowski. Baltimore: Johns Hopkins University Press, 2001.

Chin, Ko-Lin, Sheldon Zhang, and Robert J. Kelly. "Transnational Chinese Organized Crime Activities: Patterns and Emerging Trends." *Transnational Organized Crime* 4 (Autumn–Winter 1998): 127–54.

Chu, Yiu Kong. "Hong Kong Triads after 1997." *Trends in Organized Crime* 8 (Spring 2005): 5–12.

———. *The Triads as Business.* London: Routledge, 2000.

Cirincione, Joseph, Jon B. Wolfsthal, and Miriam Rajkumar. *Deadly Arsenals: Nuclear, Biological, and Chemical Threats.* 2nd ed. Washington, DC: Carnegie Endowment for International Peace, 2005.

Cockayne, James. "Transnational Organized Crime: Multilateral Responses to a Rising Threat." Coping with Crisis Working Paper, International Peace Academy, New York, April 2007. http://www.ciaonet.org/wps/ipi/0016362/f_0016362_14160.pdf.

Cockayne, James, and Christoph Mikulaschek. "Transnational Security Challenges and the United Nations: Overcoming Sovereign Walls and Institutional Silos." International Peace Academy, New York, February 2008. http://www.ipacademy.org/asset/file/253/westpoint.pdf.

"Colombia: The Cartels Reorganize." *Stratfor Global Intelligence*, February 1, 2008. http://www.stratfor.com/analysis/colombia_cartels_reorganize.

"Colombia's Drug Business: The Wages of Prohibition." *Economist*, December 24, 1994.

Connelly, Matthew, and Paul Kennedy. "Must It Be the Rest against the West?" *Atlantic Monthly*, December 1994.

Cooper, Anderson. "The War Next Door: Homeland Security Secretary Says Every American Has a Stake in Mexico's War against Murderous Gangs." *60 Minutes*, CBS, March 1, 2009. http://www.cbsnews,.com/stories/2009/02/26/60minutes/main4831806.shtml.

"The Covert Arms Trade: The Second-Oldest Profession." *Economist*, February 12, 1994.

Cukier, Wendy, and Steve Shropshire. "Domestic Gun Markets: The Licit-Illicit Links." In *Running Guns: The Global Black Market in Small Arms*, edited by Lora Lumpe. London: Zed Books, 2000.

Cukier, Wendy, and Victor W. Sidel. *The Global Gun Epidemic: From Saturday Night Specials to AK-47s.* Westport, CT: Praeger Security International, 2006.

Curtis, Glenn E., Seth L. Elan, Rexford A. Hudson, and Nina A. Kollars. "Trans-national Activities of Chinese Crime Organizations." Federal Research Division, Library of Congress, Washington, DC, April 2003. http://www.loc.gov/rr/frd/pdf-files/ChineseOrgCrime.pdf.

Curtis, Glenn E., and Tara Karacan. "The Nexus among Terrorists, Narcotics Traf-fickers, Weapons Proliferators, and Organized Crime Networks in Western Eu-rope." Federal Research Division, Library of Congress, Washington, DC, Decem-ber 2002. https://www.hsdl.org/homesec/docs/justice/nps10-071306-02.pdf&code =c2ccd3f559c7e727d5c7f852ffoab93c.

Cusimano, Maryann K., ed. *Beyond Sovereignty: Issues for a Global Agenda.* Boston: Bedford/St. Martin's Press, 2000.

Delfs, Robert. "Clash of Loyalties." *Far Eastern Economic Review,* November 21, 1991.

Desroches, Frederick J. *The Crime That Pays: Drug Trafficking and Organized Crime in Canada.* Toronto: Canadian Scholars' Press, 2005.

Dickie, John. *Cosa Nostra: A History of the Sicilian Mafia.* New York: Palgrave Mac-millan, 2004.

Dishman, Chris. "Terrorism, Crime and Transformation." *Studies in Conflict and Terrorism* 24 (January 2001): 43–58.

Dobriansky, Paula. "The Explosive Growth of Globalized Crime." *Global Issues* 6 (August 2001): 5 6.

Dovkants, Keith. "The London Connection." *Evening Standard,* November 12, 1997.

Downes, Lawrence. "The Terrible, Horrible Urgent National Disaster That Immigra-tion Isn't." *New York Times* (online version only), June 20, 2006. http://select.ny times.com/2006/06/20/opinion/21talking-points.html.

"Drug Smuggling: Stairway to Heaven." *Economist,* August 7, 1993.

Dupont, Alan. "Transnational Crime, Drugs, and Security in East Asia." *Asian Survey* 39 (May–June 1999): 433–55.

Edwards, Adam, and Peter Gill. "After Transnational Organized Crime? The Politics of Public Safety." In *Transnational Organized Crime: Perspectives on Global Secu-rity,* edited by Adam Edwards and Peter Gill. New York: Routledge, 2003.

———, eds. *Transnational Organized Crime: Perspectives on Global Security.* New York: Routledge, 2003.

Ellison, Michael. "New York Arrests Signal Resurgence of Mafia." *Guardian,* Septem-ber 8, 2000.

Emmers, Ralf. "Globalization and Non-Traditional Security Issues: A Study of Hu-man and Drug Trafficking in East Asia." Institute of Defence and Strategic Stud-ies, Singapore, March 2004. http://www.rsis.edu.sg/publications/WorkingPapers/ WP62.PDF.

Ervin, Clark Kent. *Open Target: Where America Is Vulnerable to Attack.* New York: Palgrave Macmillan, 2006.

Fackler, Martin. "Mayor's Death Forces Japan's Crime Rings into the Light." *New York Times*, April 21, 2007.

Feingold, David A. "Human Trafficking." *Foreign Policy* 150 (September–October 2005): 26–31.

Felbab-Brown, Vanda. "Drugs, Violence and Instability: A Global Perspective." Presentation at the Conference on Drug Trafficking, Violence and Instability in Mexico, Colombia and the Caribbean: Implications for US National Security, Pittsburgh, October 29–30, 2009.

———. "The Violent Drug Market in Mexico and Lessons from Colombia." Foreign Policy Paper 12, Brookings Institution, Washington, DC, March 2009.

Ferguson, Charles D. "On the Loose: The Market for Nuclear Weapons." *Harvard International Review* 27 (Winter 2006): 52–57.

Finckenauer, James O. "Meeting the Challenge of Transnational Crime." *National Institute of Justice Journal* 244 (July 2000): 2–7. http://www.ncjrs.gov/pdffiles1/jr000244b.pdf.

———. "The Russian 'Mafia.'" *Society* 41 (July–August 2004): 61–64. http://www.springerlink.com/content/t1x1dg85l7mcqeea/.

———. "Russian Transnational Organized Crime and Human Trafficking." In *Global Human Smuggling: Comparative Perspectives*, edited by David Kyle and Rey Koslowski. Baltimore: Johns Hopkins University Press, 2001.

Finckenauer, James O., and Yuri A. Voronin. "The Threat of Russian Organized Crime." Office of Justice Programs, U.S. Department of Justice, Washington, DC, June 2001. http://www.ncjrs.gov/pdffiles1/nij/187085.pdf.

Finckenauer, James O., and Elin J. Waring. *Russian Mafia in America*. Boston: Northeastern University Press, 1998.

Findlay, Mark. *The Globalisation of Crime: Understanding Transitional Relationships in Context*. Cambridge: Cambridge University Press, 1999.

Fisman, Raymond, and Edward Miguel. *Economic Gangsters: Corruption, Violence, and the Poverty of Nations*. Princeton, NJ: Princeton University Press, 2008.

Flynn, Stephen E. "The Brittle Superpower." In *Seeds of Disaster, Roots of Response: How Private Action Can Reduce Public Vulnerability*, edited by E. Auerswald, Lewis M. Branscomb, Todd M. La Porte, and Erwann O. Michel-Kerjan. Cambridge: Cambridge University Press, 2006.

———. "The Global Drug Trade versus the Nation-State: Why the Thugs Are Winning." In *Beyond Sovereignty: Issues for a Global Agenda*, edited by Maryann K. Cusimano. Boston: Bedford/St. Martin's Press, 2000.

Ford, Jess T. "U.S. Assistance Has Helped Mexican Counternarcotics Efforts, but the Flow of Illicit Drugs into the United States Remains High." U.S. Government Accountability Office Testimony Before the Subcommittee on the Western Hemisphere, Committee on Foreign Affairs, House of Representatives, Washington, DC, October 25, 2007.

Forero, Juan. "Venezuela Increasingly a Conduit for Cocaine: Smugglers Exploit Graft, Icy Relations with U.S." *Washington Post*, October 28, 2007.

Frank, Jerome D., and Andrei Y. Melville. "The Image of the Enemy and the Process of Change." In *Breakthrough—Emerging New Thinking: Soviet and Western Challenges Issue a Challenge to Build a World Beyond War*, edited by Anatoly Gromyko and Martin Hellman. New York: Walker, 1988.

Freedman, Lawrence. "Order and Disorder in the New World." *Foreign Affairs* 71 (1991/1992): 20–37.

Friman, H. Richard. "Obstructing Markets: Organized Crime Networks and Drug Control in Japan." In *The Illicit Global Economy and State Power*, edited by H. Richard Friman and Peter Andreas. Lanham, MD: Rowman & Littlefield, 1999.

Friman, H. Richard, and Peter Andreas, eds. *The Illicit Global Economy and State Power*. Lanham, MD: Rowman & Littlefield, 1999.

Fukumi, Sayaka. "Drug-Trafficking and the State: The Case of Colombia." In *Organized Crime and the Challenge to Democracy*, edited by Felia Allum and Renate Siebert. New York: Routledge, 2003.

Galeotti, Mark. "Transnational Organized Crime: Law Enforcement as a Global Battlespace." In *Non-State Threats and Future Wars*, edited by Robert J. Bunker. London: Frank Cass, 2003.

Gallagher, Anne. "Human Rights and the New UN Protocols on Trafficking and Migrant Smuggling: A Preliminary Analysis. *Human Rights Quarterly* 23 (November 2001): 975–1004.

Gambetta, Diego. *The Sicilian Mafia: The Business of Private Protection*. Cambridge, MA: Harvard University Press, 1993.

Garcés, Laura. "Colombia: The Link between Drugs and Terror." *Journal of Drug Issues* 35 (Winter 2005): 83–105.

Gershuni, Rochelle. "Trafficking in Persons for the Purpose of Prostitution: The Israeli Experience." *Mediterranean Quarterly* 15 (Fall 2004): 133–46.

Glenny, Misha. *McMafia: A Journey through the Global Criminal Underworld*. New York: Knopf, 2008.

Godson, Roy, ed. *Menace to Society: Political-Criminal Collaboration around the World*. New Brunswick, NJ: Transaction, 2003.

———. "The Political-Criminal Nexus and Global Security." In *Menace to Society: Political-Criminal Collaboration around the World*, edited by Roy Godson. New Brunswick, NJ: Transaction, 2003.

Godson, Roy, and William J. Olson. *International Organized Crime: Emerging Threat to U.S. Security*. Washington, DC: National Strategy Information Center, 1993.

———. "International Organized Crime." *Society* 32 (January–February 1995): 18–29.

Godson, Roy, and Phil Williams. "Strengthening Cooperation against Transsovereign Crime: A New Security Imperative." In *Beyond Sovereignty: Issues for a Global*

Agenda, edited by Maryann K. Cusimano. Boston: Bedford/St. Martin's Press, 2000.

Gong, Ting. "Dangerous Collusions: Corruption as a Collective Venture in Contemporary China." *Communist and Post-Communist Studies* 35 (March 2002).

Grant, Audra K. "Smuggling and Trafficking in Africa." In *Transnational Threats: Smuggling and Trafficking in Arms, Drugs, and Human Life*, edited by Kimberley L. Thachuk. Westport, CT: Praeger Security International, 2007.

Granville, Johanna. "Crime That Pays: The Global Spread of the Russian Mafia." *Australian Journal of Politics and History* 49 (2003): 446–53.

Greene, Joseph R. "U.S. and Multinational Coalition Disrupts Migrant Smuggling Operations." *Global Issues* 6 (August 2001): 12–14.

Handelman, Stephen. *Comrade Criminal: Russia's New Mafiya*. New Haven, CT: Yale University Press. 1995.

———. "The Russian 'Mafiya.'" *Foreign Affairs* 73 (March–April 1994): 83–96.

Hanson, Stephanie. "Combating Maritime Piracy." Council on Foreign Relations Backgrounder, January 7, 2010. http://www.cfr.org/publication/18376/.

Hardouin, Patrick, and Reiner Weichhardt. "Terrorist Fund Raising through Criminal Activities." *Journal of Money Laundering Control* 9 (July 2006): 303–8.

Hari, Johann. "You Are Being Lied to About Pirates." *Independent*, January 5, 2009. http://www.independent.co.uk/opinion/commentators/johann-hari/johann-hari-you-are-being-lied-to-about-pirates-1225817.html.

Harman, Danna. "The War on Drugs: Ambushed in Jamundi—Why the Massacre of an Elite US-Trained Colombian Police Team Prompted Congress to Freeze Drug-War Funding." *Christian Science Monitor*, September 27, 2006.

Harris, Robert. *Political Corruption: In and Beyond the Nation State*. London: Routledge, 2003.

Harvey, Robert. *Global Disorder: America and the Threat of World Conflict*. New York: Carroll & Graf, 2003.

Harwood, Matthew. "Italian Mafia Is Europe's Number One Business." *Security Management*, January 30, 2009. http://www.securitymanagement.com/news/italian-mafia-europes-number-one-business-005178.

Hays, Jeffrey. "Triads and Organized Crime in China." http://factsanddetails.com/china.php?itemid=300&catid=8&subcatid=50.

Henderson, David. "International Migration: Appraising Current Policies." *International Affairs* 70 (1994): 93–110.

Hess, Henner. "The Traditional Sicilian Mafia: Organized Crime and Repressive Crime." In *Organized Crime: A Global Perspective*, edited by Robert J. Kelly. Totowa, NJ: Rowman & Littlefield, 1986.

Hill, Peter B. E. *The Japanese Mafia: Yakuza, Law, and the State*. New York: Oxford University Press, 2003.

Hollis, André D. "Narcoterrorism: A Definitional and Operational Transnational Challenge." In *Transnational Threats: Smuggling and Trafficking in Arms, Drugs, and Human Life*, edited by Kimberley L. Thachuk. Westport, CT: Praeger Security International, 2007.

Holmes, Leslie. "Introduction." In *Terrorism, Organised Crime and Corruption: Networks and Linkages*, edited by Leslie Holmes. Cheltenham, UK: Edward Elgar, 2007.

——. "Some Concluding Observations: A Quadrumvirate in Future?" In *Terrorism, Organised Crime and Corruption: Networks and Linkages*, edited by Leslie Holmes. Cheltenham, UK: Edward Elgar, 2007.

——, ed. *Terrorism, Organised Crime and Corruption: Networks and Linkages*. Cheltenham, UK: Edward Elgar, 2007.

Hooper, John. "Death and Dirt Collide in Mafia Violence." *Guardian*, June 3, 2008. http://www.guardian.co.uk/world/2008/jun/03/italy.internationalcrime.

——. "Move Over, Cosa Nostra." *Guardian*, June 8, 2006.

Hughes, Donna M., and Tatyana A. Denisova. "The Transnational Political Criminal Nexus of Trafficking in Women from Ukraine." *Trends in Organized Crime* 6 (Spring–Summer 2001): 43–67.

Hunter, Robyn. "Somali Pirates Living the High Life." BBC, October 28, 2008. http://news.bbc.co.uk/1/hi/world/africa/7650415.stm.

Jamieson, Alison. "Transnational Organized Crime—A European Perspective: Trends in Transnational Crime during the 1990s." *Studies in Conflict and Terrorism* 24 (September 2001): 377–88.

Jenkins, Brian Michael. *Unconquerable Nation: Knowing Our Enemy, Strengthening Ourselves*. Santa Monica, CA: RAND Corporation, 2006.

Johnston, Eric. "Yakuza in Japan: From Rackets to Real Estate, Yakuza Multifaceted." *Japan Times*, February 14, 2007. http://search.japantimes.co.jp/cgi-bin/nn2007021 4i1.html.

Jordan, Ann. "Trafficking in Human Beings: The Slavery That Surrounds Us." *Global Issues* 6 (August 2001): 15–18.

Kan, Paul R. "Webs of Smoke: Drugs and Small Wars." *Small Wars and Insurgencies* 17 (June 2006): 148–62.

Kaplan, David E., and Alex Dubro. *Yakuza: Japan's Criminal Underworld*. Berkeley: University of California Press, 2003.

Karp, Aaron. "The Rise of Black and Gray Markets." *Annals of the American Academy of Political and Social Science* 535 (September 1994): 175–89.

Kattoulas, Velisarios. "Taking Care of Business." *Far Eastern Economic Review*, November 30, 2000.

Kay, Sean. *Global Security in the Twenty-first Century: The Quest for Power and the Search for Peace*. Lanham, MD: Rowman & Littlefield, 2006.

Kelly, Liz. "You Can Find Anything You Want: A Critical Reflection on Research on Trafficking in Persons within and into Europe." *International Migration* 43 (January 2005): 235–65.

Kelly, Robert J. "Criminal Underworlds: Looking Down on Society from Below." In *Organized Crime: A Global Perspective*, edited by Robert J. Kelly. Totowa, NJ: Rowman & Littlefield, 1986.

————, ed. *Organized Crime: A Global Perspective*. Totowa, NJ: Rowman & Littlefield, 1986.

Kenney, Michael. *From Pablo to Osama: Trafficking and Terrorist Networks, Government Bureaucracies, and Competitive Adaptation*. University Park: Pennsylvania State University Press, 2007.

Kerry, John. *The New War: The Web of Crime That Threatens America's Security*. New York: Simon & Schuster, 1997.

Kidron, Michael, and Ronald Segal. *The State of the World Atlas: New Edition*. New York: Penguin Books, 1995.

King, Gilbert. *Woman, Child for Sale: The New Slave Trade in the 21st Century*. New York: Chamberlain Brothers, 2004.

Klare, Michael T. *American Arms Supermarket*. Austin: University of Texas Press, 1984.

————. "Secret Operatives, Clandestine Trades: The Thriving Black Market for Weapons." *Bulletin of the Atomic Scientists* 44 (April 1988): 16–24.

Knipe, Michael. "British Police in Fight to Stop Mule Train." *Times* (London), August 6, 2002.

Koser, Khalif. "The Smuggling of Asylum Seekers into Western Europe: Contradictions, Conundrums, and Dilemmas." In *Global Human Smuggling: Comparative Perspectives*, edited by David Kyle and Rey Koslowski. Baltimore: Johns Hopkins University Press, 2001.

Kraska, Peter B. "Militarization and Policing—Its Relevance to 21st Century Police." *Policing* 1 (2007).

Kraul, Chris. "Colombian Drug Lord Killed: Cartel Leader, Indicted by U.S., Is Found Shot to Death in Venezuela." *Los Angeles Times*, February 2, 2000.

————. "New Colombia Drug Gangs Wreak Havoc: The Killing of a Farm Leader Suggests the Rise of Former Right-Wing Paramilitary Fighters." *Los Angeles Times*, May 4, 2008.

Krause, Keith. *Arms and the State: Patterns of Military Production and Trade*. New York: Cambridge University Press, 1992.

Kreyenbuhl, Thomas. "The Mafia and Italian Politics." *Swiss Review of World Affairs* 42 (August 1992).

Kristof, Nicholas D., and Sheryl Wudunn. *Half the Sky*. New York: Knopf, 2009.

Kumbon, Daniel. "Asian Mafia Has Grip on PNG." *PNG Post-Courier*, April 15, 2008.

Kyle, David, and John Dale. "Smuggling the State Back In: Agents of Human Smuggling Reconsidered." In *Global Human Smuggling: Comparative Perspectives*, edited by David Kyle and Rey Koslowski. Baltimore: Johns Hopkins University Press, 2001.

Lake, Anthony. *6 Nightmares: Real Threats in a Dangerous World and How America Can Meet Them*. New York: Little, Brown, 2000.

Lal, Rollie. "Japanese Trafficking and Smuggling." In *Transnational Threats: Smuggling and Trafficking in Arms, Drugs, and Human Life*, edited by Kimberley L. Thachuk. Westport, CT: Praeger Security International, 2007.

Laurance, Edward J. "The New Gunrunning." *Orbis* 33 (Spring 1989): 225–37.

———. "Political Implications of Illegal Arms Exports from the United States." *Political Science Quarterly* 107 (Fall 1992): 501–33.

Lea, John, and Kevin Stenson. "Security, Sovereignty, and Non-State Governance 'From Below.'" *Canadian Journal of Law and Society* 22 (2007): 9–27.

Lee, Rensselaer. "Nuclear Smuggling: Patterns and Responses." *Parameters* 33 (Spring 2003): 95–111.

———. *Smuggling Armageddon: The Nuclear Black Market in the Former Soviet Union and Europe*. New York: St. Martin's Press, 1998.

Lee, Rensselaer W., and James L. Ford. "Nuclear Smuggling." In *Beyond Sovereignty: Issues for a Global Agenda*, edited by Maryann K. Cusimano. Boston: Bedford/St. Martin's Press, 2000.

Lee, Rensselaer W., III, and Francisco E. Thoumi, "Drugs and Democracy in Colombia." In *Menace to Society: Political-Criminal Collaboration around the World*, edited by Roy Godson. New Brunswick, NJ: Transaction, 2003.

Lee, Shin-wha. "Human Security Aspects of International Migration: The Case of South Korea." *Global Economic Review* 32 (Fall 2003): 41–66.

Leggett, Ted. "Law Enforcement and International Gun Trafficking." In *Running Guns: The Global Black Market in Small Arms*, edited by Lora Lumpe. London: Zed Books, 2000.

Levi, Michael. "Liberalization and Transnational Financial Crime." In *Transnational Organized Crime and International Security: Business as Usual?* edited by Mats Berdal and Monica Serrano. Boulder, CO: Lynne Rienner, 2002.

Lois, Elisa. "Madrid: European Capital of Cocaine." *El Pais*, October 2, 2000.

Longrigg, Clare. "How to Do Business Like the Mafia." *Guardian*, April 9, 2008.

Lumpe, Lora, Sarah Meek, and R. T. Naylor. "Introduction to Gun-Running." In *Running Guns: The Global Black Market in Small Arms*, edited by Lora Lumpe. London: Zed Books, 2000.

Luna, David M. "Dismantling Illicit Networks and Corruption Nodes." Paper presented at the Thirteenth International Corruption Conference, Athens, November 2, 2008. http://www.13iacc.org/IACC_Workshops/Workshop_6.2.

Lutterbeck, Derek. "Between Police and Military: The New Security Agenda and the Rise of the Gendarmeries." *Cooperation and Conflict* 39 (March 2004).

———. "Blurring the Dividing Line: The Convergence of Internal and External Security in Western Europe." *European Security* 14 (June 2005): 231–53.

———. "The New Security Agenda: Transnational Organized Crime and International Security." http://se2.dcaf.ch/serviceengine/FileContent?serviceID=21&fileid=A9871ED8-363B-DB41-AB41-008D81E99CBE&lng=en.

MacAskill, Ewen. "FBI Deployed by US to Fight Mexican Drug Lords." *Guardian*, March 25, 2009.

MacDonald, Scott B. *Dancing on a Volcano: The Latin American Drug Trade*. Westport, CT: Praeger, 1988.

———. "The New 'Bad Guys': Exploring the Parameters of the Violent New World Order." In *Gray Area Phenomena: Confronting the New World Disorder*, edited by Max G. Manwaring. Boulder, CO: Westview Press, 1993.

Mair, Stephan. "The New World of Privatized Violence." In *Challenges of Globalization: New Trends in International Politics and Society*, edited by Alfred Pfaller and Marika Lerch, 47–61. New Brunswick, NJ: Transaction, 2005.

Makarenko, Tamara. "The Crime–Terror Continuum: Tracing the Interplay between Transnational Organised Crime and Terrorism." *Global Crime* 6 (February 2004): 129–45.

———. "'The Ties That Bind': Uncovering the Relationship between Organised Crime and Terrorism." In *Global Organized Crime: Trends and Developments*, edited by Dina Siegal, Henk van de Bunt, and Damian Zaitch. Boston: Kluwer, 2003.

Mandel, Robert. *The Changing Face of National Security: A Conceptual Analysis*. Westport, CT: Greenwood, 1994.

———. *Deadly Transfers and the Global Playground: Transnational Security Threats in a Disorderly World*. Westport, CT: Praeger, 1999.

———. "Distortions in the Intelligence Decision-Making Process." In *Intelligence and Intelligence Policy in a Democratic Society*, edited by Stephen J. Cimbala. Dobbs Ferry, NY: Transnational, 1987.

———. "Exploding Myths about Global Arms Transfers." *Journal of Conflict Studies* 18 (Fall 1998): 47–65.

———. "Fighting Fire with Fire: Privatizing Counterterrorism." In *Defeating Terrorism: Shaping the New Security Environment*, edited by Russell D. Howard and Reid L. Sawyer. New York: McGraw-Hill, 2003.

———. *Global Threat: Target-Centered Assessment and Management*. Westport, CT: Praeger Security International, 2008.

———. "Perceived Security Threat and the Global Refugee Crisis." *Armed Forces and Society* 24 (Fall 1997): 77–103.

Manwaring, Max G. *A Contemporary Challenge to State Sovereignty: Gangs and Other*

Illicit Transnational Criminal Organizations in Central America, El Salvador, Mexico, Jamaica, and Brazil. Carlisle, PA: Strategic Studies Institute, 2007.

———. "Gangs and Other Transnational Criminal Organizations (TCOs) as Transnational Threats to National Security and Sovereignty." http://www.gwu.edu/~clai/recent_events/2006/061024-Transnational_Crime_Manwaring_Paper.pdf.

———, ed. *Gray Area Phenomena: Confronting the New World Disorder.* Boulder, CO: Westview Press, 1993.

———. "The New Global Security Landscape: The Road Ahead." In *Networks, Terrorism and Global Insurgency*, edited by Robert J. Bunker. New York: Routledge, 2005.

Marsh, Nicholas. "Two Sides of the Same Coin? The Legal and Illegal Trade in Small Arms." *Brown Journal of World Affairs* 9 (Spring 2002): 217–28.

Martin, John M., and Anne T. Romano. *Multinational Crime: Terrorism, Espionage, Drug and Arms Trafficking.* Newbury Park, CA: Sage, 1992.

Massey, Douglas S., and Kristin E. Espinosa. "What Is Driving Mexico-U.S. Migration? A Theoretical, Empirical, and Policy Analysis." *American Journal of Sociology* 102 (January 1997): 939–99.

McFarlane, John. "Transnational Crime and Asia-Pacific Security." In *The Many Faces of Asian Security*, edited by Sheldon W. Simon. Lanham, MD: Rowman & Littlefield, 2001.

McLean, Phillip. "Colombia: Failed, Failing, or Just Weak?" *Washington Quarterly* 25 (Summer 2002): 123–34.

McMahon, Robert. "Afghanistan: UN Official Describes Effort to Track Al-Qaeda." *Radio Free Europe/Radio Liberty*, January 28, 2002. http://www.rferl.org.

"Mexico's Northern Border: Dangerous Desert, Breached Border." *Economist*, January 9, 2005.

Miko, Francis T. "International Human Trafficking." In *Transnational Threats: Smuggling and Trafficking in Arms, Drugs, and Human Life*, edited by Kimberley L. Thachuk. Westport, CT: Praeger Security International, 2007.

Miller, Mark J. "The Sanctioning of Unauthorized Migration and Alien Employment." In *Global Human Smuggling: Comparative Perspectives*, edited by David Kyle and Rey Koslowski. Baltimore: Johns Hopkins University Press, 2001.

Miller, Rose M. "The Threat of Transnational Crime in East Asia." Strategy Research Project, U.S. Army War College, Carlisle Barracks, PA, March 19, 2002. http://www.dtic.mil/cgi-bin/GetTRDoc?AD=ADA402060&Location=U2&doc=GetTRDoc.pdf.

Millett, Richard L. "Weak States and Porous Borders: Smuggling along the Andean Ridge." In *Transnational Threats: Smuggling and Trafficking in Arms, Drugs, and Human Life*, edited by Kimberley L. Thachuk. Westport, CT: Praeger Security International, 2007.

Mittleman, James H., and Robert Johnston. "Global Organized Crime." In *The Globalization Syndrome*, edited by James H. Mittleman. Princeton, NJ: Princeton University Press, 2000.

Moody-Stuart, George. *Grand Corruption in Third World Development*. Oxford: Worldview, 1997.

Moran, Theodore H. "International Economics and National Security." *Foreign Affairs* 69 (Winter 1990/1991): 74–90.

Motley, James B. "Coping with the Terrorist Threat: The U.S. Intelligence Dilemma." In *Intelligence and Intelligence Policy in a Democratic Society*, edited by Stephen J. Cimbala. Dobbs Ferry, NY: Transnational, 1987.

Mueller, Gerhard O. W. "Transnational Crime: Definitions and Concepts." *Transnational Organized Crime* 4 (1998): 13–21.

Mulholland, James. "Ferris versus the Triads." *News of the World*, April 13, 2008.

Murunga, Godwin. "Conflict in Somalia and Crime in Kenya: Understanding the Trans-Territoriality of Crime." *African and Asian Studies* 40 (April 2005): 137–62.

Nadelmann, Ethan A. *Cops across Borders: The Internationalization of U.S. Criminal Law Enforcement*. University Park: Pennsylvania State University Press, 1995.

——. "Global Prohibition Regimes: The Evolution of Norms in International Society." *International Organization* 44 (Summer 1990): 479–526.

Naim, Moises. *Illicit: How Smugglers, Traffickers, and Copycats Are Hijacking the Global Economy*. New York: Doubleday, 2005.

Nathan, Alan. "A Wall and Legalization: Coming Together and Defending U.S. Borders." *Washington Times*, April 12, 2006.

"National Security Strategy of the United States of America." White House, Washington, DC, September 2002. http://www.globalsecurity.org/military/library/policy/national/nss-020920.pdf.

Naylor, R. T. "Gunsmoke and Mirrors: Financing the Illegal Trade." In *Running Guns: The Global Black Market in Small Arms*, edited by Lora Lumpe. London: Zed Books, 2000.

——. "The Insurgent Economy: Black Market Operations of Guerrilla Organizations." *Crime, Law and Social Change* 20 (July 1993): 13–51.

——. "The Structure and Operation of the Modern Arms Black Market." In *Lethal Commerce*, edited by Jeffrey Boutwell, Michael T. Klare, and Laura W. Reed. Cambridge, MA: American Academy of Arts and Sciences, 1995.

——. *Wages of Crime: Black Markets, Illegal Finance and the Underworld Economy*. Ithaca, NY: Cornell University Press, 2002.

Negroponte, John D. "Annual Threat Assessment of the Director of National Intelligence for the Senate Select Committee on Intelligence." Office of the Director of National Intelligence, Washington, DC, February 2, 2006.

Newell, James L., and Martin J. Bull. "Introduction." In *Corruption in Contemporary*

Politics, edited by Martin J. Bull and James L. Newell. London: Palgrave Macmillan, 2003.

"The New Trade in Humans." *Economist*, August 5, 1995.

Nordstrom, Carolyn. *Global Outlaws: Crime, Money, and Power in the Contemporary World*. Berkeley: University of California Press, 2007.

O'Malley, Pat, and Steven Hutchinson. "Actual and Potential Links between Terrorism and Criminality." Canadian Centre for Intelligence and Security Studies, Norman Paterson School of International Affairs, Carleton University, Ottawa, 2006. http://www.csis.gc.ca/en/itac/itacdocs/2006-5.asp.

"Organized Crime in Russia." *Stratfor Global Intelligence*, April 16, 2008. http://www.stratfor.com/analysis/organized_crime_russia.

Orogun, Paul. "Plunder, Predation and Profiteering: The Political Economy of Armed Conflicts and Economic Violence in Modern Africa." *Perspectives on Global Development and Technology* 2 (2003): 283–313.

Owen, Richard. "Death Threats and Arson Fail to Halt Businessmen's Anti-Mafia Fight." *Times* (London), November 28, 2007.

Paoli, Letizia. "Broken Bonds: Mafia and Politics in Sicily." In *Menace to Society: Political-Criminal Collaboration around the World*, edited by Roy Godson. New Brunswick, NJ: Transaction, 2003.

———. "Crime, Italian Style." *Daedalus* 130 (Summer 2001): 157–85.

———. "The Illegal Drugs Market." *Journal of Modern Italian Studies* 9 (June 2004): 188–208.

———. "Italian Organised Crime: Mafia Associations and Criminal Enterprises." *Global Crime* 6 (February 2004): 19–31.

———. "Mafia and Organized Crime in Italy: The Unacknowledged Success of Law Enforcement." *West European Politics* 30 (September 2007).

———. *Mafia Brotherhoods: Organized Crime, Italian Style*. New York: Oxford University Press, 2003.

———. "The Paradoxes of Organized Crime." *Crime, Law and Social Change* 37 (2002): 51–97.

Papademetriou, Demetrios G. "Migration." *Foreign Policy* 109 (Winter 1997): 15–31.

Papadopoulou, Aspasia. "Smuggling into Europe: Transit Migrants in Greece." *Journal of Refugee Studies* 17 (June 2004): 167–84.

Paris, Roland. "Human Security: Paradigm Shift or Hot Air?" *International Security* 26 (Fall 2001): 87–102.

Passas, Nikos. "Cross-Border Crime and the Interface between Legal and Illegal Actors." In *Upperworld and Underworld in Cross-Border Crime*, edited by Petrus C. van Duyne, Klaus von Lampe, and Nikos Passas. Nijmegen, the Netherlands: Wolf Legal Publishers, 2002.

———. "Globalization and Transnational Crime: Effects of Criminogenic Asymmetries." In *Combating Transnational Crime: Concepts, Activities and Responses*, edited by Phil Williams and Dimitri Vlassis. London: Frank Cass, 2001.

Patrick, Stewart. "Weak States and Global Threats: Fact or Fiction?" *Washington Quarterly* 29 (Spring 2006): 27–53.

Pearson, Frederic S. *The Global Spread of Arms*. Boulder, CO: Westview Press, 1994.

Perl, Raphael F. "International Terrorism: Threat, Policy, and Response." Report for Congress, Congressional Research Service, Washington, DC, January 3, 2007.

———. "United States Andean Drug Policy: Background and Issues for Decisionmakers." *Journal of Interamerican Studies and World Affairs* 34 (Fall 1992): 13–35.

Picarelli, John T. "Transnational Organized Crime." In *Security Studies: An Introduction*, edited by Paul D. Williams, 453–67. London: Routledge, 2008.

"Poison across the Rio Grande." *Economist*, November 15, 1997.

Pollard, Neil. "Globalization's Bastards: Illegitimate Non-State Actors in International Law." In *Networks, Terrorism and Global Insurgency*, edited by Robert J. Bunker. New York: Routledge, 2005.

Popham, Peter. "Has the Italian Mafia Spread Its Tentacles throughout Europe? The Big Question." *Independent*, August 17, 2007.

Raine, Linnea P., and Frank J. Cilluffo, eds. *Global Organized Crime: The New Empire of Evil*. Washington, DC: Center for Strategic and International Studies, 1994.

Raspail, Jean. *The Camp of the Saints*. Petoskey, MI: Social Contract Press, 1994.

Reinares, Fernando, and Carlos Resa, "Transnational Organized Crime as an Increasing Threat to the National Security of Democratic Regimes: Assessing Political Impacts and Evaluating State Responses." http://nids.hq.nato.int/acad/fellow/97-99/reinares.pdf.

Renner, Michael. *Fighting for Survival*. New York: Norton, 1996.

Reuter, Peter, and Carol Petrie, eds. *Transnational Organized Crime: Summary of a Workshop*. Washington, DC: National Academy Press, 1999.

Richards, James R. *Transnational Criminal Organizations, Cybercrime, and Money Laundering: A Handbook for Law Enforcement Officers, Auditors, and Financial Investigators*. Boca Raton, FL: CRC Press, 1999.

Robinson, Jeffrey. *The Merger: The Conglomeration of International Organized Crime*. New York: Overlook Press, 2000.

Romm, Joseph J. *Defining National Security: The Nonmilitary Aspects*. New York: Council on Foreign Relations Press, 1993.

Rose-Ackerman, Susan. *Corruption and Government: Causes, Consequences, and Reform*. Cambridge: Cambridge University Press, 1999.

Saavedra, Boris O. "Transnational Crime and Small Arms Trafficking and Proliferation." In *Transnational Threats: Smuggling and Trafficking in Arms, Drugs, and Human Life*, edited by Kimberley L. Thachuk. Westport, CT: Praeger Security International, 2007.

Saija, Marcello, and Daniela Irrera. "Institutions and Mafia in Italy: The Case of Messina." *Global Crime* 6 (August–November 2004): 391–97.

Sampson, Anthony. *The Arms Bazaar*. New York: Viking Press, 1977.

Sanderson, Thomas M. "Transnational Terror and Organized Crime: Blurring the Lines." *SAIS Review* 24 (Winter–Spring 2004): 49–61.

Sanín, Francisco Gutiérrez. "Internal Conflict, Terrorism and Crime in Colombia." *Journal of International Development* 18 (January 2006): 137–50.

Schelling, Thomas C. *Choice and Consequence*. Cambridge, MA: Harvard University Press, 1984.

Schloss, Glenn. "Fears Triads Stepping Up Japan Role." *South China Morning Post*, June 21, 1998.

Schneider, Stephen, Margaret Beare, and Jeremy Hill. "Alternative Approaches to Combating Transnational Crime." Federal Transnational Crime Working Group, Ottawa, March 31, 2000. http://ww2.ps-sp.gc.ca/Publications/Policing/TransCrime_e.pdf.

Schweitzer, Glenn E. *A Faceless Enemy: The Origins of Modern Terrorism*. Cambridge, MA: Perseus, 2002.

Scott, Andrew W. *The Revolution in Statecraft: Informal Penetration*. New York: Random House, 1965.

Seindal, René. *Mafia: Money and Politics in Sicily*. Copenhagen: Museum Tusculanum Press, 1998.

Serrano, Monica. "Transnational Organized Crime and International Security: Business as Usual?" In *Transnational Organized Crime and International Security: Business as Usual?* edited by Mats Berdal and Monica Serrano. Boulder, CO: Lynne Rienner, 2002.

Serrano, Monica, and Maria Celia Toro. "From Drug Trafficking to Transnational Organized Crime in Latin America." In *Transnational Organized Crime and International Security: Business as Usual?* edited by Mats Berdal and Monica Serrano. Boulder, CO: Lynne Rienner, 2002.

Shanty, Frank G., ed. *Organized Crime: From Trafficking to Terrorism*. Santa Barbara, CA: ABC-CLIO, 2008.

Shaw, Mark. "Crime, Police and Public in Transitional Societies." *Transformation* 49 (2002): 1–24.

Shelley, Louise. *The Changing Position of Women: Trafficking, Crime, and Corruption*. Lanham, MD: Rowman & Littlefield, 2002.

———. "Crime Victimizes Both Society and Democracy." *Global Issues* 6 (August 2001): 19–21.

———. "The Rise and Diversification of Human Smuggling and Trafficking into the United States." In *Transnational Threats: Smuggling and Trafficking in Arms, Drugs, and Human Life*, edited by Kimberley L. Thachuk. Westport, CT: Praeger Security International, 2007.

——. "Russia and Ukraine: Transition or Tragedy?" In *Menace to Society: Political-Criminal Collaboration around the World*, edited by Roy Godson. New Brunswick, NJ: Transaction, 2003.

——. "Transnational Organized Crime: An Imminent Threat to the Nation-State?" *Journal of International Affairs* 48 (Winter 1995): 463–89.

——. "The Unholy Trinity: Transnational Crime, Corruption, and Terrorism." *Brown Journal of World Affairs* 11 (Winter–Spring 2005): 101–11.

Shelley, Louise I., et al. "Methods and Motives: Exploring Links between Transnational Organized Crime and International Terrorism." Document 211207, U.S. Department of Justice, Washington, DC, September 2005.

Shvarts, Alexander. "The Russian Mafia: Expulsion of Law." *Contemporary Justice Review* 6 (December 2003): 363–82.

Siegal, Dina, Henk van de Bunt, and Damian Zaitch, eds. *Global Organized Crime: Trends and Developments*. Boston: Kluwer, 2003.

Siers, Rhea. "The Implications for U.S. National Security." In *Transnational Threats: Smuggling and Trafficking in Arms, Drugs, and Human Life*, edited by Kimberley L. Thachuk. Westport, CT: Praeger Security International, 2007.

Smigielski, David. "Addressing the Nuclear Smuggling Threat." In *Transnational Threats: Smuggling and Trafficking in Arms, Drugs, and Human Life*, edited by Kimberley L. Thachuk. Westport, CT: Praeger Security International, 2007.

Smith, Dan. *The Penguin Atlas of War and Peace*. rev. ed. New York: Penguin Books, 2003.

——. *The Penguin State of the World Atlas*. 6th ed. New York: Penguin Books, 2008.

"Smuggling Chinese: Heroin Substitute." *Economist*, May 22, 1993.

Snyder, Craig A., ed. *Contemporary Security and Strategy*. London: Palgrave, 2007.

Snyder, Neil N. "Disrupting Illicit Small Arms Trafficking in the Middle East." Master's thesis, Naval Postgraduate School, Monterey, CA, 2008. http://www.dtic.mil/cgi-bin/GetTRDoc?AD=ADA493782&Location=U2&doc=GetTRDoc.pdf.

Sokolov, Vsevolod. "From Guns to Briefcases: The Evolution of Russian Organized Crime." *World Policy Journal* 21 (Spring 2004): 68–74.

Sorokin, Gerald L. "Arms, Alliances, and Security Tradeoffs in Enduring Rivalries." *International Studies Quarterly* 38 (September 1994): 421–46.

Stanislawski, Bartosz H. "Transnational 'Bads' in the Globalized World: The Case of Transnational Organized Crime." *Public Integrity* 6 (Spring 2004): 155–70.

Stanislawski, Bartosz H., and Margaret G. Hermann. "Transnational Organized Crime, Terrorism, and WMD." Discussion paper for the Conference on Non-State Actors, Terrorism, and Weapons of Mass Destruction, CIDCM, University of Maryland, College Park, October 15, 2004.

Sterling, Claire. *Thieves' World: The Threat of the New Global Network of Organized Crime*. New York: Simon & Schuster, 1994.

Sullivan, Brian. "International Organized Crime: A Growing National Security Threat." *Strategic Forum* 74 (May 1996).

Sullivan, John P., and Robert J. Bunker. "Drug Cartels, Street Gangs, and Warlords." In *Non-State Threats and Future Wars*, edited by Robert J. Bunker. London: Frank Cass, 2003.

Swartz, Bruce. "Helping the World Combat International Crime." *Global Issues* 6 (August 2001): 9–11.

Sweeney, John P. "Colombia's Narco-Democracy Threatens Hemispheric Security." Heritage Foundation Backgrounder 1028, March 21, 1995. http://www.heritage .org/Research/PoliticalPhilosophy/BG1028.cfm.

Szubin, Adam J. "Impact Report: Economic Sanctions against Colombian Drug Cartels." Office of Foreign Assets Control, U.S. Department of the Treasury, Washington, DC, March 2007.

Thachuk, Kimberley. "Corruption and International Security." *SAIS Review* 25 (Winter–Spring 2005): 143–52.

———. "An Introduction to Transnational Threats." In *Transnational Threats: Smuggling and Trafficking in Arms, Drugs, and Human Life*, edited by Kimberley L. Thachuk. Westport, CT: Praeger Security International, 2007.

———, ed. *Transnational Threats: Smuggling and Trafficking in Arms, Drugs, and Human Life*. Westport, CT: Praeger Security International, 2007.

Thomas, Troy S., Stephen D. Kiser, and William D. Casebeer. *Warlords Rising: Confronting Violent Non-State Actors*. Lanham, MD: Lexington Books, 2005.

Thompson, Tanya. "The Changing Face of Gangland Crime." *Scotsman*, March 10, 2008.

Thornton, Rod. *Asymmetric Warfare: Threat and Response in the Twenty-first Century*. Cambridge: Polity Press, 2007.

Treverton, Gregory F., Carl Matthies, Karla J. Cunningham, Jeremiah Goulka, Greg Ridgeway, and Anny Wong. "Film Piracy, Organized Crime, and Terrorism." Safety and Justice Program and the Global Risk and Security Center, RAND Corporation, Santa Monica, CA, 2009.

Tsyganov, Yuri. "The State, Business and Corruption in Russia." In *Terrorism, Organised Crime and Corruption: Networks and Linkages*, edited by Leslie Holmes. Cheltenham, UK: Edward Elgar, 2007.

Tunstall, Stanley Q. "Transnational Organized Crime and Conflict: Strategic Implications for the Military." Strategy Research Project, U.S. Army War College, Carlisle Barracks, PA, 2002. http://www.dtic.mil/cgi-bin/GetTRDoc?AD=ADA40455 2&Location=U2&doc=GetTRDoc.pdf.

United Nations Office on Drugs and Crime. "Effective Measures to Combat Transnational Organized Crime." Eleventh United Nations Congress on Crime Prevention and Criminal Justice, Bangkok, April 18–25, 2005. http://www.unodc.org.

———. "Organized Crime and Its Threat to Security: Tackling a Disturbing Consequence of Drug Control." Vienna, March 1, 2009. http://www.unodc.org/documents/commissions/CND-Uploads/CND-52-RelatedFiles/CND-52-Documents/CND52-ECN72009-ECN152009-CRP4-E.pdf.

U.S. Department of Justice. *Overview of the Law Enforcement Strategy to Combat International Organized Crime.* Washington, DC: Government Printing Office, 2008. http://www.usdoj.gov/criminal/icitap/press/room/2008/apr/04-23-08combat-intl-crime-overview.pdf.

Vagg, Jon. "Sometimes a Crime: Illegal Immigration and Hong Kong." *Crime and Delinquency* 39 (July 1993): 355–72.

van Creveld, Martin. *The Transformation of War.* New York: Free Press, 1991.

van Dijk, Jan. "Mafia Markers: Assessing Organized Crime and Its Impact upon Societies." *Trends in Organized Crime* 10 (December 2007): 39–56.

———. *The World of Crime: Breaking the Silence on Problems of Security, Justice, and Development across the World.* Thousand Oaks, CA: Sage, 2008.

van Duyne, Petrus C., Klaus von Lampe, and Nikos Passas, eds. *Upperworld and Underworld in Cross-Border Crime.* Nijmegen, the Netherlands: Wolf Legal Publishers, 2002.

van Schendel, Willem, and Itty Abraham, eds. *Illicit Flows and Criminal Things: States, Borders, and the Other Side of Globalization.* Bloomington: Indiana University Press, 2005.

van Soest, Dorothy. *The Global Crisis of Violence: Common Problems, Universal Causes, Shared Solutions.* Washington, DC: NASW Press, 1997.

Varese, Federico. *The Russian Mafia: Private Protection in a New Market Economy.* New York: Oxford University Press, 2001.

Vermonte, Philps Jusario. *Small Is (Not) Beautiful: The Problem of Small Arms in South East Asia.* Jakarta: Center for Strategic and International Studies, 2004.

Viano, Emilio C., ed. *Global Organized Crime and International Security.* Brookfield, VT: Ashgate, 1999.

Viano, Emilio C., Jose Magallanes, and Laurent Bridel, eds. *Transnational Organized Crime: Myth, Power, and Profit.* Durham, NC: Carolina Academic Press, 2003.

Volkov, Vadim. *Violent Entrepreneurs: The Use of Force in the Making of Russian Capitalism.* Ithaca, NY: Cornell University Press, 2002.

von Lampe, Klaus. "Organized Crime Research in Perspective." In *Upperworld and Underworld in Cross-Border Crime,* edited by Petrus van Duyne, Klaus von Lampe, and Nikos Passas. Nijmegen, the Netherlands: Wolf Legal Publishers, 2002.

Wagley, John R. "Transnational Organized Crime: Principal Threats and U.S. Responses." Report for Congress, Congressional Research Service, Washington, DC, March 20, 2006.

Wang, Xiangwei. "Forget Riots, Collusion between Officials and Triads Is a Bigger Danger." *South China Morning Post,* March 13, 2006.

Webster, William H., et al. *Russian Organized Crime: Crisis Task Force Report.* Washington, DC: Center For Strategic and International Studies, 1997.

Weiner, Myron. *The Global Migration Crisis.* New York: HarperCollins, 1995.

Williams, Phil. "Cooperation among Criminal Organizations." In *Transnational Organized Crime and International Security: Business as Usual?* edited by Mats Berdal and Monica Serrano. Boulder, CO: Lynne Rienner, 2002.

———. "Drugs and Guns." *Bulletin of the Atomic Scientists* 55 (January–February 1999).

———. "Human Commodity Trafficking: An Overview." In *Illegal Migration and Commercial Sex: The New Slave Trade,* edited by Phil Williams. London: Frank Cass, 1999.

———. "New Context, Smart Enemies." *Non-State Threats and Future Wars,* edited by Robert J. Bunker. London: Frank Cass, 2003.

———. "Organizing Transnational Crime: Networks, Markets and Hierarchies." In *Combating Transnational Crime: Concepts, Activities and Responses,* edited by Phil Williams and Dimitri Vlassis. London: Frank Cass, 2001.

———. "Organizing Transnational Crime: Networks, Markets and Hierarchies." Paper presented at the Workshop on Transnational Organized Crime, Committee on Law and Justice, National Research Council, Washington, DC, June 17–18, 1998.

———. "Strategy for a New World: Combating Terrorism and Transnational Organized Crime." In *Strategy in the Contemporary World,* edited by John Baylis, James L. Wirtz, Colin S. Gray, and Eliot Cohen, 192–208. 2nd ed. New York: Oxford University Press, 2007.

———. "Terrorism, Organized Crime, and WMD Smuggling: Challenge and Response." *Strategic Insights* 6 (August 2007).

———. "Transnational Criminal Organisations and International Security." *Survival* 36 (Spring 1994): 96–113.

———. *Violent Non-State Actors and National and International Security.* Zurich: Swiss Federal Institute of Technology, 2008.

Williams, Phil, and John T. Picarelli. "Combating Organized Crime in Armed Conflict." In *Profiting from Peace: Managing the Resource Dimensions of Civil War,* edited by Karen Ballentine and Heiko Nitzschke, 123–52. Boulder, CO: Lynne Rienner, 2005.

Williams, Phil, and Dimitri Vlassis, eds. *Combating Transnational Crime: Concepts, Activities and Responses.* London: Frank Cass, 2001.

Wong, Anny. "Chinese Crime Organizations as Transnational Enterprises." In *Transnational Threats: Smuggling and Trafficking in Arms, Drugs, and Human Life,* edited by Kimberley L. Thachuk. Westport, CT: Praeger Security International, 2007.

Wong, Diana. "The Rumor of Trafficking: Border Controls, Illegal Migration, and the

Sovereignty of the Nation-State." In *Illicit Flows and Criminal Things: States, Borders, and the Other Side of Globalization*, edited by Willem van Schendel and Itty Abraham. Bloomington: Indiana University Press, 2005.

Woodiwiss, Michael. "Transnational Organized Crime: The Strange Career of an American Concept." In *Critical Reflections on Transnational Organized Crime, Money Laundering, and Corruption*, edited by Margaret E. Beare. Toronto: University of Toronto Press, 2003.

Woolsey, R. James. "Global Organized Crime: Threats to U.S. and International Security." In *Global Organized Crime: The New Empire of Evil*, edited by Linnea P. Raine and Frank J. Cilluffo. Washington, DC: Center for Strategic and International Studies, 1994.

Xia, Ming. "Organizational Formations of Organized Crime in China: Perspectives from the State, Markets, and Networks." *Journal of Contemporary China* 17 (2008): 1–23.

Zaitseva, Lyudmila. "Organized Crime, Terrorism and Nuclear Trafficking." *Strategic Insights* 6 (August 2007).

Zaitseva, Lyudmila, and Kevin Hand. "Nuclear Smuggling Chains: Suppliers, Intermediaries, and End-Users." *American Behavioral Scientist* 46 (February 2003): 822–44.

Zeskind, Leonard. "The New Nativism: The Alarming Overlap between White Nationalists and Mainstream Anti-Immigrant Forces." *American Prospect*, November 2005.

Zhang, Sheldon, and Ko-Lin Chin. "Characteristics of Chinese Human Smugglers." Office of Justice Programs, U.S. Department of Justice, Washington, DC, August 2004.

INDEX

accountability, of authority structures, 6, 7, 32–33, 42, 51, 59–60, 167, 179, 183, 188–189
action-reaction cycle, 168–169, 185
anarchy, 25–31, 167
anti-crime success, 176–177
"anything goes" mentality, 126
arms transfers, illicit, 11, 93–102, causes of, 94; conventional arms, 96–98, 99–101, 102; criminal corruption versus violence, 98–99; criminal-terrorist linkages, 152; dual-use, 25, 92, 96–97; general scope and nature, 93–94; government tolerance of, 169; identity of smugglers, 8; illicit drug and human transfer linkages, 91–92; individual versus state security impacts, 99–102, 131; management challenges, 92–93, 94–95, 169; nuclear arms, 91, 94, 95–96, 98–99, 100, 102; profits, 97; relationship to violence, 53, 101; small arms and light weapons, 100–101; weapons of mass destruction, 63
Aruba, as a criminal state, 36–37
asymmetric power, 42, 50, 100, 163, 174

backfire effects, from transnational organized crime management strategies, 6, 21, 33, 116, 157, 164–167, 172–173
"black hole" states, 24, 36
blurring of legitimate and illegitimate activity, 50, 92
borders, porous or permeable, 21, 22, 30, 33, 35, 98, 117, 135

bribery. *See* corruption
bureaucracy, bloated, 29, 30, 38, 163, 195

Chinese triads, 68–71; corruption versus violence, 69–70; individual versus state security impacts, 70–71; involvement in migrant labor smuggling, 117; links to other transnational criminal organizations, 67; organizational background, 68–69; preferred tactics, 129
civil society norms, 5, 42, 44, 53, 54, 57, 64–65, 101–102, 122, 139–140, 173–174, 185, 189, 194
coercive countermeasures, changes in, 127
Cold War, 1, 5, 11–12, 19, 22, 24, 25, 84, 95
Colombian cartels, 72–76; corruption versus violence, 73–75; individual versus state security impacts, 75–76; links to other transnational criminal organizations, 67; organizational background, 71–73; preferred tactics, 129
conflict: caused by arms transfers, 94, 96, 97, 99–100, 101; caused by drug transfers, 112; disconnected from transnational organized crime, 34; ethnic, 23, 101; facilitated by transnational organized crime, 54, 146, 194; facilitating transnational organized crime, 24, 54; link to failing states, 23; link to insecurity, 139–140; low-intensity, 19; not involving states, 146; undeclared, 52
contagion of transnational organized crime, 28, 30, 182, 187